Early Stories of *Willa Cather*

Also by MILDRED R. BENNETT

The World of *Willa Cather*

Early Stories of

Willa Cather

Selected and with
commentary by

Mildred R. Bennett

Dodd, Mead & Company
NEW YORK

First published as a Dodd, Mead Quality Paperback in 1983

Published by Dodd, Mead & Company, Inc.
79 Madison Avenue, New York, N.Y. 10016

Distributed in Canada by
McClelland and Stewart Limited, Toronto

Manufactured in the United States of America

Library of Congress Cataloging in Publication Data

Cather, Willa, 1873-1947.
  Early stories of Willa Cather.

  I. Bennett, Mildred R. II. Title.
PS3505.A87A6   1983   813'.52   83-16324
ISBN 0-396-08268-8 (pbk.)

✿ Introduction

Each time Willa Cather put pen to paper she had one story to tell and that story was *sensitive man's disharmony with his environment*. This theme is as much Cather as is her distinctive signature.

The young Willa of 1892–1900 had in embryonic form everything that was to make her great. Her brain was already a "limbo" full of "ghosts" for which she was trying to find bodies.

The following stories all published before 1901 are now in the public domain and therefore available for the first time. Although they have been known to a few Cather scholars, these stories, because Willa Cather herself did not esteem them, have been largely ignored. The first five and the eighth of this group appeared in *Writings from Willa Cather's Campus Years*, edited by James R. Shively, 1950, University of Nebraska Press.

The Pittsburgh stories were first brought to my attention in 1948 by Rose Demorest, librarian of the Pennsylvania Room at the Carnegie Library in Pittsburgh. In the fall of 1955 I returned to Pittsburgh to recheck material and found one story that had been previously missed.

Edward Wagenknecht (*Cavalcade of the American Novel*, 1952, Henry Holt) points out that Willa Cather had some editorial help with the two stories "On the Divide" and "Eric Hermannson's Soul."

In the absence of Willa Cather's letters, which may never be published, no complete scholastic study of Cather can afford to ignore this material of her formative years. For this reason, these stories are presented.

❧ Contents

Early Stories of *Willa Cather*

Peter

published in *The Mahogany Tree*, May 21, 1892
published in *Hesperian*, November 24, 1892

Peter Sadelack, Father of Anton

published in *The Library*, July 21, 1900

[This story will be at once recognized as the suicide which appears in *My Ántonia*. In that book it is evident that homesickness has driven Mr. Shimerda to desperation. In this very short story, the violin stands as the symbol of Mr. Sadelack's old life. Actually, the man who killed himself was named Sadilek and Annie Sadilek was the character Ántonia.

The major differences between the two versions come in the introductory paragraphs. Following is the introduction of the first, then of the second version.]

"No, Antone, I have told thee many, many times, no, thou shalt not sell it until I am gone."

"But I need money; what good is that old fiddle to thee? The very crows laugh at thee when thou art trying to play. Thy hand trembles so that thou canst scarce hold the bow. Thou shalt go with me to the Blue to cut wood tomorrow. See to it thou art up early."

"What, on the Sabbath, Antone, when it is so cold? I get so very cold, my son, let us not go tomorrow."

"Yes, tomorrow, thou lazy old man. Do not cut wood upon the Sabbath? Care I how cold it is? Wood thou shalt cut, and haul it too, and as for the fiddle, I tell thee I will sell it yet." Antone pulled his ragged cap down over his low, heavy brow, and went out. The old man drew his stool up nearer the fire, and sat stroking his violin with trembling fingers and muttering, "Not while I live, not while I live."

> [This is the end of the first introduction. In the second we find no reference to a religious angle nor to the bitter cold. In *My Ántonia*, the oldest son, Ambrosch, is very religious, and we are made very conscious of the cold wind and the miles of snow bound prairie.
> The mother introduced in the second version is easygoing, and not at all like Mrs. Shimerda of *My Ántonia,* a woman determined to get ahead.
> Notice also in this second introduction that the familiar thee and thou have been changed to you.]

"No, Anton, I tell you again, you shall not sell the violin while I live, not the violin. It fed you while you were a child, it brought in all the money we ever saw then. It has done enough!" said Peter.

Anton kicked at a chunk in the fire place and retorted angrily:

"What good is that old fiddle to you, old man? Since your hand shakes, the very crows laugh at you when you are trying to play. The man who offered me good money for it is a fool. Fifty dollars, he said—enough to buy a new hay rake. When have we had fifty dollars in the house? When have we made fifty dollars? Can you pick fifty dollars off of the plum bushes? I met him at the store to-night and told him he could have the fiddle, and I can't go back on the bargain. He will come for it to-morrow, and he will get it; you may make up your mind to that. Maybe you'll keep the cattle out of the wheat better next spring with that plaything of yours out of the way, and maybe you won't forget to feed the pigs so often."

> [Here is the Cather theme brought out in *One of Ours:* the struggle between artistic living and materialistic living.]

Mother Sadelack got up from her spinning wheel and shuffled out into the kitchen. She knew there would be hot words between Anton and his father, and she was averse to all excitement, except the mild enthusiasm for life produced by drinking black heavy Bohemian beer. She was rather sorry on the whole that a self-important college student from Oklahoma City had taken a fancy to Peter's violin and had offered him money for it. She had threatened to break it often enough in her jealous rages long ago, when Peter had gone a-serenading this and that chorus girl in Prague, but that was all over and done, and the fiddle was well enough and had never done anyone any harm. She was also sorry that Anton ill-used his father and swore at him, but it was not in her makeup to take things very seriously. She could never remember when her children had been born or when they were going to be born, or whether she had put her bread to rise, and she managed to live altogether without mental exertion.

[Continuing first version. Note the difference in spelling of Antone—Anton.]

Five years ago they had come here, Peter Sadelack, and his wife, and oldest son Antone, and countless smaller Sadelacks, here to southwestern Nebraska, and had taken up a homestead. Antone was the acknowledged master of the premises, and people said he was a likely youth, and would do well. That he was mean and untrustworthy every one knew, but that made little difference. His corn was better tended than any in the county, and his wheat always yielded more than other men's.

[Another reference to the worship of materialism.
Note in the second version below that the state has been changed from Nebraska to Oklahoma. Also the crops and conditions are much more civilized than they are in *My Ántonia*.]

Five years ago Peter Sadelack, and his wife, and his oldest son, Anton and countless smaller Sadelacks had come to Southwestern Oaklahoma [spelling as in original], and had taken up a homestead. Anton had been moderately successful as a farmer.

He kept his corn clean, and he knew how and when to plant his wheat. He was furthermore, industrious and exceedingly parsimonious, and he worked his mother and sisters and little brothers in the fields like animals. He even got some work out of Peter, though it usually had to be done over again. Still, people said that Anton was a better man than his father.

[Now both versions are the same.]

Of Peter, no one knew much, nor had any one a good word to say for him. He drank whenever he could get out of Anton's sight long enough to pawn his hat or coat for whiskey. Indeed, there were but two things he could [First version says *would.*] not pawn, his pipe and his violin. He was a lazy, absent-minded old fellow, who liked to fiddle better than to plow, though Anton surely got work enough out of them all, for that matter. In the house of which Anton was master there was no one, from the little boy of three years old to the old man of sixty, who did not earn his bread. Still, people said that Peter was worthless, and was a great drag on Anton, his son, who never drank, and was a much better man than his father had ever been. Peter did not care what people said. He did not like the country, nor the people, least of all he liked the plowing. He was very homesick for Bohemia. [No paragraph break here in first version.]

Long ago—only eight years by the calendar, but it seemed eight centuries to Peter—he had been a second violinist in the great theatre at Prague. He had gone into the theatre very young, and had been there all his life, until he had a stroke of paralysis, which made his arm [*arms* in first version] so weak that his bowing was uncertain. Then they told him he could go. Those were great days at the theatre. He had plenty to drink then and wore a dress coat every evening, and there were always parties after the play. He could play in those days, too! [First version adds *Ay that he could!*]

[The next few sentences differ. I give the first version here.]

He could never read the notes well, so he did not play first; but his touch, he had a touch indeed, so Herr Mikilsdoff, who led the orchestra, had said. Sometimes now Peter thought he could plow better if he could only bow as he used to.

> [There is no paragraph break here in the first version as in the second. I continue with the second following the above sentence: "He could play in those days, too!"]

He had never had enough industry to acquire much technique, but he had a certain depth of tone and a strong intuition for effective execution. Sometimes Peter thought he would be willing to plow and dig for Anton forever if he could only free his crippled arm and play once as he used to.

He had seen all the lovely women of the world there, all the great singers and the great players. He was in the orchestra when Rachel played, and he heard Liszt play when the Countess d'Agoult sat in the stage box and threw the master white lilies. Once a French woman came and played for weeks, he did not remember her name now. He did not remember her face very well either, for it changed so, it was never twice the same. But the beauty of it, and the great hunger men felt at the sight of it, that he remembered. Most of all he remembered her voice. He did not speak [first version: *know*] French, and could not understand a word she said, but it seemed to him that she must be talking the music of Chopin. And her voice, he thought he should know that in the other world. The last night she played a play in which a man touched her arm, and she stabbed him. [First version begins sentence with *As*.] Peter sat among the smoking gas jets down below the footlights, with his fiddle on his knee, and looked up at [First version: *to*] her; he thought [first version] he would like to die, too, if he could touch her arm once, and have her stab him so. [Second version: *if he could touch her arm once he would be willing to have her stab him so.*] Peter went home to his wife very drunk that night. Even in those days he was a foolish fellow, who cared for nothing but music and pretty faces.

[In *My Ántonia,* Mr. Shimerda is a much more sympathetic character than we have here.]

It was all different now. He had nothing to drink and little to eat, and here there was nothing but sun, and grass, and sky. He had forgotten almost everything, but some things he remembered well enough. He loved his violin and the Holy Mary, and above all else he feared the Evil One and his son Anton.

The fire was low, and it grew cold. Still Peter sat by the fire remembering. He dared not throw more wood [first version: *cobs*] on the fire; Anton would be angry. He did not want to cut wood to-morrow, it would be Sunday, and he wanted to go to mass. Anton might let him do that and how terrible to sell the violin on a holy day! He held it under his [First version ends sentence with *let him do that* and follows with *He held the violin under*] wrinkled chin, his white hair fell over it, and he began to play "Ave Maria." His hand shook more than ever before, and at last refused to work the bow at all. He sat stupefied for awhile, then rose and, taking his violin with him, stole out into the old stable. He took Anton's shot gun down from its peg, and loaded it by the moonlight which streamed in through the door. He sat down on the dirt floor, and leaned back against the dirt wall. He heard the wolves howling in the distance, and the night wind screaming as it swept over the snow. Near him he heard the regular breathing of the horses in the dark. He put his crucifix above his heart, and folding his hands said brokenly all the Latin he had ever known, "*Pater noster, qui es in coelis.*" [First version: "*Pater noster, qui in coelum est.*"] Then he raised his head and sighed, "Not one kreutzer will Anton pay them to pray for my soul, not one kreutzer, he is so careful of his money, is Anton; he does not waste it in drink, he is a better man than I, but hard sometimes; he works the girls too hard; women were not made to work so; but he shall not sell thee, my fiddle. I can play thee no more, but they shall not part us; we have seen it all together, and we will forget it together, the French woman and all." He held his fiddle under his chin a moment, where it had lain so often, then put it across his knee and broke it through the middle. He pulled off his old boot, held the gun between his knees with the muzzle against his forehead, and pressed the trigger with his toe.

[Here is an old man, not a particularly good musician, who is willing to face—in his own considered belief—eternal damnation rather than be separated from his art—his music. This is the devotion which Cather felt it took to be an artist. She wrote friends that she would follow her art to a much hotter place than Pittsburgh if need be. She said that the god of art accepted only human sacrifices.

In *My Ántonia,* although the violin is mentioned, it does not play the significant part it docs here.]

In the morning Anton found him stiff, frozen fast in a pool of blood. They could not straighten him out enough to fit a coffin, so they buried him in a pine box. Before the funeral Anton carried to town the fiddlebow which Peter had forgotten to break. Anton was very thrifty, and a better man than his father had been.

[Here is the bitter flavor found in "The Sculptor's Funeral."

Willa Cather said that one of the first stories she heard around the fire in Nebraska was the one of Mr. Sadilek's suicide, and if she ever wrote anything she would be bound to write sometime of that.

Annie Sadilek Pavelka said, "My father wanted to bring us to this country so we would have it better here."

She went on to say that from the letters he had received about Nebraska, he expected trees and beautiful houses. He found few trees, dugouts, and shacks. The shack on the place the Sadileks bought was not fit to live in, and the first year they lived with a German family. The little Annie loved her father. He was a kind, gentle man who didn't drink, swear, or smoke. He called her "Naninka."

She continued: "One nice afternoon, it was the fifteenth of February, he told mother he was going to hunt rabbits. He brought a shot gun from the old country. He never used it there. Nobody dared to shoot there, that was all rich people's property. When he didn't return by five o'clock mother, older brother and the man we lived with went to look for him. It was dark when they found him half sitting in that old house back of the bed shot in the head and already cold, nearly frozen. The sheriff said it was suicide. There was no cemetery or nothing. One of the near neighbors had to make a wooden box and they had to make his grave in the corner of our farm. But my brother had him moved, and him and my mother and brother are sleeping in Red Cloud cemetery and they have a tombstone. I hope they are resting sweetly." (Excerpts from a letter written to Frances Samland, Omaha, Nebraska—a student who wrote asking about *My Ántonia.*) The quotation is as Mrs. Pavelka wrote it, except for insertion of some punctuation for clarity. It was written in February, 1955, two months before her death at the age of eighty-six.]

❧ Lou, the Prophet

published in *Hesperian*, October 15, 1892

[This story deals with the theme of mysticism, which some people thought madness. Lou, a homesick Dane, finds his audience among children. The early Catholic missionaries found their audiences among the childlike people of the new world. So then we find the same Willa Cather in "Lou, the Prophet" that we find in *Death Comes for the Archbishop* and *Shadows on the Rock*.]

It had been a very trying summer to every one, and most of all to Lou. He had been in the West for seven years, but he had never quite gotten over his homesickness for Denmark. Among the northern people who emigrate to the great west, only the children and the old people ever long much for the lands they have left over the water. The men only know that in this new land their plow runs across the field tearing up the fresh, warm earth, with never a stone to stay its course. That if they dig and delve the land long enough, and if they are not compelled to mortgage it to keep body and soul together, some day it will be theirs, their very own.

[This is Alexandra Bergson's feeling throughout *O Pioneers*. It is the motivating force of her life.]

They are not like the southern people; they loose [probably misprint for *lose*] their love for their fatherland quicker and have less of sentiment about them.

[Willa Cather already understood the Latin people; for example, consider Father Hector, who took the vow of perpetual stability, and his predecessor Chabanel, who did

9

the same in *Shadows on the Rock*, and Madame Auclair, who
on her deathbed wanted to leave her daughter Cecile "a feeling about life that had come down to her through so many
centuries and that she had brought with her across the wastes
of obliterating, brutal ocean. The sense of 'our way' . . ."]

They have to think too much about how they shall get bread
to care much what soil gives it to them. But among even the
most blunted, mechanical people, the youths and the aged always have a touch of romance in them.

Lou was only twenty-two; he had been but a boy when his
family left Denmark, and had never ceased to remember it. He
was a rather simple fellow, and was always considered less promising than his brothers; but last year he had taken up a claim
of his own and made a rough dug-out upon it and he lived there
all alone. His life was that of many another young man in our
country. He rose early in the morning, in the summer just before
day-break; in the winter, long before. First he fed his stock,
then himself, which was a much less important matter. He ate
the same food at dinner that he ate at breakfast, and the same
at supper that he ate at dinner. His bill of fare never changed the
year round; bread, coffee, beans and sorghum molasses, sometimes a little salt pork. After breakfast he worked until dinner
time, ate, and then worked again. He always went to bed soon
after the sunset, for he was always tired, and it saved oil. Sometimes, on Sundays, he would go over home after he had done his
washing and house cleaning, and sometimes he hunted. His life
was as sane and as uneventful as the life of his plow horses, and
it was as hard and thankless. He was thrifty for a simple, thick-
headed fellow, and in the spring he was to have married Nelse
Sorenson's daughter, but he had lost all his cattle during the
winter, and was not so prosperous as he had hoped to be; so,
instead she married her cousin, who had an "eighty" of his
own. That hurt Lou more than anyone ever dreamed.

[An "eighty" was eighty acres of land.]

A few weeks later his mother died. He had always loved his mother. She had been kind to him and used to come over to see him sometimes, and shake up his hard bed for him, and sweep, and make his bread. She had a strong affection for the boy, he was her youngest, and she always felt sorry for him; she had danced a great deal before his birth, and an old woman in Denmark had told her that was the cause of the boy's weak head.

Perhaps the greatest calamity of all was the threatened loss of his corn crop. He had bought a new corn planter on time that spring, and had intended that his corn should pay for it. Now, it looked as though he would not have corn enough to feed his horses. Unless rain fell within the next two weeks, his entire crop would be ruined; it was half gone now.

[Willa Cather thought there was a correlation between the dryness of the weather and the number of suicides.]

All these things together were too much for poor Lou, and one morning he felt a strange loathing for the bread and sorghum which he usually ate as mechanically as he slept. He kept thinking about the strawberries he used to gather on the mountains after the snows were gone, and the cold water in the mountain streams.

[Denmark is a flat country. Willa Cather was probably thinking of Scandinavia without separating Denmark from Sweden and Norway.]

He felt hot someway, and wanted cold water. He had no well, and he hauled his water from a neighbor's well every Sunday, and it got warm in the barrels those hot summer days. He worked at his haying all day; at night, when he was through feeding, he stood a long time by the pig stye with a basket on his arm. When the moon came up, he sighed restlessly and tore the buffalo pea flowers with his bare toes. After a while, he put his basket away, and went into his hot close, little dug-out. He did not sleep well, and he dreamed a horrible dream. He thought he saw the Devil and all his angels in the air holding back the rain clouds, and they loosed all the damned in Hell, and they came, poor tortured things, and drank up whole clouds of rain. Then he thought a strange light shone from the south, just over the river bluffs, and the clouds parted, and Christ and all his angels were descending. They were coming, coming, myriads and myriads of them, in a great blaze of glory. Then he felt something give way in his poor, weak head, and with a cry of pain he awoke. He lay shuddering a long time in the dark, then got up and lit his lantern and took from the shelf his mother's Bible. It opened of itself at Revelation and Lou began to read, slowly indeed, for it was hard work for him. Page by page, he read those burning, blinding, blasting words, and they seemed to shrivel up his poor brain altogether. At last the book slipped from his hands and he sank down upon his knees in prayer, and stayed so until the dull gray dawn stole over the land and he heard the pigs clamoring for their feed.

[Crazy Ivar in *O Pioneers* reads the Norwegian Bible, but he gets comfort from it. He is supposed to run about the country and howl (according to gossip), but he is clean, cures sick animals, and protects birds.]

He worked about the place until noon, and then prayed and read again. So he went on several days, praying and reading and fasting, until he grew thin and haggard. Nature did not comfort him any, he knew nothing about nature, he had never seen her; he had only stared into a black plow furrow all his life. Before, he had only seen in the wide, green lands and the open blue the possibilities of earning his bread; now, he only saw in them a great world ready for the judgment, a funeral pyre ready for the torch.

One morning, he went over to the big prairie dog town, where several little Danish boys herded their fathers' cattle. The

boys were very fond of Lou; he never teased them as the other
men did, but used to help them with their cattle, and let them
come over to his dug-out to make sorghum taffy. When they saw
him coming, they ran to meet him and asked him where he had
been all these days. He did not answer their questions, but
said: "Come into the cave, I want to see you."

Some six or eight boys herded near the dog town every
summer, and by their combined efforts they had dug a cave in
the side of a high bank. It was large enough to hold them all
comfortably, and high enough to stand in. There the boys used
to go when it rained or when it was cold in the fall. They followed Lou silently and sat down on the floor. Lou stood up
and looked tenderly down into the little faces before him. They
were old-faced little fellows, though they were not over twelve
or thirteen years old; hard work matures boys quickly.

"Boys," he said earnestly, "I have found out why it don't rain,
it's because of the sins of the world. You don't know how wicked
the world is, it's all bad, all, even Denmark. People have been
sinning a long time, but they won't much longer.

> [Crazy Ivar of *O Pioneers* wanted to stay away from
> people so that he would not be tempted. Moreover, he just
> didn't like civilization. Cather's sympathies are all for the
> Ivars and the Lous—the ones who are different, even if that
> difference doesn't mean superior gifts as in her stories of
> artists.]

God has been watching and watching for thousands of years, and
filling up the phials of wrath, and now he is going to pour out
his vengeance and let Hell loose upon the world. He is burning
up our corn now, and worse things will happen; for the sun
shall be as sack-cloth, and the moon shall be like blood, and
the stars of heaven shall fall, and the heavens shall part like a
scroll, and the mountains shall be moved out of their places, and
the great day of his wrath shall come, against which none may
stand. Oh, boys! the floods and the flames shall come down upon

us together and the whole world shall perish." Lou paused for breath, and the little boys gazed at him in wonder. The sweat was running down his haggard face, and his eyes were staring wildly. Presently, he resumed in a softer tone, "Boys, if you want rain, there is only one way to get it, by prayer. The people of the world won't pray, perhaps if they did God would not hear them, for they are so wicked; but he will hear you, for you are little children and are likened unto the kingdom of heaven, and he loved ye."

Lou's haggard, unshaven face bent toward them and his blue eyes gazed at them with terrible earnestness.

"Show us how, Lou," said one little fellow in an awed whisper. Lou knelt down in the cave, his long, shaggy hair hung down over his face, and his voice trembled as he spoke:

"Oh God, they call thee many long names in thy book, thy prophets; but we are only simple folk, the boys are all little and I am weak headed ever since I was born, therefore, let us call thee Father, for thy other names are hard to remember. O Father, we are so thirsty, all the world is thirsty; the creeks are all dried up, and the river is so low that the fishes die and rot in it; the corn is almost gone; the hay is light; and even the little flowers are no more beautiful. O God! our corn may yet be saved. O, give us rain! Our corn means so much to us, if it fails, all our pigs and cattle will die, and we ourselves come very near it; but if you do not send rain, O Father, and if the end is indeed come, be merciful to thy great, wicked world. They do many wrong things, but I think they forget thy word, for it is a long book to remember, and some are little and some are born weak headed, like me, and some are born very strong headed, which is near as bad. Oh, forgive them their abominations in all the world, both in Denmark and here, for the fire hurts so, O God! Amen."

The little boys knelt and each said a few blundering words. Outside, the sun shone brightly and the cattle nibbled at the short, dry grass, and the hot wind blew through the shriveled corn; within the cave, they knelt as many another had knelt before them, some in temples, some in prison cells, some in the caves of earth, and One, indeed, in the garden, praying for the sin of the world.

> [Think of all the scenes of prayer that Cather was to write: in *Death Comes for the Archbishop,* particularly the chapter called "December Night," when Bishop Latour finds Sada in the doorway and takes her into the church to pray; or in *Shadows on the Rock,* especially the story of Jeanne Le Ber, the recluse. Cather is never contemptuous of simple-hearted worship, as she is of assumed and pretentious piety such as Brother Weldon's in *One of Ours.*]

The next day, Lou went to town, and prayed in the streets. When the people saw his emaciated frame and wild eyes, and heard his wild words, they told the sheriff to do his duty, the man must be mad. Then Lou ran away; he ran for miles, then walked and limped and stumbled on, until he reached the cave; there the boys found him in the morning. The officials hunted him for days, but he hid in the cave, and the little Danes kept his secret well. They shared their dinners with him, and prayed with him all day long. They had always liked him, but now they would have gone straight through fire for him, any one of them, they almost worshipped him. He had about him that mysticism which always appeals so quickly to children. I have always thought that bear story which the Hebrews used to tell their children very improbable. If it was true, then I have my doubts about the prophet; no one in the world will hoot at in-sincere and affected piety sooner than a child, but no one feels the true prophetic flame quicker, no one is more readily touched by simple goodness. A very young child can tell a sincere man better than any phrenologist.

> [Little Jacques in *Shadows on the Rock* says, "Cecile, all the saints in this church like children, don't they?" There is also the scene where Bishop Laval finds Jacques freezing in the street one night, takes him home, bathes him, feeds him, and puts him in his own bed while he sits up all night.

[The crowning point—the scene where Cather characterizes
this high-handed man whom many feared—is his kissing
first one foot, then the other, of this little waif.]

One morning, he told the boys that he had had another
"true dream." He was not going to die like other men, but God
was going to take him to himself as he was. The end of the
world was close at hand, too very close. He prayed more than
usual that day, and when they sat eating their dinner in the sunshine, he suddenly sprang to his feet and stared wildly south,
crying, "See, see, it is the great light! the end comes!! and they
do not know it; they will keep on sinning, I must tell them, I
must!"

"No, no, Lou, they will catch you; they are looking for
you, you must not go!"

[Crazy Ivar in *O Pioneers* had the same problem: the
people wanted to have him locked up because he was different. But he had Alexandra to protect him.]

"I must go, my boys; but first let me speak once more to
you. Men would not heed me, or believe me, because my head
is weak, but you have always believed in me, that God has
revealed his word to me, and I will pray God to take you to
himself quickly, for ye are worthy. Watch and pray always,
boys, watch the light over the bluffs, it is breaking, breaking,
and shall grow brighter. Good bye, my boys, I must leave ye in
the world yet awhile." He kissed them all tenderly and blessed
them, and started south. He walked at first, then he ran, faster
and faster he went, all the while shouting at the top of his voice,
"The sword of the Lord and of Gideon!"

The police officers heard of it, and set out to find him. They
hunted the country over and even dragged the river, but they
never found him again, living or dead. It is thought that he was
drowned and the quicksands of the river sucked his body under.
But the little Dane boys in our country firmly believe that he was

translated like Enoch of old. On stormy nights, when the great winds sweep down from the north they huddle together in their beds and fancy that in the wind they still hear that wild cry, "The sword of the Lord and of Gideon."

A Tale of the White Pyramid

published in *Hesperian*, December 22, 1892

[This shows, in spite of its stiffness, certain Cather characteristics: It is told in first person. The hero is of great physical perfection—a quality that many of the Cather heroes of this period show—and he is resented by the populace, those inferior beings who do not share his superiority.

The background shows a great love of and interest in antiquity, and certainly an ability to recreate it for our sight. Ptah was the chief god of ancient Memphis; Khufu, the first king of the Fourth or Memphite dynasty of Egypt. Therefore reference to Houris, the beautiful maidens of Moslem paradise, is anachronistic.]

(I Kakau, son of Ramenka, high priest of Phtahah in the great temple at Memphis, write this, which is an account of what I, Kakau, saw on the first day of my arrival at Memphis, and the first day of my sojourn in the home of Rui, my uncle, who was a priest of Phtahah before me.)

As I drew near the city the sun hung hot over the valley which wound like a green thread toward the south. On either side the river lay the fields of grain, and beyond was the desert of yellow sand which stretched away to where the low line of Lybian hills rose against the sky. The heat was very great, and the breeze scarce stirred the reeds which grew in the black mud down where the Nile, like a great tawny serpent, crept lazily away through the desert. Memphis stood as silent as the judgment hall of Osiris. The shops and even the temples were deserted, and no man stirred in the streets save the watchmen of the city. Early in the morning the people had arisen and washed the ashes from their faces, shaved their bodies, taken off the robes of mourning, and had gone out into the plain, for the seventy-two days of mourning were now over.

Senefrau the first, Lord of the Light and Ruler of the Upper and Lower Kingdoms, was dead and gathered unto his fathers. His body had passed into the hands of the embalmers, and lain for the allotted seventy days in niter, and had been wrapped in gums and spices and white linen and placed in a golden mummy case, and to-day it was to be placed in the stone sarcophagus in the white pyramid, where it was to await its soul.

Early in the morning, when I came unto the house of my uncle, he took me in his chariot and drove out of the city into the great plain which is north of the city, where the pyramid stood. The great plain was covered with a multitude of men. There all the men of the city were gathered together, and men from all over the land of Khem. Here and there were tethered many horses and camels of those who had come from afar. The army was there, and the priesthood, and men of all ranks; slaves, and swineherds, and the princes of the people. At the head of the army stood a tall dark man in a chariot of ivory and gold, speaking with a youth who stood beside the chariot.

"It is Kufu, the king," said Rui, "men say that before the Nile rises again he will begin to build a pyramid, and that it will be such a one as men have never seen before, nor shall we afterwards."

"Who is he that stands near unto the king, and with whom the king speaks?" I asked. Then there came a cloud upon the face of Rui, the brother of my father, and he answered and said unto me:

"He is a youth of the Shepherd people of the north, he is a builder and has worked upon the tomb. He is cunning of hand and wise of heart, and Kufu has shown him great favor, but the people like him not, for he is of the blood of strangers."

I spoke no more of the youth, for I saw that Rui liked him not, but my eyes were upon him continually, for I had seen no other man like unto him for beauty of face or of form.

After a time it came to pass that the great tumult ceased throughout the plain, and the words of men died upon their lips. Up from the shore of the sacred lake wound the funeral procession toward the tomb, and by the Lord of Truth I then thought the glory of Isis could be no grander. There were boys clad in white and wreathed with lotus flowers, and thousands of slaves clad in the skins of leopards, bearing bread and wine and oil, and carrying the images of the gods. There were maidens, bands of harpers and of musicians, and the captives which the king had taken in war leading tigers and lions of the desert. There was the sacred ark drawn by twenty white oxen, and there were many priests, and the guards of the king, and the sacred body of Senefrau, borne by carriers. After the body of the king came all the women of his household, beating their hearts, and weeping bitterly. As the train approached men fell upon their faces and prayed to Pthahah, the Great South Wall, and Kufu bowed his head. At the foot of the pyramid the train halted, and the youths clothed in white, and the priests, and those who bore the body began to ascend the pyramid, singing as they went:

Enter into thy rest, oh Pharaoh!
Enter into thy kingdom.
For the crown of the two lands was heavy,
And thy head was old,
And thou hast laid it aside forever.
Thy two arms were weak,
And the scepter was a great weight,
And thou hast put it from thee.
Enter thou into thy new reign,
Longer than the eternities.
Darkness shall be thy realm, O King,
And sleep thy minion.
The chariots of Ethiopia shall surround thee no more,

Nor the multitudes of the mighty encompass thee in battle,
For thou, being dead, art become as a god;
Good thou knowest, oh king;
And evil has been nigh unto thee,
Yet neither approach thee now,
For thou art dead, and like unto the gods.

They bore him down into the pyramid, and left him to sleep, and to wait. Then I saw a multitude of men gather about a great white stone that lay at the base of the tomb, and I questioned Rui concerning it, and he answered me:

"This pyramid as thou seest opens not at the side, but from the top down. That great slab of stone is to cover the top of the tomb. See, even now the workmen spread mortar upon the top of the tomb, and fasten ropes about the great stone to lift it into place. Neith grant that they harm not the stone, for it has taken a thousand men ten years to cut and polish it and to bring it thither."

I saw slaves bending over the great stone, fastening about it ropes which hung from the great pulleys built upon the shafts which rose from the upper stage of the pyramid. While they did this, companies of slaves began to ascend the sides of the tomb, each company with its master. The men were all fashioned like the men of the north, and their strength was like ribbed steel, for these were the mightiest men in Egypt. After a time there was silence in the plain. The slaves took hold of the ropes that swung from the pulleys, and every voice was hushed. It was as still without the pyramid as it was within. At last the sound of the Sistrum [a noisemaker used in the worship of Isis] broke the stillness, the master builders waved their lashes, and the two thousand slaves who were upon the pyramid set their feet firmly upon the polished stone and threw the weight of their bodies upon the ropes. Slowly, slowly, amid the creaking and groaning of the ropes, the great stone left the earth. The musicians played and the people shouted, for never before in all Egypt had so

great a stone been raised. But suddenly the shouting ceased, and
the music was hushed, and a stillness like the sleep of Nut fell
over the plain. All the people gazed upward, and the heart of
Khem grew sick as they looked. The great stone had risen half
way, the lifting ropes were firm as the pillars of heaven, but
one of the ropes which held the stone in place gave way and
stretched, and the great stone which was the pride of the land,
was settling at one end and slipping from its fastenings. The
slaves crouched upon the pyramid, the builders spoke no word,
and the people turned their eyes from the stone, that they might
not see it fall. As I looked up, I saw a man running rapidly along
the tier of the pyramid opposite the rocking stone. I knew his
face to be the face of the stranger whom I saw speaking with the
king. He threw off his garments as he ran, and at the edge of
the stone tier he paused for a moment, he crouched low, gathering all his strength, then suddenly straightening his body he
threw back his head and shot straight forward, like an arrow
shot from the bow, over eighteen cubits, and fell lightly upon
his feet on the uppermost end of the stone. He stood with both
hands clenched at his side, his right foot a little before his left,
erect and fair as the statue of Houris, watching the farther end
of the stone. For a little the stone stood still, then swung back
and lay evenly as when all was well, and then the end upon
which the youth stood, sank. He thrust his right foot further forward, his toes clinging to the polished stone, and clasping his
hands about his waist above the hips, slowly bowed his great
frame forward. The stone slab felt its master and swung slowly
back, and again the end on which the youth stood was uppermost. So he stood, his dusky limbs showing clear against the
white stone, his every muscle quivering, the sweat pouring from
his body, swaying the great stone. The great white desert seemed
to rock and sway, the sun grew hotter and stood still in heaven,
the sky and the sea of faces seemed to whirl and reel, then blend
into one awful face, grinning horribly. The slaves, not daring to
breathe, crouched upon the tomb, the multitude stood still and

gazed upward, and earth and heaven and men were as dumb as if the gods had smitten them mad with thunder. Then a great cry rang out:

"In the name of Phtahah and of your fathers' souls, pull!"

It was the voice of Kufu. Slowly, like men awakened from a dream, the slaves drew up that swinging stone, and he stood upon it. Below the king stood, his hands clutching the front of his chariot, and his eyes strained upon the stone. When the slab reached the top of the shaft on which the pulley hung, it was swung back over the pyramid, and the descent began. The slaves, sick with fear, lost control of it, and the great stone plunged down faster and faster. I wondered if the mortar spread upon the top was thick enough to break its fall. Just as it struck the top in safety, he who stood upon it, gathering all his strength leaped high into the air to break the shock and fell motionless upon the stone. Then such a cry as went up, never before roused old Nilus from his dreams, or made the walls of the city to tremble. They bore him down from the tomb and placed him in the chariot of the king. Then the king's trumpeter sounded, and then Kufu spake:

"We have this day seen a deed the like of which we have never seen before, neither have our fathers told us of such a thing. Know, men of Egypt that he, the Shepherd stranger, who has risen upon the swinging stone, shall build the great pyramid, for he is worthy in my sight. The king has said."

Then the people cheered, but their faces were dark. And the charioteer of the king lashed his horses across the plain toward the city.

Of the great pyramid and of the mystery thereof, and of the strange builder, and of the sin of the king, I may not speak, for my lips are sealed.

A Son of the Celestial:
A Character

published in *Hesperian*, January 15, 1893

[The problem of the immigrant fascinated Cather from
the beginning, and we can see from this and later stories
that she was interested in the Chinese. That she did not write
more of these people is probably due to her belief expressed
in a sketch of a Chinese laundryman, published in the *Lincoln State Journal*, November 19, 1893: "It is as impossible
to graft into him the life and energy of this generation as
it is to transfuse living blood into the dried veins of the mummies who have slept in their mummy pits these two thousand years."

It is possible that her interest in the Orient was augmented by her reading of Lafcadio Hearn and Rudyard
Kipling, and by her natural love of antiquity.]

Ah lie me dead in the sunrise land,
Where the sky is blue and the hills are gray,
Where the camels doze in the desert sun,
And the sea gulls scream o'er the big blue bay.

Where the Hwang-Ho glides through the golden sand,
And the herons play in the rushes tall,
Where pagoda rise upon every hill
And the peach trees bloom by the Chinese wall.

Where the great grim gods sit still in the dark,
And lamps burn dim at their carven feet,

And their eyes like the eyes of the serpent king
Flash green through the dusk of the incense sweet.

Though deep under ground I shall see the sun,
And shall feel the stretch of the blue overhead,
And the gems that gleam on the breast of the god,
And shall smell the scent of the peach—though dead.

[This little word picture like an old silk print gives us
an early example of Cather's ability to write about that
which she hadn't actually seen or experienced, to convey
her feeling for that "terrible antiquity" which may seem cold
and lifeless but which her words bring to the mellow glow
of something always vital but only today remembered.]

Most of the world knew him only as Yung Le Ho, one of
the few white-haired Chinamen who were to be seen about the
streets of San Francisco. His cue was as long as that of any
other John, and with the exception of wearing spectacles, he
adhered strictly to his national costume. He sat all day long in
an open bazaar where he worked in silk and ivory and sandal
wood. Americans who had lived there long said he must be
worth a vast deal of money, for Yung was the best workman in
the city. All the ladies who were enthusiastic over Chinese art
bought his painted silken birds, and beautiful lacquered boxes,
his bronze vases, his little ivory gods and his carved sandal wood,
and paid him whatsoever he demanded for them. Had he possessed a dozen hands he might have sold the work of all of
them; as it was, he was very skillful with two. Yung was like
Michel Angelo, he allowed no one to touch his work but himself;
he did it all, rough work and delicate. When the ship brought
him strange black boxes with a sweet spicy odor about them, he
opened them with his own hands and took out the yellow ivory
tusks, and the bales of silk, and the blocks of shining ebony.
And no hands but his touched them until they were fashioned
into the beautiful things with which the ladies of San Francisco
loved to adorn their drawing rooms.

Day after day he sat in his stall, cross-legged and silent like
the gods of his country, carving his ivory into strange images and
his sandal wood into shapes of foliage and birds. Sometimes he
cut it into the shapes of foliage of his own land; the mulberry
and apricot and chestnut and juniper that grew about the sacred
mountain; the bamboo and camphor tree, and the rich Indian
bean, and the odorous camellias and japonicas that grew far to
the south on the low banks of the Yang-Tse-Kiang. Sometimes
he cut shapes and leaves that were not of earth, but were things
he had seen in his dreams when the Smoke was on him.

[This idea of carving things seen in dreams or night-
mares comes out a little later in "On the Divide."]

There were some people beside the artistic public who knew
Yung; they were the linguistic scholars of the city—there are a
few of them, even so far west as San Francisco. The two or three
men who knew a little Sanskrit and attacked an extract from
the Vedas now and then, used often to go to Yung to get help.
For the little whitehaired Chinaman knew Sanskrit as thoroughly
as his own tongue. The professors had a good deal of respect
for Yung, though they never told anyone of it, and kept him
completely obscured in the background as professors and doctors
of philosophy always do persons whom they consider "doubtful"
acquaintances.

[This reflection on the scholars of the west as against
those of the east gives Willa Cather a chance to get even a
little with the professors at the University of Nebraska who
considered her and her talents "doubtful." Yung found American schoolmen distasteful. So, in certain cases, did Cather.]

Yung never pushed himself forward, nor courted the learned
gentlemen. He always gave them what they wanted, then shut
up like a clam and no more could be gotten out of him. Perhaps
Yung did not have quite as much respect for the gentlemen as
they had for him. He had seen a good many countries and a

good many people, and he knew knowledge from pedantry. He found American schoolmen distasteful. "Too muchee good to know muchee," he once sarcastically remarked. Of course Yung was only a heathen Chinee who bowed down to wood and stone, his judgment in this and other matter does not count for much.

There was one American whom Yung took to his heart and loved, if a Chinaman can love, and that was old Ponter. Ponter was one of the most learned men who ever drifted into 'Frisco, but his best days were over before he came. He had held the chair of Sanskrit in a western university for years, but he could drink too much beer and was too good a shot at billiards to keep that place forever, so the college had requested his resignation. He went from place to place until at last he drifted into San Francisco, where he stayed.

[We have already seen Lou, who dies for an ideal—mad though it be, mad because other people do not tolerate him. We have seen Peter, who destroys himself because he can't stand the loss of the artistic and the substitution of the materialistic. Now we have the scholar who is likewise a misfit—too cosmopolitan, too broad for his contemporaries. We meet this type again in the lawyer of "A Sculptor's Funeral" and in the alcoholic musician Wunsch of *Song of the Lark*. And in a way poor Ponter is a forerunner of St. Peter, the professor of *The Professor's House*. The professor has no excesses except study; he is a misfit, nevertheless, because of the delicacy of his feeling and the acuteness of his perceptions.]

He went clear down to the mud sills there. How he lived no one knew. He did some copying for the lawyers, and he waited on the table in a third-rate boarding house, and he smoked a great deal of opium. Yung, too, loved the Smoke; perhaps it was that as much as Sanskrit that drew the two men together. At any rate, as soon as Yung's bazaar was closed, they went together down to his dark little den in the Chinese quarters, and there they talked Buddha and Confucius and Lao-tse till midnight. Then they went across the hall to the Seven Portals of Paradise. There they each took a mat and each his own sweet pipe with bowls of jade and mouthpieces of amber—Yung had given Ponter one— and pulled a few steady puffs and were in bliss till morning.

To Ponter, Yung told a good deal of his history. Not in regular narrative form, for he never talked about himself long, but he let it out bit by bit. When he was a boy he lived in Nanking, the oldest city of the oldest empire, where the great schools are and the tallest pagoda in the world rears its height of shining porcelain. There he had been educated, and had learned all the wisdom of the Chinese. He became tired of all that after awhile; tired of the rice paper books and of the masters in their black gowns, of the blue mountains and of the shadows of the great tower that fell sharp upon the yellow pavement in the glare of the sun. He went south; down the great canal in a red barge with big sails like dragon's wings. He came to Soutcheofou that is built upon the water-ways among the hills of Lake Taihoo. There the air smelt always of flowers, and the bamboo woods were green, and the rice fields shook in the wind. There the actors and jugglers gather the year around, and the Mandarins come to find brides for their harems. For once a god had loved a woman of that city, and he gave to her the charms of heaven, and since then the maidens of Soutcheofou have been the most beautiful in the Middle Kingdom, and have lived but to love and be loved. There Yung dwelt until he tired of pleasure. Then he went on foot across the barren plains of Thibet and the snow-capped Himalayas into India. He spent ten years in a temple there among the Brahamin priests, learning the sacred books. Then he fell in with some high caste Indian magicians and went with them. Of the next five years of his life Yung never spoke. Once, when Ponter questioned him about them, he laughed an ugly laugh which showed his broken yellow teeth and said:

"I not know what I did then. The devil he know, he and the fiends."

At last Yung came to California. There he took to carving and the Smoke.

Yung was rich; he might have dwelt in a fine house, but he

preferred to live among his own people in a little room across from the Seven Portals. He celebrated all the feasts and festivals with the other Chinamen, and bowed down to the gods in the joss house. He explained this to Ponter one day by saying:
"It is to keep us together, keep us Chinamen."

Wise Yung! It was not because of the cheapness of Chinese labor that the Chinese bill was enacted. It was because church and state feared this people who went about unproselyting and unproselyted. Who had printed centuries before Gutenberg was born, who had used anesthetics before chloroform was ever dreamed of. Who, in the new west, settled down and ate and drank and dressed as men had done in the days of the flood. Their terrible antiquity weighed upon us like a dead hand upon a living heart.

Yung did not know much about English literature. He liked the Bible, and he had picked up a copy of Hiawatha and was very fond of it. I suppose the artificialness of the poem appealed to his natural instinct and his training. Ponter was much disgusted with his taste, and one night he read the whole of Hamlet aloud to him, translating the archaic phrases into doggerel Chinese as he read. When he finished, Yung stared at him with a troubled look and said in Chinese:

"Yes, it is a great book, but I do not understand. If I were a young man I might try, but it is different. We cut our trees into shape, we bind our women into shape, we make our books into shape by rule. Your trees and women and books just grow, and yet they have shape. I do not understand. Come, let us smoke, the Smoke is good."

Ponter threw the book on the floor and arose and paced the floor shouting angrily:

"O yes, d—n you! You are a terrible people! I have come as near losing all human feeling and all human kinship as ever a white man did, but you make me shudder, every one of you. You live right under the sun's face, but you cannot feel his fire. The breast of God heaves just over you, but you never know it. You ought to be a feeling, passionate people, but you are as heartless and devilish as your accursed stone gods that leer at you in your Pagodas. Your sages learn rites, rites, rites, like so many parrots. They have forgotten how to think so long ago that they have forgotten they ever forgot. Your drama has outlived pathos, your science has outlived investigation, your poetry has outlived passion. Your very roses do not smell, they have forgotten how to give odor ages and ages ago. Your devilish gods have cursed you with immortality and you have outlived your souls. You are so old that you are born yellow and wrinkled and blind. You ought to have been buried centuries before Europe was civilized. You ought to have been wrapped in your mort cloth ages before our swaddling clothes were made. You are dead things that move!"

[This is quite a tirade just because the Chinese does not appreciate Hamlet, but it is about the way Willa Cather would feel. In her newspaper writings of this period, she scores the Lincoln people in just such a fashion when they fail to rise to an artistic occasion. She was vitriolic over those who failed to share her enthusiasm over *Camille;* she even abused Mark Twain because he didn't admire French novelists.

In "The Affair at Grover Station," we find the villain with yellow wrinkled finger tips—the sign of the ancient blood in his veins.]

Yung answered never a word, but smiled his hideous smile and went across to the Portals of Paradise, and lay down upon his mat, and drew long whiffs from his mouth piece, slowly, solemnly, as though he were doing sacrifice to some god. He dreams of his own country, dreams of the sea and the mountains and forests and the slopes of sunny land. When he awakes there is not much of his dream left, only masses and masses of color that haunt him all day.

"Ponter," said Yung one day as he sat cutting a little three-faced Vishnu in ivory, "when I die do not even bury me here. Let them go through the rites and then send me home. I must lie there while the flesh is yet on my bones. Let the funeral be grand. Let there be many mourners, and roast pigs, and rice and gin. Let the gin bowls be of real China, and let the coffin be a costly one like the coffins of Liauchau, there is money enough. Let my pipe stay in my hand, and put me on the first ship that sails."

Not long after that, Ponter arose from his mat one morning, and went over to waken Yung. But Yung would not waken any more. He had tasted his last ounce of the Smoke, and he lay with the mouthpiece in his mouth, and his fingers clutched about the bowl. Ponter sat down by him and said slowly:

"A white man has got pretty low down, Yung, when he takes to the Smoke and runs with a heathen. But I liked you, Yung, as much as a man can like a stone thing. You weren't a bad fellow, sir. You knew more Sanskrit than Muller dreamed of knowing, and more ethics than Plato, a long sight, and more black art than the devil himself. You knew more than any man I ever saw, more good and more evil. You could do a neater job with a knife and a piece of bone than any man in civilization, and you got away with more Smoke than any yaller man I ever saw. You were not a bad fellow Yung, but your heart has been dead these last six thousand years, and it was better for your carcass to follow suit."

He went out and got the finest lacquered coffin in 'Frisco and he put old Yung inside with a pound of rice and his pipe and a pound of the best opium in the market. Then he nailed him up singing: "*Ibimus, Ibimus, Utcumque praecedes, supernum, Carpere iter comites parati,*" softly as he hammered away.

He took the body to the graveyard where the Chinamen went through the rites. Then they loaded Yung on an outbound steamer. Next day Ponter stood on the docks and watched her plowing her way toward the Celestial shore.

🦢 The Clemency of the Court

published in *Hesperian*, October 26, 1893

[Willa Cather visited the state penitentiary in Lincoln at least twice while she was in the university and reported favorably on the administration. Therefore one would conclude that this story did not come out of what she saw there. Serge is a forerunner of Frank Shabata of *O Pioneers* who killed his wife Marie and Emil Bergson, and whom Alexandra visited at the state prison. But the episode of Frank Shabata does not carry the brutal flavor of "The Clemency of the Court." Serge is a serf, treated like a serf, a slave. His treatment reminds one of the treatment of Jean Valjean in *Les Misérables*. The story seems born of Willa's reading of Hugo, Maupassant, and probably Turgenev. The latter wrote a story in which a serf split open his master's skull with an axe. The futility of Serge's existence is borrowed from Maupassant. But the love of nature and the distrust of organized society are Cather's own.

The same type of incident appears in *Shadows on the Rock*, the tale of poor Bichet who was hanged for stealing two pots.]

"Damn you! What do you mean by giving me hooping like that?"

Serge Povolitchky folded his big workworn hands and was silent. That helpless, doglike silence of his always had a bad effect on the guard's temper, and he turned on him afresh.

"What do you mean by it, I say? Maybe you think you are some better than the rest of us; maybe you think you are too good to work. We'll see about that."

Serge still stared at the ground, muttering in a low, husky voice, "I could make some broom, I think. I would try much."

"O, you would, would you? So you don't try now? We will see about that. We will send you to a school where you can learn to hoop barrels. We have a school here, a little, dark school, a night school, you know, where we teach men a great many things."

Serge looked up appealingly into the man's face and his eyelids quivered with terror, but he said nothing, so the guard continued:

"Now I'll sit down here and watch you hoop them barrels, and if you don't do a mighty good job, I'll report you to the warden and have you strung up as high as a rope can twist."

Serge turned to his work again. He did wish the guard would not watch him; it seemed to him that he could hoop all right if he did not feel the guard's eye on him all the time. His hands had never done anything but dig and plow and they were so clumsy he could not make them do right. The guard began to swear and Serge trembled so he could scarcely hold his hammer. He was very much afraid of the dark cell. His cell was next to it and often at night he had heard the men groaning and shrieking when the pain got bad, and begging the guards for water. He heard one poor fellow get delirious when the rope cut and strangled him, and talk to his mother all night long, begging her not to hug him so hard, for she hurt him.

The guard went out and Serge worked on, never even stopping to wipe the sweat from his face. It was strange he could not hoop as well as the other men, for he was as strong and stalwart as they, but he was so clumsy at it. He thought he could work in the broom room if they would only let him. He had handled straw all his life, and it would seem good to work at the broom corn that had the scent of outdoors about it. But they said the broom room was full. He felt weak and sick all over, someway. He could not work in the house, he had never been indoors a whole day in his life until he came here.

Serge was born in the western part of the State, where he did not see many people. His mother was a handsome Russian girl, one of a Russian colony that a railroad had brought West to build grades. His father was supposed to be a railroad contractor, no one knew surely. At any rate by no will of his own or wish of his own, Serge existed. When he was a few months old, his mother had drowned herself in a pond so small that no one ever quite saw how she managed to do it.

Baba Skaldi, an old Russian woman of the colony, took Serge and brought him up among her own children. A hard enough life he had of it with her. She fed him what her children would not eat, and clothed him in what her children would not wear.

> [His situation sounds like that of Cosette in Victor
> Hugo's *Les Misérables*.]

She used to boast to *baba* Konach that she got a man's work out of the young rat. There was one pleasure in Serge's life with her. Often at night after she had beaten him and he lay sobbing on the floor in the corner, she would tell her children stories of Russia. They were beautiful stories, Serge thought. In spite of all her cruelty he never quite disliked *baba* Skaldi because she could tell such fine stories. The story told oftenest was one about her own brother. He had done something wrong, Serge could never make out just what, and had been sent to Siberia. His wife had gone with him. The *baba* told all about the journey to Siberia as she had heard it from returned convicts; all about the awful marches in the mud and ice, and how on the boundary line the men would weep and fall down and kiss the soil of Russia. When her brother reached the prison, he and his wife used to work in the mines. His wife was too good a woman to get on well in the prison, the *baba* said, and one day she had been knouted to death at the command of an officer. After that her husband tried in many ways to kill himself, but they always caught him at it.

At last, one night, he bit deep into his arm and tore open the veins with his teeth and bled to death. The officials found him dead with his teeth still set in his lacerated arm.

[Here is the story within a story which Cather was to use so often. The story here, though not the same as that of Peter and Pavel in *My Ántonia*, is just as horrible.

The Russian settlement in Webster County was in the northwest part, not too far from the Cather farm.]

When she finished the little boys used to cry out at the awfulness of it, but their mother would soothe them and tell them that such things could not possibly happen here, because in this country the State took care of people. In Russia there was no State, only the great Tzar. Ah, yes, the State would take care of the children! The *baba* had heard a Fourth-of-July speech once, and she had great ideas about the State.

Serge used to listen till his eyes grew big, and play that he was that brother of the *baba's* and that he had been knouted by the officials and that was why his little legs smarted so. Sometimes he would steal out in the snow in his bare feet and take a sunflower stalk and play he was hunting bears in Russia, or would walk about on the little frozen pond where his mother had died and think it was the Volga. Before his birth his mother used to go off alone and sit in the snow for hours to cool the fever in her head and weep and think about her own country. The feeling for the snow and the love for it seemed to go into the boy's blood, somehow. He was never so happy as when he saw the white flakes whirling.

When he was twelve years old a farmer took him to work for his board and clothes. Then a change came into Serge's life. That first morning as he stood, awkward and embarrassed, in the Davis kitchen, holding his hands under his hat and shuffling his bare feet over the floor, a little yellow cur came up to him and began to rub its nose against his leg. He held out his hand and the dog licked it. Serge bent over him, stroking him and calling him Russian pet names. For the first time in his lonely loveless life, he felt that something liked him.

The Davises gave him enough to eat and enough to wear and they did not beat him. He could not read or talk English, so they treated him very much as they did the horses. He stayed there seven years because he did not have enough sense to know that he was utterly miserable and could go somewhere else, and because the Slavonic instinct was in him to labor and keep silent. The dog was the only thing that made life endurable. He called the dog Matushka, which was the name by which he always thought of his mother. He used to go to town sometimes, but he did not enjoy it, people frightened him so. When the town girls used to pass him dressed in their pretty dresses with their clean, white hands, he thought of his bare feet and his rough, tawny hair and his ragged overalls, and he would slink away behind his team with Matushka. On the coldest winter nights he always slept in the barn with the dog for a bedfellow. As he and the dog cuddled up to each other in the hay, he used to think about things, most often about Russia and the State. Russia must be a fine country but he was glad he did not live there, because the State was much better. The State was so very good to people. Once a man came there to get Davis to vote for him, and he asked Serge who his father was. Serge said he had none. The man only smiled and said, "Well, never mind, the State will be a father to you, my lad, and a mother."

Serge had a vague idea that the State must be an abstract thing of some kind, but he always thought of her as a woman with kind eyes, dressed in white with a yellow light about her head, and a little child in her arms, like the picture of the virgin in the church. He always took off his hat when he passed the court house in town, because he had an idea that it had something to do with the State someway. He thought he owed the State a great deal for something, he did not know what; that the State would do something great for him some day, because he had no one else. After his chores he used to go and sit down in the corral with his back against the wire fence and his chin on his knees and look at the sunset. He never got much pleasure out of it, it was always like watching something die. It made him feel desolate and lonesome to see so much sky, yet he always sat there, irresistibly fascinated. It was not much wonder that his eyes grew dull and his brain heavy, sitting there evening after evening with his dog, staring across the brown, windswept prairies that never lead anywhere, but always stretch on and on in a great yearning for something they never reach. He liked the plains because he thought they must be like the Russian steppes, and because they seemed like himself, always lonely and empty-handed.

One day when he was helping Davis top a haystack, Davis got angry at the dog for some reason and kicked at it. Serge threw out his arm and caught the blow himself. Davis, angrier than before, caught the hatchet and laid the dog's head open. He threw down the bloody hatchet and, telling Serge to go clean it, he bent over his work. Serge stood motionless, as dazed and helpless as if he had been struck himself. The dog's tail quivered and its legs moved weakly, its breath came through its throat in faint, wheezing groans and from its bleeding head its two dark eyes, clouded with pain, still looked lovingly up at him. He dropped on his knees beside it and lifted its poor head against his heart. It was only for a moment. It laid its paw upon his arm and then was still. Serge laid the dog gently down and rose. He took the bloody hatchet and went up behind his master. He did not hurry and he did not falter. He raised the weapon and struck down, clove through the man's skull from crown to chin, even as the man had struck the dog. Then he went to the barn to get a shovel to bury the dog. As he passed the house, the woman called out to him to tell her husband to come to dinner. He answered simply, "He will not come to dinner today. I killed him behind the haystack."

She rushed from the house with a shriek and when she caught sight of what lay behind the haystack, she started for the nearest farm house. Serge went to the barn for the shovel. He had no consciousness of having done wrong. He did not even think about the dead man. His heart seemed to cling to the side of his chest, the only thing he had ever loved was dead. He went to the hay-mow where he and Matushka slept every night and took a box from under the hay from which he drew a red silk handkerchief, the only "pretty thing," and indeed, the only handkerchief he had ever possessed. He went back to the hay-stack and never once glancing at the man, took the dog in his arms.

There was one spot on the farm that Serge liked. He and Matushka used often to go there on Sundays. It was a little, marshy pool, grown up in cat-tails and reeds with a few scraggy willows on the banks. The grass used to be quite green there, not red and gray like the buffalo grass. There he carried Matushka. He laid him down and began to dig a grave under the willows. The worst of it was that the world went on just as usual. The winds were laughing away among the rushes, sending the water slapping against the banks. The meadow larks sang in the corn field and the sun shone just as it did yesterday and all the while Matushka was dead and his own heart was breaking in his breast. When the hole was deep enough, he took the handkerchief from his pocket and tied it neatly about poor Matushka's mangled head. Then he pulled a few wild roses and laid them on its breast and fell sobbing across the body of the little yellow cur. Presently he saw the neighbors coming over the hill with Mrs. Davis, and he laid the dog in the grave and covered him up.

About his trial Serge remembered very little, except that they had taken him to the court house and he had not found the State. He remembered that the room was full of people, and some of them talked a great deal, and that the young lawyer who defended him cried when his sentence was read. The lawyer seemed to understand it all, about Matushka and the State, and everything. Serge thought he was the handsomest and most learned man in the world. He had fought day and night for Serge, without sleeping and almost without eating. Serge could always see him as he looked when he paced up and down the platform, shaking the hair back from his brow and trying to get it through the heads of the jurymen that love was love, even if it was for a dog. The people told Serge that his sentence had been commuted from death to imprisonment for life by the clemency of the court, but he knew well enough that it was by the talk of that lawyer. He had not deserted Serge after the trial even, he had come with him to the prison and had seen him put on his convict clothing.

"It's the State's badge of knighthood, Serge," he said, bitterly, touching one of the stripes. "The old emblem of the royal garter, to show that your blood is royal."

[On the whole, Cather's pictures of lawyers are quite favorable. In "The Sculptor's Funeral," Laird, although a drunkard, is in a way admirable. Judge Pommeroy in *A Lost Lady* was a close friend of Captain Forrester.]

Just as the six o'clock whistle was blowing, the guard returned.

"You are to go to your cell tonight, and if you don't do no better in the morning, you are to be strung up in the dark cell, come along."

Serge laid down his hammer and followed him to his cell. Some of the men made little book shelves for their cells and pasted pictures on the walls. Serge had neither books nor pictures, and he did not know how to ask for any, so his cell was bare. The cells were only six by four, just a little larger than a grave.

As a rule, the prisoners suffered from no particular cruelty, only from the elimination of all those little delicacies that make men men. The aim of the prison authorities seemed to be to make everything unnecessarily ugly and repulsive. The little things in which fine feeling is most truly manifest received no respect at all. Serge's bringing up had been none of the best, but it took him some time to get used to eating without knife or fork the indifferent food thrust in square tin bowls under the door of his cell. Most of the men read at night, but he could not read, so he lay tossing on his iron bunk, wondering how the fields were looking. His greatest deprivation was that he could not see the fields. The love of the plains was strong in him. It had always been so, ever since he was a little fellow, when the brown grass was up to his shoulders and the straw stacks were the golden mountains of fairyland. Men from the cities on the hills never understand this love, but the men from the plain country know what I mean. When he had tired himself out with longing, he turned over and fell asleep. He was never impatient, for he believed that the State would come some day and explain, and take him to herself. He watched for her coming every day, hoped for it every night.

In the morning the work went no better. They watched him all the time and he could do nothing. At noon they took him into the dark cell and strung him up. They put his arms behind him and tied them together, then passed the rope about his neck, drawing arms up as high as they could be stretched, so that if he let them "sag" he would strangle, and so they left him. The cell was perfectly bare and was not long enough for a man to lie at full length in. The prisoners were told to stand up, so Serge stood. At night his arms were let down long enough for him to eat his bread and water, then he was roped up again. All night long he stood there. By the end of the next day the pain in his arms was almost unendurable. They were paralyzed from the shoulder down so that the guard had to feed him like a baby. The next day and the next night and the next day he lay upon the floor of the cell, suffering as though every muscle were being individually wrenched from his arms. He had not been out of the bare cell for four days. All the ventilation came through some little augur holes in the door and the heat and odor were becoming unbearable. He had thought on the first night that the pain would kill him before morning, but he had endured over eighty-four hours of it and when the guard came in with his bread and water he found him lying with his eyes closed and his teeth set on his lip. He roused him with a kick and held the bread and water out to him, but Serge took only the water.

"Rope too tight?" growled the guard. Serge said nothing. He was almost dead now and he wanted to finish for he could not hoop barrels.

"Gittin' so stuck up you can't speak, are you? Well, we'll just stretch you up a bit tighter." And he gave the stick in the rope another vicious twist that almost tore the arms from their sockets and sent a thrill of agony through the man's whole frame. Then Serge was left alone. The fever raged in his veins and about midnight his thirst was intolerable. He lay with his mouth open and his tongue hanging out. The pain in his arms made his whole body tremble like a man with a chill. He could no longer keep his arms up and the ropes were beginning to strangle him. He did not call for help. He had heard poor devils shriek for help all night long and get no relief. He suffered, as the people of his mother's nation, in hopeless silence. The blood of the serf was in him, blood that has cowered beneath the knout for centuries and uttered no complaint. Then the State would surely come soon, she would not let them kill him. His mother, the State!

He fell into a half stupor. He dreamed about what the *baba* used to tell about the bargemen in their bearskin coats coming down the Volga in the spring when the ice had broken up and gone out; about how the wolves used to howl and follow the sledges across the snow in the starlight.

[See the story of Peter and Pavel in *My Ántonia*.]

That cold, white snow, that lay in ridges and banks! He thought he felt it in his mouth and he awoke and found himself licking the stone floor. He thought how lovely the plains would look in the morning when the sun was up; how the sunflowers would shake themselves in the wind, how the corn leaves would shine and how the cob-webs would sparkle all over the grass and the air would be clear and blue, the birds would begin to sing, the colts would run and jump in the pasture and the black bull would begin to bellow for his corn.

The rope grew tighter and tighter. The State must come soon now. He thought he felt the dog's cold nose against his throat. He tried to call its name, but the sound only came in an inarticulate gurgle. He drew his knees up to his chin and died.

And so it was that this great mother, the State, took this willful, restless child of hers and put him to sleep in her bosom.

✣ "The Fear That Walks by Noonday"

published in *Sombrero*, 1895 (First Prize Story)

[At a football game one afternoon Dorothy Canfield happened to see Willa Cather on the bleachers behind her. After the game she waited for Willa and said, "I just had a good idea. What about the ghost of a football player that comes back and wins the game for his team?"

"Wonderful," Willa said. "I'll use it."

Dorothy thought no more of it until the story appeared. Of the ten-dollar prize which it won, Willa gave Dorothy five.

When, after both women were famous, this story was republished, Dorothy Canfield Fisher was amused, Willa Cather distressed. In response to inquiry at that time, Miss Cather said that when she wrote the story, nobody seemed so wonderful as Henry James. At another time she said, "I began by imitating Henry James."]

"Where is my shin guard? Horton, you lazy dog, get your duds off, won't you? Why didn't you dress at the hotel with the rest of us? There's got to be a stop to your blamed eccentricities some day," fumed Reggie, hunting wildly about in a pile of overcoats.

Horton began pulling off his coat with that air of disinterested deliberation he always assumed to hide any particular nervousness. He was to play two positions that day, both half and full, and he knew it meant stiff work.

"What do you think of the man who plays in Morrison's place, Strike?" he asked as he took off his shoes.

"I can tell you better in about half an hour; I suppose the

'Injuns' knew what they were about when they put him there."

"They probably put him there because they hadn't another man who could even look like a full back. He played quarter badly enough, if I remember him."

"I don't see where they get the face to play us at all. They would never have scored last month if it hadn't been for Morrison's punting. That fellow played a great game, but the rest of them are light men, and their coach is an idiot. That man would have made his mark if he'd lived. He could play different positions just as easily as Chum-Chum plays different roles—pardon the liberty, Fred—and then there was that awful stone wall strength of his to back it; he was a mighty man."

"If you are palpitating to know why the 'Injuns' insist on playing us, I'll tell you; it's for blood. Exhibition game be damned! It's to break our bones they're playing. We were surprised when they didn't let down on us harder as soon as the fellow died, but they have been cherishing their wrath, they haven't lost an ounce of it, and they are going into us to-day for vengeance."

"Well, their sentiments are worthy, but they haven't got the players."

"Let up on Morrison there, Horton," shouted Reggie, "we sent flowers and sympathies at the time, but we are not going to lose this game out of respect to his memory: shut up and get your shin guard on. I say, Nelson, if you don't get out of here with that cigarette I'll kick you out. I'll get so hungry I'll break training rules. Besides, the coach will be in here in a minute going around smelling our breaths like our mammas used to do, if he catches a scent of it. I'm humming glad it's the last week of training; I couldn't stand another day of it. I brought a whole pocket full of cigars, and I'll have one well under way before the cheering is over. Won't we see the town to-night, Freddy?"

Horton nodded and laughed one of his wicked laughs. "Training has gone a shade too far this season. It's all nonsense to say that nobody but hermits and anchorites can play foot ball. A Methodist parson don't have to practice half such rigid abstinence as a man on the eleven." And he kicked viciously at the straw on the floor as he remembered the supper parties he had renounced, the invitations he had declined, and the pretty faces he had avoided in the last three months.

"Five minutes to three!" said the coach, as he entered, pounding on the door with his cane. Strike began to hunt frantically for the inflater, one of the tackles went striding around the room seeking his nose protector with lamentations and profanity, and the rest of the men got on their knees and began burrowing in the pile of coats for things they had forgotten to take out of their pockets. Reggie began to hurry his men and make the usual encouraging remarks to the effect that the universe was not created to the especial end that they should win that foot ball game, that the game was going to the men who kept the coolest heads and played the hardest ball. The coach rapped impatiently again, and Horton and Reggie stepped out together, the rest following them. As soon as Horton heard the shouts which greeted their appearance, his eyes flashed, and he threw his head back like a cavalry horse that hears the bugle sound a charge. He jumped over the ropes and ran swiftly across the field, leaving Reggie to saunter along at his leisure, bowing to the ladies in the grand stand and on the tally-hos as he passed.

When he reached the lower part of the field he found a hundred Marathon college men around the team yelling and shouting their encouragement. Reggie promptly directed the policemen to clear the field, and, taking his favorite attitude, his feet wide apart and his body very straight, he carelessly tossed the quarter into the air.

"Line 'em up, Reggie, line 'em up. Let us into it while the divine afflatus lasts," whispered Horton.

The men sprang to their places, and Reggie forgot the ladies on the tally-hos; the color came to his face, and he drew himself up and threw every sinew of his little body on a tension. The crowd outside began to cheer again, as the wedge started off for north goal. The western men were poor on defensive work, and the Marathon wedge gained ground on the first play. The first impetus of success was broken by Horton fumbling and losing the ball. The eleven looked rather dazed at this, and Horton was the most dazed looking man of them all, for he did not indulge in that kind of thing often. Reggie could scarcely believe his senses, and stood staring at Horton in unspeakable amazement, but Horton only spread out his hands and stared at them as though to see if they were still there. There was little time for reflection or conjecture. The western men gave their Indian yell and prepared to play; their captain sang out his signals, and the rushing began. In spite of the desperate resistance on the part of Reggie's men, the ball went steadily south, and in twelve minutes the "Injuns" had scored. No one quite knew how they did it, least of all their bewildered opponents. They did some bad fumbling on the five-yard line, but though Reggie's men fell all over the ball, they did not seem to be able to take hold of it.

"Call in a doctor," shouted Reggie; "they're paralyzed in the arms, every one of 'em."

Time was given to bandage a hurt, and half a dozen men jumped over the ropes and shot past the policemen and rushed up to Reggie, pitifully asking what the matter was.

"Matter! I don't know! They're all asleep or drunk. Go kick them, pound them, anything to get them awake." And the little captain threw his sweater over his shoulder and swore long and loud at all mankind in general and Frederick Horton in particular. Horton turned away without looking at him. He was a younger man than Reggie, and, although he had had more experiences, they were not of the kind that counted much with the men of the eleven. He was very proud of being the captain's right-hand man, and it cut him hard to fail him.

"I believe I've been drugged, Black," he said, turning to the right tackle. "I am as cold as ice all over and I can't use my arms at all; I've a notion to ask Reggie to call in a sub."

"Don't, for heaven's sake, Horton; he is almost frantic now; believe it would completely demoralize the team; you have never laid off since you were on the eleven, and if you should now when you have no visible hurt it would frighten them to death."

"I feel awful, I am so horribly cold."

"So am I, so are all the fellows; see how the "Injuns" are shivering over there, will you? There must be a cold wave; see how Strike's hair is blowing down in his eyes."

"The cold wave seems to be confined to our locality," remarked Horton in a matter-of-fact way; but in somewhat strained tones. "The girls out there are all in their summer dresses without wraps, and the wind which is cutting our faces all up don't even stir the ribbon on their hats."

"Y-a-s, horribly draughty place, this," said Black blankly.

"Horribly draughty as all out doors," said Horton with a grim laugh.

"Bur-r-r!" said Strike, as he handed his sweater over to a substitute and took his last pull at a lemon, "this wind is awful; I never felt anything so cold; it's a raw, wet cold that goes clear into the marrow of a fellow's bones. I don't see where it comes from; there is no wind outside the ropes apparently."

"The winds blow in such strange directions here," said Horton, picking up a straw and dropping it. "It goes straight down with force enough to break several camels' backs."

"Ugh! it's as though the firmament had sprung a leak and the winds were sucking in from the other side."

"Shut your mouths, both of you," said Reggie, with an emphatic oath. "You will have them all scared to death; there's a panic now, that's what's the matter, one of those quiet, stupid panics that are the worst to manage. Laugh, Freddie, laugh hard; get up some enthusiasm; come, you, shut up, if you can't do any better than that. Start the yell, Strike, perhaps that will fetch them."

A weak yell that sounded like an echo rose from the field and the Marathon men outside the ropes caught it up and cheered till the air rang. This seemed to rouse the men on the field, and they got to their places with considerable energy.

Reggie gave an exultant cry, as the western men soon lost the ball, and his men started it north and kept steadily gaining. They were within ten yards of the goal, when suddenly the ball rose serenely out of a mass of struggling humanity and flew back twenty, forty, sixty, eighty yards toward the southern goal! But the half was versed in his occupation; he ran across and stood under the ball, waiting for it with out-stretched arms. It seemed to Horton that the ball was all day in falling; it was right over him and yet it seemed to hang back from him, like Chum-Chum when she was playing with him. With an impatient oath he ground his teeth together and bowed his body forward to hold it with his breast, and even his knees if need be, waiting with strength and eagerness enough in his arm to burst the ball to shreds. The crowd shouted with delight, but suddenly caught its breath; the ball fell into his arms, between them, through them, and rolled on the ground at his feet. Still he stood there with his face raised and his arms stretched upward in an attitude ridiculously suggestive of prayer. The men rushed fiercely around him shouting and reviling; his arms dropped like lead to his side, and he stood without moving a muscle, and in his face there was a look that a man might have who had seen what he loved best go down to death through his very arms and had not been able to close them and save. Reggie came up with his longest oaths on his lip, but when he saw Horton's face he checked himself and said with that sweetness of temper that always came to him when he saw the black bottom of despair,

"Keep quiet, fellows, Horton's all right, only he is a bit nervous." Horton moved for the first time and turned on the little captain, "You can say anything else you like, Reggie, but if you say I am scared I'll knock you down."

"No, Fred, I don't mean that; we must hang together, man, every one of us, there are powers enough against us," said Reggie, sadly. The men looked at each other with startled faces. So long as Reggie swore there was hope, but when he became gentle all was lost.

In another part of the field another captain fell on his full-back's neck and cried, "Thomas, my son, how did you do it? Morrison in his palmiest days never made a better lift than that."

"I-I didn't do it, I guess; some of the other fellows did; Towmen, I think."

"Not much I didn't," said Towmen, "you were so excited you didn't know what you were doing. You did it, though; I saw it go right up from your foot."

"Well, it may be," growled the "Injun" half, "but when I make plays like that I'd really like to be conscious of them. I must be getting to be a darned excitable individual if I can punt eighty yards and never know it."

"Heavens! how cold it is. This is a great game, though; I don't believe they'll score."

"I don't; they act like dead men; I would say their man Horton was sick or drunk if all the others didn't act just like him."

The "Injuns" lost the ball again, but when Reggie's men were working it north the same old punting scheme was worked somewhere by someone in the "Injuns'" ranks. This time Amack, the right half, ran bravely for it; but when he was almost beneath it he fell violently to the ground, for no visible reason, and lay there struggling like a man in a fit. As they were taking him off the field, time was called for the first half. Reggie's friends and several of his professors broke through the gang of policemen and rushed up to him. Reggie stepped in front of his men and spoke to the first man who came up, "If you say one word or ask one question I'll quit the field. Keep away from me and from my men. Let us alone." The paleness that showed through the dirt on Reggie's face alarmed the visitors, and they went away as quickly as they had come. Reggie and his men lay down and covered themselves with their overcoats, and lay there shuddering under that icy wind that sucked down upon them. The men were perfectly quiet and each one crept off by himself. Even the substitutes who brought them lemons and water did not talk much; they had neither disparagement nor encouragement to offer; they sat around and shivered like the rest. Horton hid his face on his arm and lay like one stunned. He muttered the score, 18 to 0, but he did not feel the words his lips spoke, nor comprehend them. Like most dreamy, imaginative men, Horton was not very much at home in college. Sometimes in his loneliness he tried to draw near to the average man, and be on a level with him, and in so doing made a consummate fool of himself, as dreamers always do when they try to get themselves awake.

[Horton now becomes a typical Cather character, like Claude Wheeler, who is too fine, too sensitive for his environment.]

He was awkward and shy among women, silent and morose among men. He was tolerated in the societies because he could write good poetry, and in the clubs because he could play foot ball. He was very proud of his accomplishments as a half back, for they made him seem like other men. However ornamental and useful a large imagination and sensitive temperament may be to a man of mature years, to a young man they are often very like a deformity which he longs to hide. He wondered what the captain would think of him and groaned. He feared Reggie as much as he adored him. Reggie was one of those men who, by the very practicality of their intellects, astonish the world. He was a glorious man for a college. He was brilliant, adaptable, and successful; yet all his brains he managed to cover up by a pate of tow hair, parted very carefully in the middle, and his iron strength was generally very successfully disguised by a very dudish exterior. In short, he possessed the one thing which is greater than genius, the faculty of clothing genius in such boundless good nature that it is offensive to nobody. Horton felt to a painful degree his inferiority to him in most things, and it was not pleasant to him to lose ground in the one thing in which he felt they could meet on an equal footing.

[Here is the situation of Claude Wheeler again—his feeling of inferiority to and admiration for the Erlichs and later David Gerhardt.]

Horton turned over and looked up at the leaden sky, feeling the wind sweep into his eyes and nostrils. He looked about him and saw the other men all lying down with their heads covered, as though they were trying to get away from the awful cold and the sense of Reggie's reproach. He wondered what was the matter with them; whether they had been drugged or mesmerized. He tried to remember something in all the books he had read that would fit the case, but his memory seemed as cold and dazed as the rest of him; he only remembered some hazy Greek, which read to the effect that the gods sometimes bring madness upon those they wish to destroy. And here was another proof that the world was going wrong—it was not a normal thing for him to remember any Greek.

He was glad when at last he heard Reggie's voice calling the men together; he went slowly up to him and said rather feebly, "I say, a little brandy wouldn't hurt us, would it? I am so awfully cold I don't know what the devil is the matter with me, Reggie, my arms are so stiff I can't use 'em at all."

Reggie handed him a bottle from his grip, saying briefly, "It can't make things any worse."

In the second half the Marathon men went about as though they were walking in their sleep. They seldom said anything, and the captain was beyond coaxing or swearing; he only gave his signals in a voice as hollow as if it came from an empty church. His men got the ball a dozen times, but they always lost it as soon as they got it, or, when they had worked it down to one goal the "Injun" would punt it back to the other. The very spectators sat still and silent, feeling that they were seeing something strange and unnatural. Every now and then some "Injun" would make a run, and a Marathon man would dash up and run beside him for a long distance without ever catching him, but with his hands hanging at his side. People asked the physicians in the audience what was the matter; but they shook their heads.

It was at this juncture that Freddie Horton awoke and bestirred himself. Horton was a peculiar player; he was either passive or brilliant. He could not do good line work; he could not help other men play. If he did anything he must take matters into his own hands, and he generally did; no one in the northwest had ever made such nervy, dashing plays as he; he seemed to have the faculty of making sensational and romantic situations in foot ball just as he did in poetry. He played with his imagination. The second half was half over, and as yet he had done nothing but blunder. His honor and the honor of the team had been trampled on. As he thought of it the big veins stood out in his forehead and he set his teeth hard together. At last his opportunity came, or rather he made it. In a general scramble for the ball he caught it in his arms and ran. He held the ball tight against his breast until he could feel his heart knocking against the hard skin; he was conscious of nothing but the wind whistling in his ears and the ground flying under his feet, and the fact that he had ninety yards to run. Both teams followed him as fast as they could, but Horton was running for his honor, and his feet scarcely touched the earth. The spectators, who had waited all afternoon for a chance to shout, now rose to their feet and all the lungs full of pent-up enthusiasm burst forth. But the gods are not to be frustrated for a man's honor or his dishonor, and when Freddie Horton was within ten yards of the goal he threw his arms over his head and leaped into the air and fell. When the crowd reached him they found no marks of injury except the blood and foam at his mouth where his teeth had bitten into his lip. But when they looked at him the men of both teams turned away shuddering. His knees were drawn up to his chin; his hands were dug into the ground on either side of him; his face was the livid, bruised blue of a man who dies with apoplexy; his eyes were wide open and full of unspeakable horror and fear, glassy as ice, and still as though they had been frozen fast in their sockets.

It was an hour before they brought him to, and then he lay perfectly silent and would answer no questions. When he was stretched obliquely across the seats of a carriage going home he spoke for the first time.

"Give me your hand, Reggie; for God's sake let me feel

something warm and human. I am awful sorry, Reggie; I tried
for all my life was worth to make that goal, but—" he drew the
captain's head down to his lips and whispered something that
made Reggie's face turn white and the sweat break out on his
forehead. He drew big Horton's head upon his breast and stroked
it as tenderly as a woman.

PART II

There was silence in the dining room of the Exeter house
that night when the waiters brought in the last course. The evening had not been a lively one. The defeated men were tired
with that heavy weariness which follows defeat, and the victors
seemed strained and uneasy in their manners. They all avoided
speaking of the game and forced themselves to speak of things
they could not fix their minds upon. Reggie sat at the head of
the table correct and faultless. Reggie was always correct, but
to-night there was very little of festal cheer about him. He was
cleanly shaved, his hair was parted with the usual mathematical
accuracy. A little strip of black court plaster covered the only
external wound defeat had left. But his face was as white as
the spotless expanse of his shirt bosom, and his eyes had big
black circles under them like those of a man coming down with
the fever. All evening he had been nervous and excited; he had
not eaten anything and was evidently keeping something under.
Every one wondered what it was, and yet feared to hear it.
When asked about Horton he simply shuddered, mumbled something, and had his wine glass filled again.

Laughter or fear are contagious, and by the time the last
course was on the table every one was as nervous as Reggie. The
talk started up fitfully now and then but it soon died down, and
the weakly attempts at wit were received in silence.

Suddenly every one became conscious of the awful cold
and inexplicable downward draught that they had felt that afternoon. Every one was determined not to show it. No one pre-
tended to even notice the flicker of the gas jets, and the fact that

their breath curled upward from their mouths in little wreaths of vapor. Every one turned his attention to his plate and his glass stood full beside him. Black made some remarks about politics, but his teeth chattered so he gave it up. Reggie's face was working nervously, and he suddenly rose to his feet and said in a harsh, strained voice,

"Gentlemen, you had one man on your side this afternoon who came a long journey to beat us. I mean the man who did that wonderful punting and who stood before the goal when Mr. Horton made his run. I propose the first toast of the evening to the twelfth man, who won the game. Need I name him?"

The silence was as heavy as before. Reggie extended his glass to the captain beside him, but suddenly his arm changed direction; he held the glass out over the table and tipped it in empty air as though touching glasses with some one. The sweat broke out on Reggie's face; he put his glass to his lips and tried to drink, but only succeeded in biting out a big piece of the rim of his wine glass. He spat the glass out quickly upon his plate and began to laugh, with the wine oozing out between his white lips. Then everyone laughed; leaning upon each other's shoulders, they gave way to volleys and shrieks of laughter, waving their glasses in hands that could scarcely hold them. The negro waiter, who had been leaning against the wall asleep, came forward rubbing his eyes to see what was the mattter. As he approached the end of the table he felt that chilling wind, with its damp, wet smell like the air from a vault, and the unnatural cold that drove to the heart's center like a knife blade.

"My Gawd!" he shrieked, dropping his tray, and with an inarticulate gurgling cry he fled out of the door and down the stairway with the banqueters after him, all but Reggie, who fell to the floor, cursing and struggling and grappling with the powers of darkness. When the men reached the lower hall they stood without speaking, holding tightly to each other's hands like frightened children. At last Reggie came down the stairs, steadying himself against the banister. His dress coat was torn, his hair was rumpled down over his forehead, his shirt front was stained with wine, and the ends of his tie were hanging to his waist. He stood looking at the men and they looked at him, and no one spoke.

Presently a man rushed into the hall from the office and shouted "McKinley has carried Ohio by eighty-one thousand majority!" and Regiland Ashton, the product of centuries of democratic faith and tradition, leaped down the six remaining stairs and shouted, "Hurrah for Bill McKinley."

In a few minutes the men were looking for a carriage to take Regiland Ashton home.

✥ *On the Divide*

published in *Overland*, January, 1896

[Canute is a Norwegian. Although *O Pioneers* and *Song of the Lark* deal chiefly with Swedes, the setting of "On the Divide" is the same as that of *O Pioneers* and part of *My Ántonia*.]

Near Rattlesnake Creek, on the side of a little draw stood Canute's shanty. North, east, south, stretched the level Nebraska plain of long rust-red grass that undulated constantly in the wind. To the west the ground was broken and rough, and a narrow strip of timber wound along the turbid, muddy little stream that had scarcely ambition enough to crawl over its black bottom.

["Norway Creek, a shallow, muddy stream that sometimes flowed, and sometimes stood still, at the bottom of a winding ravine with steep, shelving sides overgrown with brush and cottonwoods and dwarf ash." *O Pioneers*, a description of the Bergson homestead.

The rust-red grass is mentioned in *My Ántonia* and in the description of the graveyard in "Neighbour Rosicky."]

If it had not been for the few stunted cottonwoods and elms that grew along its banks, Canute would have shot himself years ago. The Norwegians are a timber-loving people, and if there is even a turtle pond with a few plum bushes around it they seem irresistibly drawn toward it.

As to the shanty itself, Canute had built it without aid of any kind, for when he first squatted along the banks of Rattlesnake Creek there was not a human being within twenty miles. It was built of logs split in halves, the chinks stopped with mud and plaster. The roof was covered with earth and was supported by one gigantic beam curved in the shape of a round arch. It was almost impossible that any tree had ever grown in that shape. The Norwegians used to say that Canute had taken the log across his knee and bent it into the shape he wished. There were two rooms, or rather there was one room with a partition made of ash saplings interwoven and bound together like big straw basket work. In one corner there was a cook stove, rusted and broken. In the other a bed made of unplaned planks and poles. It was fully eight feet long, and upon it was a heap of dark bed clothing. There was a chair and a bench of colossal proportions. There was an ordinary kitchen cupboard with a few cracked dirty dishes in it, and beside it on a tall box a tin wash-basin. Under the bed was a pile of pint flasks, some broken, some whole, all empty. On the wood box lay a pair of shoes of almost incredible dimensions. On the wall hung a saddle, a gun, and some ragged clothing, conspicuous among which was a suit of dark cloth, apparently new, with a paper collar carefully wrapped in a red silk handkerchief and pinned to the sleeve. Over the door hung a wolf and a badger skin, and on the door itself a brace of thirty or forty snake skins whose noisy tails rattled ominously every time it opened. The strangest things in the shanty were the wide window-sills. At first glance they looked as though they had been ruthlessly hacked and mutilated with a hatchet, but on closer inspection all the notches and holes in the wood took form and shape. There seemed to be a series of pictures. They were, in a rough way, artistic, but the figures were heavy and labored, as though they had been cut very slowly and with very awkward instruments. There were men plowing with little horned imps sitting on their shoulders and on their horses' heads. There were men praying with a skull hanging over their heads and little demons behind them mocking their attitudes. There were men fighting with big serpents, and skeletons dancing together. All about these pictures were blooming vines and foliage such as never grew in this world, and coiled among the branches of the vines there was always the scaly body of a serpent, and behind every flower there was a serpent's head. It was a veritable Dance of Death by one who had felt its sting. In the wood box lay some boards, and every inch of them was cut up in the same manner. Sometimes the work was very rude and careless, and looked as though the hand of the workman had trembled. It would sometimes have been hard to distinguish the men from their evil geniuses but for one fact, the men were always grave and were either toiling or praying, while the devils were always smiling and dancing. Several of these boards had been split for kindling and it was evident that the artist did not value his work highly.

[The inarticulate must express themselves in some way. One is reminded of the primitive religious wooden carvings mentioned so often in *Death Comes for the Archbishop*. Canute's symbolism goes back to the primitive terrors of mankind.]

It was the first day of winter on the Divide. Canute stumbled into his shanty carrying a basket of cobs, and after filling the stove, sat down on a stool and crouched his seven foot frame over the fire, staring drearily out of the window at the wide gray sky. He knew by heart every individual clump of bunch grass in the miles of red shaggy prairie that stretched before his cabin. He knew it in all the deceitful loveliness of its early summer, in all the bitter barrenness of its autumn. He had seen it smitten by all the plagues of Egypt. He had seen it parched by drought, and sogged by rain, beaten by hail, and swept by fire, and in the grasshopper years he had seen it eaten as bare and clean as bones that the vultures have left. After the great fires he had seen it stretch for miles and miles, black and smoking as the floor of hell.

[Bergson in *O Pioneers* has much the same soliloquy over his land.]

He rose slowly and crossed the room, dragging his big feet heavily as though they were burdens to him. He looked out of the window into the hog corral and saw the pigs burying themselves in the straw before the shed. The leaden gray clouds were beginning to spill themselves, and the snow flakes were settling down over the white leprous patches of frozen earth where the hogs had gnawed even the sod away. He shuddered and began to walk, trampling heavily with his ungainly feet. He was the wreck of ten winters on the Divide and he knew what that meant. Men fear the winters of the Divide as a child fears night or as men in the North Seas fear the still dark cold of the polar twilight.

[This calls to mind a sentence from *My Ántonia:* "In the winter bleakness a hunger for color came over people, like the Laplander's craving for fats and sugar."]

His eyes fell upon his gun, and he took it down from the wall and looked it over. He sat down on the edge of his bed and held the barrel towards his face, letting his forehead rest upon it, and laid his finger on the trigger. He was perfectly calm, there was neither passion nor despair in his face, but the thoughtful look of a man who is considering. Presently he laid down the gun, and reaching into the cupboard, drew out a pint bottle of raw white alcohol. Lifting it to his lips, he drank greedily. He washed his face in the tin basin and combed his rough hair and shaggy blond beard. Then he stood in uncertainty before the suit of dark clothes that hung on the wall. For the fiftieth time he took them in his hands and tried to summon courage to put them on. He took the paper collar that was pinned to the sleeve of the coat and cautiously slipped it under his rough beard, looking with timid expectancy into the cracked, splashed glass that hung over the bench. With a short laugh he threw it down on the bed, and pulling on his old black hat, he went out, striking off across the level.

It was a physical necessity for him to get away from his cabin once in a while. He had been there for ten years, digging and plowing and sowing, and reaping what little the hail and the hot winds and the frosts left him to reap. Insanity and suicide are very common things on the Divide. They come on like an epidemic in the hot wind season. Those scorching dusty winds that blow up over the bluffs from Kansas seem to dry up the blood in men's veins as they do the sap in the corn leaves. Whenever the yellow scorch creeps down over the tender inside leaves about the ear, then the coroners prepare for active duty; for the oil of the country is burned out and it does not take long for the flame to eat up the wick. It causes no great sensation there when a Dane is found swinging to his own windmill tower, and most of the Poles after they have become too careless and discouraged to shave themselves keep their razors to cut their throats with.

[Suicides have their fascination for Willa Cather. Besides Mr. Shimerda in *My Ántonia*, there is the transient who jumps into a threshing machine; and in *Song of the Lark* the tramp who jumps into the water tower.]

It may be that the next generation on the Divide will be very happy, but the present one came too late in life. It is useless for men that have cut hemlocks among the mountains of Sweden for forty years to try to be happy in a country as flat and gray and as naked as the sea. It is not easy for men that have spent their youth fishing in the Northern seas to be content with following a plow, and men that have served in the Austrian army hate hard work and coarse clothing on the loneliness of the plains, and long for marches and excitement and tavern company and pretty barmaids. After a man has passed his fortieth birthday it is not easy for him to change the habits and conditions of his life.

[The age of forty seems to have had special significance for Cather, hence her later title *Not Under Forty*.]

Most men bring with them to the Divide only the dregs of the lives that they have squandered in other lands and among other peoples.

[This was literally true of many of those who settled in Webster County, Nebraska, after the Civil War.]

Canute Canuteson was as mad as any of them, but his madness did not take the form of suicide or religion but of alcohol. He had always taken liquor when he wanted it, as all Norwegians do, but after his first year of solitary life he settled down to it steadily. He exhausted whisky after a while, and went to alcohol, because its effects were speedier and surer. He was a big man and with a terrible amount of resistant force, and it took a great deal of alcohol even to move him. After nine years of drinking, the quantities he could take would seem fabulous to an ordinary drinking man. He never let it interfere with his work, he generally drank at night and on Sundays. Every night, as soon as his chores were done, he began to drink. While he was able to sit up he would play on his mouth harp or hack away at his window sills with his jack knife. When the liquor went to his head he would lie down on his bed and stare out of the window until he went to sleep. He drank alone and in solitude not for pleasure or good cheer, but to forget the awful loneliness and level of the Divide. Milton made a sad blunder when he put mountains in hell. Mountains postulate faith and aspiration. All mountain peoples are religious. It was the cities of the plains that, because of their utter lack of spirituality and the mad caprice of their vice, were cursed of God.

[Mountains or high places become a symbol in Cather's writings. The Archbishop dies thinking of his home mountains. Myra Henshawe dies on a high cliff, watching "the morning break over the sea." Willa Cather's grave overlooks a valley leading to a mountain.]

Alcohol is perfectly consistent in its effects upon man. Drunkenness is merely an exaggeration. A foolish man drunk becomes maudlin; a bloody man, vicious; a coarse man, vulgar. Canute was none of these, but he was morose and gloomy, and liquor took him through all the hells of Dante. As he lay on his giant's bed all the horrors of this world and every other were laid bare to his chilled senses. He was a man who knew no joy, a man who toiled in silence and bitterness. The skull and the serpent were always before him, the symbols of eternal futileness and of eternal hate.

When the first Norwegians near enough to be called neighbors came, Canute rejoiced, and planned to escape from his bosom vice. But he was not a social man by nature and had not the power of drawing out the social side of other people. His new neighbors rather feared him because of his great strength and size, his silence and his lowering brows. Perhaps, too, they knew that he was mad, mad from the eternal treachery of the plains, which every spring stretch green and rustle with the promises of Eden, showing long grassy lagoons full of clear water and cattle whose hoofs are stained with wild roses. Before autumn the lagoons are dried up, and the ground is burnt dry and hard until it blisters and cracks open.

> [Willa Cather preferred autumn to spring. In *Lucy Gayheart* she speaks of brutal spring rain; in fact that whole book is filled with the bitter taste of a promising but unfulfilled spring.]

So instead of becoming a friend and neighbor to the men that settled about him, Canute became a mystery and a terror. They told awful stories of his size and strength and of the alcohol he drank. They said that one night, when he went out to see to his horses just before he went to bed, his steps were unsteady and the rotten planks of the floor gave way and threw him behind the feet of a fiery young stallion. His foot was caught fast in the floor, and the nervous horse began kicking frantically. When Canute felt the blood trickling down into his eyes from a scalp wound in his head, he roused himself from his kingly indifference, and with the quiet stoical courage of a drunken man leaned forward and wound his arms about the horse's hind legs and held them against his breast with crushing embrace. All through the darkness and cold of the night he lay there, matching strength against strength. When little Jim Peterson went over the next morning at four o'clock to go with him to the Blue to cut wood, he found him so, and the horse was on its fore knees, trembling and whinnying with fear. This is the story the Norwegians tell of him, and if it is true it is no wonder that they feared and hated this Holder of the Heels of Horses.

[Here she makes Canute almost a mythical figure—the strong earth symbol. Later she does in a more subtle manner the same thing with Alexandra of *O Pioneers*, and Ántonia of *My Ántonia*.]

One spring there moved to the next "eighty" a family that made a great change in Canute's life. Ole Yensen was too drunk most of the time to be afraid of any one, and his wife Mary was too garrulous to be afraid of any one who listened to her talk, and Lena, their pretty daughter, was not afraid of man nor devil. So it came about that Canute went over to take his alcohol with Ole oftener than he took it alone. After a while the report spread that he was going to marry Yensen's daughter, and the Norwegian girls began to tease Lena about the great bear she was going to keep house for. No one could quite see how the affair had come about, for Canute's tactics of courtship were somewhat peculiar. He apparently never spoke to her at all: he would sit for hours with Mary chattering on one side of him and Ole drinking on the other and watch Lena at her work. She teased him, and threw flour in his face and put vinegar in his coffee, but he took her rough jokes with silent wonder, never even smiling. He took her to church occasionally, but the most watchful and curious people never saw him speak to her. He would sit staring at her while she giggled and flirted with the other men.

[The Lena who lives in the pages of *My Ántonia* is a much deeper person than this Lena. This very shallow type female is found in several of these early stories. There are plenty of them throughout the later books, but they do not stand out much in memory. Take Alexandra's sisters-in-law in *O Pioneers*, or Lily Fisher of *Song of the Lark*.]

Next spring Mary Lee went to town to work in a steam laundry. She came home every Sunday, and always ran across

to Yensens to startle Lena with stories of ten cent theaters, fire-
men's dances, and all the other esthetic delights of metropolitan
life. In a few weeks Lena's head was completely turned, and she
gave her father no rest until he let her go to town to seek her
fortune at the ironing board. From the time she came home on
her first visit she began to treat Canute with contempt. She
had bought a plush cloak and kid gloves, had her clothes made
by the dress-maker, and assumed airs and graces that made the
other women of the neighborhood cordially detest her. She generally brought with her a young man from town who waxed his
mustache and wore a red necktie, and she did not even intro-
duce him to Canute.

The neighbors teased Canute a good deal until he knocked
one of them down. He gave no sign of suffering from her neglect
except that he drank more and avoided the other Norwegians
more carefully then ever. He lay around in his den and no one
knew what he felt or thought, but little Jim Peterson, who had
seen him glowering at Lena in church one Sunday when she
was there with the town man, said that he would not give an
acre of his wheat for Lena's life or the town chap's either; and
Jim's wheat was so wondrously worthless that the statement was
an exceedingly strong one.

Canute had bought a new suit of clothes that looked as
nearly like the town man's as possible. They had cost him half a
millet crop; for tailors are not accustomed to fitting giants and
they charge for it. He had hung those clothes in his shanty two
months ago and had never put them on, partly from fear of ridi-
cule, partly from discouragement, and partly because there was
something in his own soul that revolted at the littleness of the
device.

Lena was at home just at this time. Work was slack in the
laundry and Mary had not been well, so Lena stayed at home,
glad enough to get an opportunity to torment Canute once more.

She was washing in the side kitchen, singing loudly as she
worked. Mary was on her knees, blacking the stove and scolding
violently about the young man who was coming out from town

that night. The young man had committed the fatal error of laughing at Mary's ceaseless babble and had never been forgiven.

"He is no good, and you will come to a bad end by running with him! I do not see why a daughter of mine should act so. I do not see why the Lord should visit such a punishment upon me as to give me such a daughter. There are plenty of good men you can marry."

Lena tossed her head and answered curtly, "I don't happen to want to marry any man right away, and so long as Dick dresses nice and has plenty of money to spend, there is no harm in my going with him."

"Money to spend? Yes, and that is all he does with it I'll be bound. You think it very fine now, but you will change your tune when you have been married five years and see your children running naked and your cupboard empty. Did Anne Hermanson come to any good end by marrying a town man?"

"I don't know anything about Anne Hermanson, but I know any of the laundry girls would have Dick quick enough if they could get him."

"Yes, and a nice lot of store clothes huzzies you are too. Now there is Canuteson who has an 'eighty' proved up and fifty head of cattle and—"

"And hair that ain't been cut since he was a baby, and a big dirty beard, and he wears overalls on Sundays, and drinks like a pig. Besides he will keep. I can have all the fun I want, and when I am old and ugly like you he can have me and take care of me. The Lord knows there ain't nobody else going to marry him."

Canute drew his hand back from the latch as though it were red hot. He was not the kind of man to make a good eavesdropper, and he wished he had knocked sooner. He pulled himself together and struck the door like a battering ram. Mary jumped and opened it with a screech.

"God! Canute, how you scared us! I thought it was crazy Lou—he has been tearing around the neighborhood trying to convert folks. I am afraid as death of him. He ought to be sent off, I think. He is just as liable as not to kill us all, or burn the barn, or poison the dogs.

[See "Lou, The Prophet," published 1892.]

He has been worrying even the poor minister to death, and he laid up with the rheumatism, too! Did you notice that he was too sick to preach last Sunday? But don't stand there in the cold, come in. Yensen isn't here, but he just went over to Sorenson's for the mail; he won't be gone long. Walk right in the other room and sit down."

Canute followed her, looking steadily in front of him and not noticing Lena as he passed her. But Lena's vanity would not allow him to pass unmolested. She took the wet sheet she was wringing out and cracked him across the face with it, and ran giggling to the other side of the room. The blow stung his cheeks and the soapy water flew in his eyes, and he involuntarily began rubbing them with his hands. Lena giggled with delight at his discomfiture, and the wrath in Canute's face grew blacker than ever. A big man humiliated is vastly more undignified than a little one. He forgot the sting of his face in the bitter consciousness that he had made a fool of himself. He stumbled blindly into the living room, knocking his head against the door jamb because he forgot to stoop. He dropped into a chair behind the stove, thrusting his big feet back helplessly on either side of him.

Ole was a long time in coming, and Canute sat there, still and silent, with his hands clenched on his knees, and the skin of his face seemed to have shriveled up into little wrinkles that trembled when he lowered his brows. His life had been one long lethargy of solitude and alcohol, but now he was awakening, and it was as when the dumb stagnant heat of summer breaks out into thunder.

When Ole came staggering in, heavy with liquor, Canute rose at once.

"Yensen," he said quietly, "I have come to see if you will let me marry your daughter today."

"Today!" gasped Ole.

"Yes, I will not wait until tomorrow. I am tired of living alone."

Ole braced his staggering knees against the bedstead, and stammered eloquently: "Do you think I will marry my daughter to a drunkard? a man who drinks raw alcohol? a man who sleeps with rattle snakes? Get out of my house or I will kick you out for your impudence." And Ole began looking anxiously for his feet.

Canute answered not a word, but he put on his hat and went out into the kitchen. He went up to Lena and said without looking at her, "Get your things on and come with me!"

The tones of his voice startled her, and she said angrily, dropping the soap, "Are you drunk?"

"If you do not come with me, I will take you—you had better come," said Canute quietly.

She lifted a sheet to strike him, but he caught her arm roughly and wrenched the sheet from her. He turned to the wall and took down a hood and shawl that hung there, and began wrapping her up. Lena scratched and fought like a wild thing. Ole stood in the door, cursing, and Mary howled and screeched at the top of her voice. As for Canute, he lifted the girl in his arms and went out of the house. She kicked and struggled, but the helpless wailing of Mary and Ole soon died away in the distance, and her face was held down tightly on Canute's shoulder so that she could not see whither he was taking her. She was conscious only of the north wind whistling in her ears, and of rapid steady motion and of a great breast that heaved beneath her in quick, irregular breaths.

[Alexandra in *O Pioneers* often has the "illusion of being lifted up bodily and carried lightly by some one very strong . . . carried swiftly off across the fields . . . carried by a strong being who took from her all bodily weariness." When finally Alexandra saw him, "His shoulders seemed strong as

the foundations of the world . . . she knew at once that it
was the arm of the mightiest of all lovers . . ." Judging
from Cather's work, that lover would be Life, and here in
the simple story of Canute she has cast Life in a Norse mold
of heroic physical proportions.]

The harder she struggled the tighter those iron arms that had
held the heels of horses crushed about her, until she felt as if
they would crush the breath from her, and lay still with fear.
Canute was striding across the level fields at a pace at which man
never went before, drawing the stinging north winds into his
lungs in great gulps. He walked with his eyes half closed and
looking straight in front of him, only lowering them when he
bent his head to blow away the snow flakes that settled on her
hair. So it was that Canute took her to his home, even as his
bearded barbarian ancestors took the fair frivolous women of the
South in their hairy arms and bore them down to their war ships.
For ever and anon the soul becomes weary of the conventions
that are not of it, and with a single stroke shatters the civilized
lies with which it is unable to cope, and the strong arm reaches
out and takes by force what it cannot win by cunning.

When Canute reached his shanty he placed the girl upon a
chair, where she sat sobbing. He stayed only a few minutes. He
filled the stove with wood and lit the lamp, drank a huge swallow of alcohol and put the bottle in his pocket. He paused a moment, staring heavily at the weeping girl, then he went off
and locked the door and disappeared in the gathering gloom of
the night.

Wrapped in flannels and soaked with turpentine, the little
Norwegian preacher sat reading his Bible, when he heard a
thundering knock at his door, and Canute entered, covered with
snow and his beard frozen fast to his coat.

"Come in, Canute, you must be frozen," said the little man,
shoving a chair towards his visitor.

Canute remained standing with his hat on and said quietly,
"I want you to come over to my house tonight to marry me to
Lena Yensen."

"Have you got a license, Canute?"

"No, I don't want a license. I want to be married."

"But I can't marry you without a license, man. It would not be legal."

A dangerous light came in the big Norwegian's eye. "I want you to come over to my house to marry me to Lena Yensen."

"No, I can't, it would kill an ox to go out in a storm like this, and my rheumatism is bad tonight."

"Then if you will not go I must take you," said Canute with a sigh.

He took down the preacher's bearskin coat and bade him put it on while he hitched up his buggy. He went out and closed the door softly after him. Presently he returned and found the frightened minister crouching before the fire with his coat lying beside him. Canute helped him put it on and gently wrapped his head in his big muffler. Then he picked him up and carried him out and placed him in his buggy. As he tucked the buffalo robes around him he said: "Your horse is old, he might flounder or lose his way in this storm. I will lead him."

The minister took the reins feebly in his hands and sat shivering with the cold. Sometimes when there was a lull in the wind, he could see the horse struggling through the snow with the man plodding steadily beside him. Again the blowing snow would hide them from him altogether. He had no idea where they were or what direction they were going. He felt as though he were being whirled away in the heart of the storm, and he said all the prayers he knew. But at last the long four miles were over, and Canute set him down in the snow while he unlocked the door. He saw the bride sitting by the fire with her eyes red and swollen as though she had been weeping. Canute placed a huge chair for him, and said roughly,—

"Warm yourself."

Lena began to cry and moan afresh, begging the minister to take her home. He looked helplessly at Canute. Canute said simply,

"If you are warm now, you can marry us."

"My daughter, do you take this step of your own free will?" asked the minister in a trembling voice.

"No, sir, I don't, and it is disgraceful he should force me into it! I won't marry him."

"Then, Canute, I cannot marry you," said the minister, standing as straight as his rheumatic limbs would let him.

"Are you ready to marry us now, sir?" said Canute, laying one iron hand on his stooped shoulder. The little preacher was a good man, but like most men of weak body he was a coward and had a horror of physical suffering, although he had known so much of it. So with many qualms of conscience he began to repeat the marriage service. Lena sat sullenly in her chair, staring at the fire. Canute stood beside her, listening with his head bent reverently and his hands folded on his breast. When the little man had prayed and said amen, Canute began bundling him up again.

"I will take you home, now," he said as he carried him out and placed him in his buggy, and started off with him through the fury of the storm, floundering among the snow drifts that brought even the giant himself to his knees.

After she was left alone, Lena soon ceased weeping. She was not of a particularly sensitive temperament, and had little pride beyond that of vanity. After the first bitter anger wore itself out, she felt nothing more than a healthy sense of humiliation and defeat. She had no inclination to run away, for she was married now, and in her eyes that was final and all rebellion was useless. She knew nothing about a license, but she knew that a preacher married folks. She consoled herself by thinking that she had always intended to marry Canute someday, any way.

She grew tired of crying and looking into the fire, so she got up and began to look about her. She had heard queer tales about the inside of Canute's shanty, and her curiosity soon got the better of her rage. One of the first things she noticed was the new black suit of clothes hanging on the wall. She was dull, but it did not take a vain woman long to interpret anything so decidedly flattering, and she was pleased in spite of herself. As she looked through the cupboard, the general air of neglect and discomfort made her pity the man who lived there.

"Poor fellow, no wonder he wants to get married to get somebody to wash up his dishes. Batchin's pretty hard on a man."

It is easy to pity when once one's vanity has been tickled. She looked at the window sill and gave a little shudder and wondered if the man were crazy. Then she sat down again and sat a long time wondering what her Dick and Ole would do.

"It is queer Dick didn't come right over after me. He surely came, for he would have left town before the storm began and he might just as well come right on as go back. If he'd hurried he would have gotten here before the preacher came. I suppose he was afraid to come, for he knew Canuteson could pound him to jelly, the coward!" Her eyes flashed angrily.

The weary hours wore on and Lena began to grow horribly lonesome. It was an uncanny night and this was an uncanny place to be in. She could hear the coyotes howling hungrily a little way from the cabin, and more terrible still were all the unknown noises of the storm. She remembered the tales they told of the big log overhead and she was afraid of those snaky things on the window sills. She remembered the man who had been killed in the draw, and she wondered what she would do if she saw crazy Lou's white face glaring into the window. The rattling of the door became unbearable, she thought the latch must be loose and took the lamp to look at it. Then for the first time she saw the ugly brown snake skins whose death rattle sounded every time the wind jarred the door.

"Canute, Canute!" she screamed in terror.

Outside the door she heard a heavy sound as of a big dog getting up and shaking himself. The door opened and Canute stood before her, white as a snow drift.

"What is it?" he asked kindly.

"I am cold," she faltered.

He went out and got an armful of wood and a basket of cobs and filled the stove. Then he went out and lay in the snow before the door. Presently he heard her calling again.

"What is it?" he said, sitting up.

"I'm so lonesome, I'm afraid to stay in here all alone."

"I will go over and get your mother." And he got up.

"She won't come."

"I'll bring her," said Canute grimly.

"No, no. I don't want her, she will scold all the time."

"Well, I will bring your father."

She spoke again and it seemed as though her mouth was close up to the key-hole. She spoke lower than he had ever heard her speak before, so low that he had to put his ear up to the lock to hear her.

"I don't want him either, Canute,—I'd rather have you."

For a moment she heard no noise at all, then something like a groan. With a cry of fear she opened the door, and saw Canute stretched in the snow at her feet, his face in his hands, sobbing on the door step.

🌿 A Night at Greenway Court

published in the *Nebraska Literary Magazine*, June, 1896
published in *The Library*, April 21, 1900

[Twice only did Willa Cather use a Virginia background, here and over forty years later in *Sapphira and the Slave Girl*. The date of this adventure, 1752, is over one hundred years prior to the 1856 date of *Sapphira*, but both stories touch on Cather's family history. Jeremiah Smith, one of Willa's ancestors four generations back, had received land grants from Lord Fairfax, Baron of Cameron, dated September 30, 1762. In this short story we see the beginning of her historical sense which later made possible *Death Comes for the Archbishop* and *Shadows on the Rock*.

This story is told from the viewpoint of a young man, a Catherism well illustrated by Jim Burden in *My Ántonia* and Niel Herbert in *A Lost Lady*.

Cather said she began by imitating writers she admired. Here we find a reflection of the French writers (intrigue, courtesans, jewels), particularly of Alexandre Dumas, the elder, and something of Henry James.

The greatest variation between the two versions occurs in the opening paragraph.]

[First version:]

I, Richard Morgan, of the town of Winchester, county of Frederick, of the Commonwealth of Virginia, having been asked by my friend Josiah Goodrich, who purports making a history of this valley, to set down all I know concerning the death of

M. Philip Marie Maurepas, a gentleman, it seems, of considerable importance in his own country, will proceed to do so briefly
and with what little skill I am master of.

[Second version:]

I have been asked by my friend, Josiah Goodrich, who purports making a history of the valley of Virginia, to set down all I
know concerning the death of M. Philip Marie Maurepas, a gentleman, it seems, of considerable importance in his own country,
and whose disappearance was the subject of much conjecture
at Versailles, where even the disfavor of the king was not
enough to blot out all recollection of a man whose brilliancy
and daring had for one summer blinded the eyes of the Marquise
de Pompadour, had made a guardsman's sword outweigh a
crown, and the most selfish and crafty woman since the old
Medici seem like to sicken upon the source of her luxury and
power.

[Continuing the second version which in all respects
coincides with the first, except wherein noted:]

The incident which I am about to relate occurred in my
early youth, but so deeply did it fix itself upon my memory that
the details are as clear as though it had happened yesterday.

[This is exactly the type memory Willa Cather had, particularly in regard to happenings of her early youth.]

Indeed, of all the stirring events that have happened in my
time, those nights spent at Greenway Court in my youth stand
out most boldly in my memory. It was, I think, one evening late
in October, in the year 1752, that my Lord Fairfax sent his man
over to my father's house at Winchester

[Willa Cather was born in Frederick County. Her
father's house was near Winchester.]

to say that on the morrow his master desired my company at the Court. My father, a prosperous tobacco merchant, greatly regretted that I should be brought up in a new country, so far from the world of polite letters and social accomplishments, and contrived that I should pass much of my leisure in the company of one of the most gracious gentlemen and foremost scholars of his time, Thomas, Lord Fairfax. Accordingly, I was not surprised at my lord's summons. Late in the afternoon of the following day I rode over to the Court, and was first shown into my lord's private office, where for some time we discussed my lord's suit, then pending with the sons of Joist Hite, concerning certain lands beyond the Blue Ridge, then held by them, which my lord claimed through the extension of his grant from the crown. Our business being dispatched, he said:

"Come, Richard, in the hall I will present you to some gentlemen who will entertain you until supper time. There is a Frenchman

[This is Cather's first treatment of a Frenchman in the new world. It is a great stride from this to *Death Comes For the Archbishop* and, *Shadows on the Rock*.]

stopping here, M. Maurepas, a gentleman of most engaging conversation. The Viscount Chillingham you will not meet until later, as he has gone out with the hounds."

We crossed the yard and entered the hall where the table was already laid with my lord's silver platters and thin glass goblets, which never ceased to delight me when I dined with him, and though since, in London, I have drunk wine at a king's table, I have seen no [In the first version the word is *none,*] finer. At the end of the room, by the fire place, sat two men over their cards. One was a clergyman, whom I had met before, the other a tall, spare gentleman whom my lord introduced as M. Philip Marie Maurepas. As I sat down, the gentleman addressed me in excellent English. The bright firelight gave me an excellent opportunity to observe [The first version says *for observing.*] this man, which I did, for with us strangers were too few not to be of especial interest, and in a way their very appearance spoke to us of an older world beyond the seas for which the hearts of all of us still hungered.

[This old world hunger was to give depth and direction to Cather's best books—a hunger for antiquity which she shared with Flaubert, one of the authors she most admired.]

He was, as I have said, a tall man, narrow chested and with unusually long arms. His forehead was high, and his chin sharp, his skin was dark, tanned, as I later learned, by his long service in the Indies. [In the first version spelled *Indes*.] He had a pair of restless black eyes and thin lips shaded by a dark mustache. His hair was coal black and grew long upon his shoulders; later I noticed that it was slightly touched with gray. His dress had once been fine, but had seen considerable service and was somewhat the worse for the weather. He wore breeches of dark blue velvet and leather leggins. His shirt and vest were of dark red and had once been worked with gold.

In his belt he wore a long knife, with a slender blade, and a handle of gold curiously wrought in the form of a serpent, with eyes of pure red stones which sparkled mightily in the firelight. I must confess that in the very appearance of this man there was something that both interested and attracted me, and I fell to wondering what strange sights those keen eyes of his had looked upon.

[This is something Willa Cather wondered about every interesting stranger from the time she was able to wonder at all, a curiosity she used to the fullest.]

"M. Maurepas intends spending the winter in our wilderness, Richard, and I fear he will find that our woods offer a cold welcome to a stranger."

"Well, my lord, all the more to my taste. Having seen how hot the world can be, I am willing to see how cold."

"To see that sir," said I, "you should go to Quebec,

[This is spelled *Quebeck* in the first version. Here is the first indication of interest in the background which was to figure in *Shadows on the Rock* some thirty years later.]

where I have been with trappers. There I have thrown a cup full of water in the air and seen it descend solid ice."

[Compare this with a passage from *Sapphira*: ". . . in Canada where it was so cold, Till said, if you threw a tin-cupful of water into the air, it came down ice."]

"I fear it will be cold enough here for my present attire," said he, laughing, "yet it may be that I will taste the air of Quebec before quitting this wilderness of yours."

My lord then excused himself and withdrew, leaving me alone with the gentlemen.

"Come join me in a game of hazard, Master Morgan; it is yet half an hour until supper time," said the clergyman, who had little thought for anything but his cards and his dinner.

[This clergyman, although Church of England, seems to have come out of the pages of Dumas or Balzac. He bears little relation to the clergy of whom Cather wrote later in *Death Comes for the Archbishop* and *Shadows on the Rock*. He is, though, as distasteful as Brother Weldon in *One of Ours*.]

"And I will look at the portraits; you have fleeced me quite enough for one day, good brother of the church. I have nothing left but my diamond that I cut from the hand of a dead Rajpoot, finger and all, and it is a lucky stone, and I have no mind to lose it."

"With your permission, M. Maurepas, I will look at the portraits with you, as I have no mind to play tonight; besides, I think this is the hour for Mr. Courtney's devotions," said I, for I had no liking for the fat Churchman. He, like so many of my lord's guests, was in a sense a refugee from justice; having fallen into disgrace with the heads of the English Church, he had fled to our country and sought out Lord Fairfax, whose door was closed against no man. He had been there then three months, dwelling in shameful idleness, one of that band of renegades who continually ate at my lord's table and hunted with his dogs and devoured his substance, waiting for some turn of fortune, like the suitors in the hall of Penelope. So we left the clergyman counting his gains, and repaired to the other end of the hall, where, above the mahogany bookcases, the portraits hung. Of these there were a considerable number, and I told the Frenchman the names of as many as I knew. There was my lord's father and mother, and his younger brother, to whom he had given his English estate. There was his late Majesty George I, and old Firnando Fairfax. Hanging under the dark picture of the king he had deposed, and yet loved, was Firnando's son, fighting Thomas Fairfax, third Lord and Baron of Cameron, the great leader of the Commoners with Cromwell, who rode after Charles at Heyworth Moore and thrust the people's petition in the indignant monarch's saddle bow; who defeated the king's forces at Naseby, and after Charles was delivered over to the commissioners of Parliament, met him at Nottingham and kissed his fallen sovereign's hand, refusing to sit in judgment over God's anointed.

Among these pictures there was one upon which I had often gazed in wonderment. It was the portrait of a lady, holding in her hand a white lily. Some heavy instrument had been thrust through the canvas, marring the face beyond all recognition,

[Both the expression "portrait of a lady" and the marred painting are reminiscent of Henry James.]

but the masses of powdered hair, and throat and arms were enough to testify to the beauty of the original. The hands especially were of surpassing loveliness, and the thumb was ornamented with a single emerald, as though to call attention to its singular perfection. The costume was the court dress of the then present reign, and with the eagerness of youthful imagination I had often fancied that could that picture speak it might tell something of that upon which all men wondered; why, in the

prime of his manhood and success at court, Lord Fairfax had
left home and country, friends, and all that men hold dear, renounced the gay society in which he had shone and his favorite
pursuit of letters, and buried himself in the North American
wilderness. Upon this canvas the Frenchman's eye was soon fixed.

"And this?" he asked.

"I do not know, sir; of that my lord has never told me."

"Well, let me see; what is a man's memory good for, if not
for such things? I must have seen those hands before, and that
coronet."

[A secret in someone's background is more like Henry
James than like Willa Cather.]

He looked at it closely, and then stood back and looked at it
from a distance. Suddenly an exclamation broke from him, and
a sharp light flashed over his features.

"Ah, I thought so! So your lord has never told you of this!
Parbleu, il a beaucoup de cause! Look you, my boy, that emerald
is the only beautiful thing that ever came out of Herrenhausen—
that, and she who wears it. Perhaps you will see that emerald,
too, some day; how many and how various they will yet be, God
alone knows. How long, O Lord, how long? as your countrymen
say."

So bitter was his manner that I was half afraid, yet had a
mind to question him, when my lord returned. He brought with
him a young man of an appearance by no means distinguished,
yet kindly and affable, whom he introduced me to

[Obviously this should read *to me*. The words do not
occur in the first version.]

as the Viscount Chillingham.

"You've a good country here, Master Morgan, and better
sport than we, for all our game laws. Hang laws, I say, they're
naught but a trouble to them that make 'em and them that break
'em, and it's little good they do any of us. My Lord, you must

sell me your deer hound, Fanny; I want to take her home with me, and show 'em what your dogs are made of over here."

"You are right welcome to her, or any of the pack."

At this juncture my lord's housekeeper, Mistress Crawford, brought in the silver candlesticks, and the servants smoking dishes of bear's meat and venison, and many another delicacy for which my lord's table was famous, besides French wines and preserved cherries from his old estates in England.

[Remember the preserved cherries in Daudet's "Les Viéux"?]

The viscount flung himself into his chair, still flushed from his chase after the hounds, and stretched his long limbs.

"This is a man's life you have here, my lord. I tell you, you do well to be away from London now; it's as dull there as Mr. Courtney's church without its spiritual pastor."

The clergyman lifted his eyes from his venison long enough to remark, slyly, "Or as Hampton Court without its cleverest gamester," at which the young man reddened under his fresh coat of tan, for he had been forced to leave England because of some gaming scandal which cast grave doubts upon his personal honor.

The talk drifted to the death of the Queen of Denmark, the king's last visit to Hanover, and various matters of court gossip. Of these the gentlemen spoke freely, more freely, perhaps, than they would have dared do at home. As I have said, my lord's guests were too often gentlemen who had left dark histories behind them, and had fled into the wilds where law was scarce more than a name, and man had to contend only with the savage condition of nature, and a strong arm stood in better stead than a tender conscience. I have met many a strange man at Greenway Court, men who had cheated at play, men who had failed in great political plots, men who fled from a debtor's prison, and men charged with treason, and with a price upon their heads. For in some respects Lord Fairfax was a strangely conservative man, slow to judge and slow to anger, having seen much of the world, and thinking its conditions hard and its temptations heavy, deeming, I believe, all humanity more sinned against than sinning. And yet I have seldom known his confidence to be misplaced or his trust to be ill repaid. Whatever of information I may have acquired in my youth, I owe to the conversation of these men, for about my lord's board exiles and outlaws of all nations gathered, and unfolded in the friendly solitude of the wilderness plots and intrigues then scarce known in Europe.

[In Webster County Willa Cather had known at least the poor—sometimes almost outcasts—of many nations. Because of her reading in European, particularly French literature, she could transform them into the group described above.]

On all the matters that were discussed the Frenchman seemed the best versed man present, even touching the most minute details of the English court. At last the viscount, who was visibly surprised, turned upon him sharply:

"Have you been presented at court, monsieur?"

"Not in England, Viscount, [count, in the first version] but I have seen something of your king in Hanover; there, I think, on the banks of the stupid Leine, is his proper court, and 'tis there he sends the riches of your English. But in exchange I hear that he has brought you his treasure of Herrenhausen in her private carriage with a hundred postillions to herald her advent."

His eyes were fixed keenly on my lord's face, but Fairfax only asked, coldly:

"And where, monsieur, have you gained so perfect a mastery of the English tongue?"

"At Madras, your lordship, under Bourdonnais, where I fought your gallant countrymen, high and low, for the empire of the Indies. They taught me the sound of English speech well enough, and the music of English swords."

"Faith," broke in the viscount, "then they taught you better than they know themselves, though it's their mother tongue.

You've seen hot service there, I warrant?"

"Well, what with English guns sweeping our decks by sea, and the Indian sun broiling our shins

[The first version says *skin* and probably the word intended here is *skins.*]

by land, and the cholera tearing our entrails, we saw hot service, indeed."

"Were you in the Indian service after the return of Governor Bourdonnais to France, M. Maurepas?"

"After his return to the Bastille, you mean, my lord. Yes, I was less fortunate than my commander. There are worse prisons on earth than the Bastille, and Madras is one of them. When France sends a man to the Indies, she has no intention that [In the first version the word *that* is omitted.] he shall return alive. How I did so is another matter. Yes, I served afterward under Dupleix [In the first version the name is spelled *Duplix.*], who seized Bourdonnais' troops as well as his treasure. I was with him in the Deccan when he joined his troops with Murzapha Jung against the Nabob of the Carnatic, and white men were set to fight side by side with heathen. And I say to you, gentlemen, that the bravest man in all that melee was the old Nabob himself. He was a hundred and seven years old, and he had been a soldier from his mother's knee. He was mounted on the finest elephant in the Indian army, and he led his soldiers up into the thick of the fight in full sweep of the French bullets, ordering his bodyguard back and attended only by his driver. And when he saw his old enemy, Tecuda Sahib [In the first version the name is *Tecunda Sahib.*], in the very midst of the French guards, he ordered his driver to up and at him, and he prodded the beast forward with his own hand. When the beast came crashing through our lines a bullet struck the old man in the breast, but still he urged him on. And when the elephant was stopped the driver was gone and the old Nabob was stone dead, sitting bolt upright in his curtained cage with a naked scimitar in his hand, ready for his vengeance. And I tell ye now, gentlemen, that I for one was right sorry that the bullet went home, for I am not the man who would see a brave soldier balked of his revenge."

[This device of a story within a story is one which Cather used notably in *My Ántonia, Death Comes for the Archbishop,* and *Shadows on the Rock,* and in many of her other stories, to create depth and a feeling of historical validity. In *The Professor's House,* it reaches a new dimension.]

It is quite impossible with the pen to give any adequate idea of the dramatic manner in which he related this. I think it stirred the blood of more than one of us. The viscount struck the table with his hand, and cried:

"That's talking, sir; you see the best of life, you French.

[Willa Cather felt the same way about the French.]

As for us, we are so ridden by king-craft and state-craft we are as good as dead men. Between Walpole and the little German we have forgot the looks of a sword, and we never hear a gun these times but at the christening of some brat or other."

The clergyman looked up reproachfully from his preserved cherries, and Lord Fairfax, who seldom suffered any talk that savored of disloyalty, rose to his feet and lifted his glass.

"Gentlemen, the king's health."

"The king's health," echoed we all, rising. But M. Maurepas sat still in his chair, and his glass stood full beside him. The viscount turned upon him fiercely.

"Monsieur, you do not drink the king's health?"

"No, sir; your king, nor my king, nor no man's king. I have no king. May the devil take them one and all, and that's my health to them."

"Monsieur," cried my lord, sternly, "I am surprised to hear a soldier of the King of France speak in this fashion."

"Yes, my lord, I have been a soldier of the king, and I know the wages of kings. What were they for Bourdonnais, the bravest general who ever drew a sword? The Bastille! What were they for all my gallant comrades? Cholera, massacre, death in the rotten marshes of Pondicherry. *Le diable!* I know them well: prison, the sword, the stake, the recompense of kings!" He laughed terribly and struck his forehead with his hand.

"Monsieur," said my lord, "it may be that you have suffered much, and for that reason only do I excuse much that you say. Human justice is often at fault, and kings are but human. Nevertheless, they are ordained of heaven, and so long as there is breath in our bodies we owe them loyal service."

The Frenchman rose and stood, his dark eyes flashing like coals of fire and his hands trembling as he waved them in the air. And methought the prophets of Israel must have looked so when they cried out unto the people, though his words were as dark blasphemy as ever fell from human lips.

"I tell you, sir, that the day will come, and is now at hand, when there will be no more kings. When a king's blood will be cheaper than pothouse wine and flow as plentifully. When crowned heads will pray for a peasant's cap, and princes will hide their royal lineage as lepers hide their sores. Ordained by God! Look you, sir, there is a wise man of France—so wise, indeed, that he dare not dwell in France, but hides among the Prussians —who says that there is no God! No Jehovah with his frying pan of lost souls! That [The first version inserts here the word *it.*] is all a tale made up by kings to terrify their vassals; [The first version says *slaves.*] that instead of God making kings, the kings made God."

We were all struck with horror, and the viscount rose to his feet again and threw himself into an attitude of attack, while Mr. Courtney, whose place it was to speak, cowered in his seat and continued to look wistfully at the cherries.

"Stop, sir," bawled the viscount, "we have not much faith left in England, thanks to such as Mr. Courtney here, but we've enough still to fight for. Little George may have his faults, but he's a brave man and a soldier. Let us see whether you can be as much."

But the Frenchman did not so much as look at him. He was well sped with wine, and in his eyes there was a fierce light as of some ancient hatred woke anew. Staggering down the hall he pointed to the canvas which had so interested him in the afternoon.

"My lord, I wonder at you that you should dare to keep that picture here, though three hundred

[The first version says *three thousand* and is of course what was intended here.]

miles of perilous sea, and savagery, and forests, and mountains impassable lie between you and Hampton Court. If you are a man, I think you have no cause to love the name of king. Yet is not your heart as good as any man's, and will not your money buy as many trinkets? I tell you, this wilderness is not dark enough to hide that woman's face! And she carries a lily in her hand, the lilies of Herrenhausen!

[In *A Lost Lady*, when Niel hears the subdued laughter in Mrs. Forrester's bedroom and realizes the truth about her, he says, "Lilies that fester, lilies that fester smell far worse than weeds."]

Justice de Dieu—." But he got no further, for my lord's hand had struck him in the mouth.

It all came about so quickly that even then it was but a blur of sudden action to me. We sprang between them, but Fairfax had no intention of striking twice.

"We can settle this in the morning, sir," he said, quietly. As he turned away M. Maurepas drew himself together with the litheness of a cat, and before I could catch his arm he had seized the long knife from his belt and thrown it after his host. It whizzed past my lord and stuck quivering in the oak wainscoting, while the man who threw it sank upon the floor, a pitiable heap of intoxication. My lord turned to his man, who still stood behind his chair, "Joseph [In the first version the name is *Henry*.] call me at five; at six I shall kill a scoundrel."

With that he left us to watch over the drunken slumbers of the Frenchman.

In the morning they met on the level stretch before the court. At my lord's request I stood as second to M. Maurepas. My principal was much shaken by his debauch of last night, and I thought when my lord looked upon him he was already dead. For in Lord Fairfax's face was a purpose which it seemed no human will could thwart. Never have I seen him look the noble, Christian gentleman as he looked it then. Just as the autumn mists were rising from the hills, their weapons crossed, and the rising sun shot my lord's blade with fire until it looked the sword of righteousness indeed. It lasted but a moment. M. Maurepas, so renowned in war and gallantry, who had been the shame of two courts and the rival of two kings, fell, unknown and friend-less, in the wilderness.

Two years later, after I had been presented and, through my father, stood in favor at court, I once had the honor to dine with His Majesty at Hampton Court. At his right sat a woman known to history only too well, the Duchess of Yarmouth, most beautiful of the women of Herrenhausen, who had been given an English title to cover the ill name she had brought with her,

> [In the first version the part of the sentence beginning with "the Duchess of Yarmouth. . . . brought with her," is omitted.]

still brilliant, still beautiful, as she was unto the end. By her side I was seated. When the dishes were removed, as we sat over our wine, the king bade me tell him some of the adventures that had befallen in my own land.

"I can tell you, Your Majesty, how Lord Fairfax fought and killed M. Maurepas about a woman's picture."

"That sounds well; tell on," said the monarch in his heavy German accent. [In the first version the word *German* is omitted.]

Then upon my hand under the table I felt a clasp, cold and trembling. I glanced down and saw there a white hand of wondrous beauty, the thumb ornamented with a single emerald. I sat still in amazement, for the lady's face was smiling and gave no sign.

The king clinked his glass impatiently with his nail.

"Well, go on with your story. Are we to wait for [In the first version the word *on* is used instead of *for*.] you all day?"

Again I felt that trembling pressure in mute entreaty on my hand.

"I think there is no story to tell, Your Majesty."

"And I think you are a very stupid young man," said His Majesty, testily, as he rose from the table.

"Perhaps he is abashed," laughed my lady, but her bosom heaved with a deep sigh of relief.

So my day of royal favor was a short one, nor was I sorry, for I had kept my friend's secret and shielded a fair lady's honor, which are the two first duties of a Virginian.

❧ Nanette: An Aside

published in *The Home Monthly*, August, 1896

[Here we find Cather's first treatment of the opera singer who was to be the center of interest in many of her short stories and in *Song of the Lark* and *Lucy Gayheart*. And here are her theories of art, her conviction so often expressed later, that no artist can have a happy marriage, that an artist can scarcely have happiness at all.]

Of course you do not know Nanette. You go to hear Tradutorri, go every night she is in the cast perhaps, and rave for days afterward over her voice, her beauty, her power, and when all is said the thing you most admire is a something which has no name, the indescribable quality which is Tradutorri herself.

[Compare with the following from *Song of the Lark:* "There's the voice itself, so beautiful and individual, and then there's something else; the thing in it which responds to every shade of thought and feeling, spontaneously, almost unconsciously."—"What one strives for is so far away, so beautiful that there's nothing one can say about it."]

But of Nanette, the preserver of Madame's beauty, the mistress of Madame's finances, the executrix of Madame's affairs, the power behind the scenes, of course, you know nothing.

It was after twelve o'clock when Nanette entered Madame's sleeping apartments at the Savoy and threw up the blinds, for Tradutorri always slept late after a performance. Last night it was Cavalleria Rusticana, and *Santuzza* is a trying role when it is enacted not merely with the emotions but with the soul, and it is this peculiar soul-note that has made Tradutorri great and unique among the artists of her generation.

[From *Song of the Lark:* "Her secret. It is every artist's secret. Passion. That is all. It is an open secret, and perfectly safe."]

"Madame has slept well, I hope?" inquired Nanette respectfully, as she presented herself at the foot of the bed.

"As well as usual, I believe," said Tradutorri rather wearily. "You have brought my breakfast? Well, you may put it here and put the ribbons in my gown while I eat. I will get up afterward."

Nanette took a chair by the bed and busied herself with a mass of white tulle.

"We leave America next week, Madame?"

"Yes, Friday; on the *Paris,*" said Madame, absently glancing up from her strawberries. "Why, Nanette, you are crying! One would think you had sung 'Voi lo sapete' yourself last night. What is the matter, my child?"

"Oh, it is nothing worthy of Madame's notice. One is always sorry to say good bye, that is all."

"To one's own country, perhaps, but this is different. You have no friends here; pray why should you be sorry to go?"

"Madame is mistaken when she says I have no friends here."

"Friends! Why, I thought you saw no one. Who, for example?"

"Well, there is a gentleman—"

"Bah! Must there always be a 'gentleman' even with you? But who is this fellow? Go on."

"Surely Madame has noticed?"

"Not I; I have noticed nothing. I have been very absentminded, rather ill, and abominally busy. Who is it?"

"Surely Madame must have noticed Signor Luongo, the head waiter?"

"The tall one, you mean, with the fine head like poor Sandro Salvini's? Yes, certainly I have noticed him; he is a very impressive piece of furniture. Well, what of him?"

"Nothing, Madame, but that he is very desirous that I should marry him."

"Indeed! And you?"

"I could wish for no greater happiness on earth, Madame."

Tradutorri laid a strawberry stem carefully upon her plate.

"Um-m-m, let me see; we have been here just two months and this affair has all come about. You have profited by your stage training, Nanette."

"O, Madame! Have you forgotten last season? We stopped here for six weeks then."

"The same 'gentleman' for two successive seasons? You are very disappointing, Nanette. You have not profited by your opportunities after all."

"Madame is pleased to jest, but I assure her that it is a very serious affair to me."

"O, yes, they all are. *Affaires tres sérieux.* That is scarcely an original remark, Nanette. I think I remember having made it once myself."

The love of bitter unbelief that Nanette feared came over Madame's face. Presently, as Nanette said nothing, Tradutorri spoke again.

"So you expect me to believe that this is really a serious matter?"

"No, Madame," said Nanette quietly. "He believes it and I believe. It is not necessary that any one else should."

Madame glanced curiously at the girl's face, and when she spoke again it was in a different tone.

"Very well: I do not see any objection. I need a man. It is not a bad thing to have your own porter in London, and after our London engagement is over we will go directly to Paris. He can take charge of my house there, my present steward is not entirely satisfactory, you know. You can spend the summer together there and doubtless by next season you can endure to be separated from him for a few months. So stop crying and send this statuesque signor to me tomorrow, and I will arrange matters. I want you to be happy, my girl—at least to try."

"Madame is good—too good, as always. I know your great heart. Out of your very compassion you would burden yourself with this man because I fancy him, as you once burdened yourself with me. But that is impossible, Madame. He would never leave New York. He will have his wife to himself or not at all. Very many professional people stay here, not all like Madame, and he has his prejudices. He would never allow me to travel, not even with Madame. He is very firm in these matters."

"O, ho! So he has prejudices against our profession, this *garçon?* Certainly you have contrived to do the usual thing in a very usual manner. You have fallen in love with a man who objects to your work."

Tradutorri pushed the tray away from her and lay down laughing a little as she threw her arms over her head.

"You see, Madame, that is where all the trouble comes. For of course I could not leave you."

Tradutorri looked up sharply, almost pleadingly, into Nanette's face.

"Leave me? Good Heavens, no! Of course you can not leave me. Why, who could ever learn all the needs of my life as you know them? What I may eat and what I may not, when I may see people and when they will tire me, what costumes I can wear and at what temperature I can have my baths. You know I am as helpless as a child in these matters. Leave me? The possibility has never occurred to me. Why, girl, I have grown fond of you! You have come entirely into my life. You have been my confidante and friend, the only creature I have trusted these last ten years. Leave me? I think it would break my heart. Come, brush out my hair, I will get up. The thing is impossible!"

[In *Lucy Gayheart,* "She [Lucy] almost wished she were Giuseppe [the valet], after all, it was people like that who counted with artists—more than their admirers."]

"So I told him, Madame," said Nanette tragically. "I said to him: 'Had it pleased Heaven to give me a voice I should have given myself wholly to my art, without one reservation, without one regret, as Madame has done. As it is, I am devoted to

Madame and her art as long as she has need of me.' Yes, that is what I said."

Tradutorri looked gravely at Nanette's face in the glass. "I am not at all sure that either I or my art are worth it, Nanette."

II

Tradutorri had just returned from her last performance in New York. It had been one of those eventful nights when the audience catches fire and drives a singer to her best, drives her beyond herself until she is greater than she knows or means to be.

> [From *The Song of the Lark:* "That afternoon nothing new came to Thea Kronborg, no enlightenment, no inspiration. She merely came into full possession of things she had been refining and perfecting for so long."—"If you love the good thing vitally, enough to give up for it all that one must give up, then you must hate the cheap thing just as hard. I tell you, there is such a thing as creative hate! A contempt that drives you through fire, makes you risk everything and lose everything, makes you a long sight better than you ever knew you could be."]

Now that it was over she was utterly exhausted and the life-force in her was low.

> [Compare this with Thea's exhaustion the night Dr. Archie comes to see her.]

I have said she is the only woman of our generation who sings with the soul rather than the senses, the only one indeed since Malibran, who died of that prodigal expense of spirit.

> [Thea in *Song of the Lark* has to give up all that is dear except art. She gives up Ottenburg—he wants a son. She doesn't return when her mother dies. "Your work becomes your personal life. . . It takes you up, and uses you, and spins you out; and that is your life."]

Other singers there are who feel and vent their suffering. Their methods are simple and transparent: they pour out their self-inflicted anguish and when it is over they are merely tired as children are after excitement. But Tradutorri holds back her suffering within herself; she suffers as the flesh and blood women of her century suffer. She is intense without being emotional. She takes this great anguish of hers and lays it in a tomb and rolls a stone before the door and walls it up. You wonder that one woman's heart can hold a grief so great. It is this stifled pain that wrings your heart when you hear her, that gives you the impression of horrible reality. It is this too, of which she is slowly dying now.

See, in all great impersonation there are two stages. One in which object is the generation of emotional power; to produce from one's own brain a whirlwind that will sweep the common-places of the world away from the naked souls of men and women and leave them defenseless and strange to each other. The other is the conservation of all this emotional energy; to bind the whirlwind down within one's straining heart, to feel the tears of many burning in one's eyes and yet not to weep, to hold all these chaotic faces still and silent within one's self until out of this tempest of pain and passion there speaks the still, small voice unto the soul of man. This is the theory of "repression." This is classical art, art exalted, art deified.

> [In "The Novel Démeublé" Cather says, "Whatever is felt upon the page without being specifically named there— that, one might say, is created. It is the inexplicable presence of the thing not named, of the overtone divined by the ear but not heard by it, the verbal mood, the emotional aura of the fact or the thing or the deed, that gives high quality to the novel or the drama, as well as to poetry itself."]

And of all the mighty artists of her time Tradutorri is the only woman who has given us art like this. And now she is dying of it, they say.

Nanette was undoing Madame's shoes. She had put the mail

silently on the writing desk. She had not given it to her before
the performance as there was one of those blue letters from
Madame's husband, written in an unsteady hand with the post-
mark of Monte Carlo, which always made Madame weep and
were always answered by large drafts.

[Cressida Garnet in "The Diamond Mine" is exploited
by her husbands, her family, and her worthless son. Clement
Sebastian in *Lucy Gayheart* has a greedy and heartless wife.]

There was also another from Madame's little crippled daughter
hidden away in a convent in Italy.

"I will see to my letters presently, Nanette. With me news is
generally bad news. I wish to speak with you tonight. We leave
New York in two days, and the glances of this signor statuesque
of yours is more than I can endure. I feel a veritable *mère Capu-
let.*"

"Has he dared to look impertinently at Madame? I will see
that this is stopped."

"You think that you could be really happy with this man,
Nanette?"

Nanette was sitting upon the floor with the flowers from
Madame's corsage in her lap. She rested her sharp little chin on
her hand.

"Is any one really happy, Madame? But this I know, that I
could endure to be very unhappy always to be with him." Her
saucy little French face grew grave and her lips trembled.

Madame Tradutorri took her hand tenderly.

"Then if you feel like that I have nothing to say. How
strange that this should come to you, Nanette; it never has to
me.

[Cather had the conviction throughout her life that it
was impossible for an artist to be happy. Thea couldn't have
married anyone and been happy. Cressida Garnet is never
happy in marriage. Nor Clement Sebastian. Nor any of the
singers or painters of Cather's pages.

Ordinary people like maids or farmers (*My Ántonia*)
may have happy marriages, although they are not common
in Cather lore. When Thea (*Song of the Lark*) saw a poor
old German couple at Paderewski's recital, knew they'd sacri-
ficed for their tickets, and saw the old lady put her hand on
her husband's arm, with a look of recognition like forget-
me-nots, she wanted to ask them how they'd kept that feeling
like a bouquet in a glass of water.]

"Listen: Your mother and I were friends once when we
both sang in the chorus in a miserable little theatre in Naples.
She sang quite as well as I then, and she was a handsome girl
and her future looked brighter than mine. But somehow in the
strange lottery of art I rose and she went under with the wheel.
She had youth, beauty, vigor, but was one of the countless thousands who fail. When I found her years afterward, dying in a
charity hospital in Paris, I took you from her. You were scarcely
ten years old then. If you had sung I should have given you the
best instruction; as it was I was only able to save you from that
most horrible of fates, the chorus. You have been with me so
long. Through all my troubles you were the one person who
did not change toward me. You have become indispensable to
me, but I am no longer so to you. I have inquired as to the repu-
tation of this signor of yours from the proprietors of the house
and I find it excellent. Ah, Nanette, did you really think I could
stand between you and happiness? You have been a good girl,
Nanette. You have stayed with me when we did not stop at
hotels like this one, and when your wages were not paid you for
weeks together."

"Madame, it is you who have been good! Always giving
and giving to a poor girl like me with no voice at all. You know
that I would not leave you for anything in the world but this."

"Are you sure you can be happy so? Think what it means!
No more music, no more great personages, no more plunges from
winter to summer in a single night, no more Russia, no more
Paris, no more Italy. Just a little house somewhere in a strange
country with a man who may have faults of his own, and per-

haps little children growing up about you to be cared for always. You have been used to changes and money and excitement, and those habits of life are hard to change, my girl."

[At about the time this story was written, Willa Cather wrote a friend that she did not want to get married. Her objections were approximately the ones Madame cites above—the things Nanette will miss, particularly independence.]

"Madame, you know how it is. One sees much and stops at the best hotels, and goes to the best milliners—and yet one is not happy, but a stranger always. That is, I mean"—
"Yes, I know too well what you mean. Don't spoil it now you have said it. And yet one is not happy! You will not be lonely, you think, all alone in this big strange city, so far from our world?"
"Alone! Why, Madame, Arturo is here!"
Tradutorri looked wistfully at her shining face.
"How strange that this should come to you, Nanette. Be very happy in it, dear. Let nothing come between you and it; no desire, no ambition. It is not given to every one. There are women who wear crowns who would give them for an hour of it."

[Madame's skepticism is Cather's own. In a 1921 interview she said: "After all, it is the little things that really matter most, the unfinished things, the things that never quite come to birth. Sometimes a man's wedding day is the happiest day in his life; but usually he likes most of all to look back upon some quite simple, quite uneventful day, when nothing in particular happened but all the world seemed touched with gold. Sometimes it is a man's wife who sums up to him his ideal of all that a woman can be; but how often it is some girl whom he scarcely knows, whose beauty and kindliness have caught at his imagination without cloying it!"]

"O, Madame, if I could but see you happy before I leave you!"

"Hush, we will not speak of that. When the flowers thrown me in my youth shall live again, or when the dead crater of my own mountain shall be red once more—then, perhaps. Now go and tell your lover that the dragon has renounced her prey."

"Madame, I rebel against this loveless life of yours! You should be happy. Surely with so much else you should at least have that."

Tradutorri pulled up from her dressing case the score of the last great opera written in Europe which had been sent her to originate the title role.

"You see this, Nanette? When I began life, between me and this lay everything dear in life—every love, every human hope. I have had to bury what lay between. It is the same thing florists do when they cut away all the buds that one flower may blossom with the strength of all.

[This is exactly what Thea has to do in *Song of the Lark*.]

God is a very merciless artist, and when he works out his purposes in the flesh his chisel does not falter. But no more of this, my child. Go find your lover. I shall undress alone tonight. I must get used to it. Good night, my dear. You are the last of them all, the last of all who have brought warmth into my life. You must let me kiss you to-night. No, not that way—on the lips. Such a happy face to-night, Nanette! May it be so always!"

After Nanette was gone Madame put her head down on her dressing case and wept, those lonely tears of utter wretchedness that a homesick girl sheds at school. And yet upon her brow shone the coronet that the nations had given her when they called her queen.

🌿 Tommy, the Unsentimental

published in *The Home Monthly*, August, 1896

[Willa Cather went to Pittsburgh as managing editor of *The Home Monthly* in July of 1896. Almost immediately Mr. Axtell, the man who was responsible for the new magazine, took off for the west and left Willa with the whole responsibility of getting out the first, the August, issue. She wrote at least half of it herself, under several names. This light story gives us an idea of Miss Cather's ideas on her young contemporaries.]

"Your father says he [Jay] has no business tact at all, and of course that's dreadfully unfortunate."

"Business," replied Tommy, "he's a baby in business; he's good for nothing on earth but to keep his hair parted straight and wear that white carnation in his buttonhole. He has 'em sent down from Hastings twice a week as regularly as the mail comes, but the drafts he cashes lie in his safe until they are lost, or somebody finds them. I go up occasionally and send a package away for him myself. He'll answer your notes promptly enough, but his business letters—I believe he destroys them unopened to shake the responsibility of answering them."

"I am at a loss to see how you can have such patience with him, Tommy, in so many ways he is thoroughly reprehensible."

"Well, a man's likeableness don't depend at all on his virtues or acquirements, nor a woman's either, unfortunately. You like them or you don't like them, and that's all there is to it. For the why of it you must appeal to a higher oracle than I. Jay is a likeable fellow, and that's his only and sole acquirement, but after all it's a rather happy one."

[This is a genuine Cather sentiment. She uses a character, Victor Morse in *One of Ours,* very similar to Jay. Victor had been a bank clerk in Crystal Lake, Iowa, and had little to commend him except that he was, like Jay, likeable.]

"Yes, he certainly is that," replied Miss Jessica, as she deliberately turned off the gas jet and proceeded to arrange her toilet articles. Tommy watched her closely and then turned away with a baffled expression.

Needless to say, Tommy was not a boy, although her keen gray eyes and wide forehead were scarcely girlish, and she had the lank figure of an active half grown lad. Her real name was Theodosia, but during Thomas Shirley's frequent absences from the bank she had attended to his business and correspondence signing herself "T. Shirley," until everyone in Southdown called her "Tommy." That blunt sort of familiarity is not unfrequent in the west, and is meant well enough. People rather expect some business ability in a girl there, and they respect it immensely.

[Willa called "Willie" by her friends and family helped in her father's abstract office. She also helped the local doctors in their rounds and, besides, went every week to the courthouse to read the weekly court proceedings.]

That, Tommy undoubtedly had, and if she had not, things would have gone at sixes and sevens in the Southdown National. For Thomas Shirley had big land interests in Wyoming that called him constantly away from home, and his cashier, little Jay Ellington Harper, was, in the local phrase, a weak brother in the bank. He was the son of a friend of old Shirley's, whose papa had sent him West, because he had made a sad mess of his college career, and had spent too much money and gone at too

giddy a pace down East. Conditions changed the young gentleman's life, for it was simply impossible to live either prodigally
or rapidly in Southdown, but they could not materially affect
his mental habits or inclinations. He was made cashier of Shirley's bank because his father bought in half the stock, but
Tommy did his work for him.

The relation between these two young people was peculiar;
Harper was, in his way, very grateful to her for keeping him
out of disgrace with her father, and showed it by a hundred
little attentions which were new to her and much more agreeable
than the work she did for him was irksome. Tommy knew that
she was immensely fond of him, and she knew at the same time
that she was thoroughly foolish for being so. As she expressed
it, she was not of his sort, and never would be. She did not often
take pains to think, but when she did she saw matters pretty
clearly, and she was of a peculiarly unfeminine mind that could
not escape meeting and acknowledging a logical conclusion. But
she went on liking Jay Ellington Harper, just the same. Now
Harper was the only foolish man of Tommy's acquaintance. She
knew plenty of active young business men and sturdy ranchers,
such as one meets about live Western towns, and took no particular interest in them, probably just because they were practical
and sensible and thoroughly of her own kind. She knew almost
no women, because in those days there were few women in
Southdown who were in any sense interesting, or interested in
anything but babies and salads. Her best friends were her father's old business friends, elderly men who had seen a good
deal of the world, and who were very proud and fond of Tommy.
They recognized a sort of squareness and honesty of spirit in
the girl that Jay Ellington Harper never discovered, or, if he did,
knew too little of its rareness to value highly. Those old specu-
lators and men of business had always felt a sort of responsibility
for Tom Shirley's little girl, and had rather taken her mother's
place, and been her advisers on many points upon which men
seldom feel at liberty to address a girl.

[So many of the satisfactory man-woman relationships
in Cather's writings are the father-daughter or older man-
young girl type of friendship. Take, for example, the hero
worship Lucy Gayheart feels for Sebastian, or Thea's friendship with Dr. Archie, Alexandra's for Ivar, the feeling between Neighbour Rosicky and his city-bred daughter-in-law,
to name a few.]

She was just one of them; she played whist and billiards with
them, and made their cocktails for them, not scorning to take
one herself occasionally. Indeed, Tommy's cocktails were things
of fame in Southdown, and the professional compounders of
drinks always bowed respectfully to her as though acknowledging a powerful rival.

Now all these things displeased and puzzled Jay Ellington
Harper, and Tommy knew it full well, but clung to her old
manner of living with a stubborn pertinacity, feeling somehow
that to change would be both foolish and disloyal to the Old
Boys. And as things went on, the seven Old Boys made greater
demands upon her time than ever, for they were shrewd men,
most of them, and had not lived fifty years in this world without learning a few things and unlearning many more. And while
Tommy lived on in the blissful delusion that her role of indifference was perfectly played and without a flaw, they suspected
how things were going and were perplexed as to the outcome.
Still, their confidence was by no means shaken, and as Joe
Elsworth said to Joe Sawyer one evening at billiards, "I think
we can pretty nearly depend on Tommy's good sense."

They were too wise to say anything to Tommy, but they
said just a word or two to Thomas Shirley, Sr., and combined
to make things very unpleasant for Mr. Jay Ellington Harper.

At length their relations with Harper became so strained
that the young man felt it would be better for him to leave town,
so his father started him in a little bank of his own up in Red
Willow. Red Willow, however, was scarcely a safe distance, being
only some twenty-five miles north, upon the Divide, and Tommy

occasionally found excuse to run up on her wheel to straighten out the young man's business for him.

[A fifty-mile round trip by bicycle would not, in those days, have been considered unusual.]

So when she suddenly decided to go East to school for a year, Thomas, Sr., drew a sigh of great relief. But the seven Old Boys shook their heads; they did not like to see her gravitating toward the East; it was a sign of weakening, they said, and showed an inclination to experiment with another kind of life, Jay Ellington Harper's kind.

But to school Tommy went, and from all reports conducted herself in a most seemly manner; made no more cocktails, played no more billiards. She took rather her own way with the curriculum, but she distinguished herself in athletics, which in Southdown counted for vastly more than erudition.

Her evident joy on getting back to Southdown was appreciated by everyone. She went about shaking hands with everybody, her shrewd face, that was so like a clever wholesome boy's, held high with happiness. As she said to old Joe Elsworth one morning, when they were driving behind his stud through a little thicket of cottonwood scattered along the sun-parched bluffs,

"It's all very fine down East there, and the hills are great, but one gets mighty homesick for this sky, the old intense blue of it, you know. Down there the skies are all pale and smoky. And this wind, this hateful, dear, old everlasting wind that comes down like the sweep of cavalry and is never tamed or broken, O Joe, I used to get hungry for this wind! I couldn't sleep in that lifeless stillness down there."

[Willa Cather had been away from Nebraska about a month when she wrote this, but already she had that ambivalent feeling: the love and hate, the blessing and the curse of Nebraska that was to follow her throughout her life.

Actually her letters from this period do not mention
homesickness, rather a joy at getting back to trees that God
planted, and hills; and it is possible that she was not herself conscious of how she felt about the skies and the "hateful, dear, old everlasting wind."]

"How about the people, Tom?"

"O, they are fine enough folk, but we're not their sort, Joe,
and never can be."

"You realize that, do you, fully?"

"Quite fully enough, thank you, Joe." She laughed rather
dismally, and Joe cut his horse with the whip.

[The feeling of not fitting in haunted Willa Cather quite
as much as it did Claude Wheeler in *One of Ours*. In fact,
she definitely identified herself with him in that respect. For
this information I am indebted to Cather's letters to Dorothy
Canfield Fisher.]

The only unsatisfactory thing about Tommy's return was
that she brought with her a girl she had grown fond of at
school, a dainty, white, languid bit of a thing, who used violet
perfumes and carried a sunshade. The Old Boys said it was a
bad sign when a rebellious girl like Tommy took to being sweet
and gentle to one of her own sex, the worst sign in the world.

The new girl was no sooner in town than a new complica-
tion came about. There was no doubt of the impression she made
on Jay Ellington Harper. She indisputably had all those little
evidences of good breeding that were about the only things
which could touch the timid, harassed young man who was so
much out of his element. It was a very plain case on his part,
and the souls of the seven were troubled within them. Said Joe
Elsworth to the other Joe,

"The heart of the cad is gone out to the little muff, as is
right and proper and in accordance with the eternal fitness of
things. But there's the other girl who has the blindness that
may not be cured, and she gets all the rub of it. It's no use. I

can't help her, and I am going to run down to Kansas City for awhile. I can't stay here and see the abominable suffering of it." He didn't go, however.

There was just one other person who understood the hopelessness of the situation quite as well as Joe, and that was Tommy. That is, she understood Harper's attitude. As to Miss Jessica's she was not quite so certain, for Miss Jessica, though pale and languid and addicted to sunshades was a maiden most discreet. Conversations on the subject usually ended without any further information as to Miss Jessica's feelings, and Tommy sometimes wondered if she were capable of having any at all.

At last the calamity which Tommy had long foretold descended upon Jay Ellington Harper. One morning she received a telegram from him begging her to intercede with her father; there was a run on his bank and he must have help before noon. It was then ten thirty, and the one sleepy little train that ran up to Red Willow daily had crawled out of the station an hour before. Thomas Shirley, Sr., was not at home.

"And it's a good thing for Jay Ellington he's not, he might be more stony hearted than I," remarked Tommy, as she closed the ledger and turned to the terrified Miss Jessica. "Of course we're his only chance, no one else would turn their hand over to help him. The train went an hour ago and he says it must be there by noon. It's the only bank in the town, so nothing can be done by telegraph. There is nothing left but to wheel for it. I may make it, and I may not. Jess, you scamper up to the house and get my wheel out, the tire may need a little attention. I will be along in a minute."

"O Theodosia, can't I go with you? I must go!"

"You go! O, yes, of course, if you want to. You know what you are getting into, though. It's twenty-five miles uppish grade and hilly, and only an hour and a quarter to do it in."

[Such a distance in that length of time would be almost impossible.]

"O, Theodosia, I can do anything now!" cried Miss Jessica, as she put up her sunshade and fled precipitately. Tommy smiled as she began cramming bank notes into a canvas bag. "May be you can, my dear, and may be you can't."

The road from Southdown to Red Willow is not by any means a favorite bicycle road; it is rough, hilly and climbs from the river bottoms up to the big Divide by a steady up grade, running white and hot through the scorched corn fields and grazing lands where the long-horned Texan cattle browse about in the old buffalo wallows. Miss Jessica soon found that with the peddling that had to be done there was little time left for emotion of any sort, or little sensibility for anything but the throbbing, dazzling heat that had to be endured. Down there in the valley the distant bluffs were vibrating and dancing with the heat, the cattle, completely overcome by it, had hidden under the shelving banks of the "draws" and the prairie dogs had fled to the bottom of their holes that are said to reach to water. The whirr of the seventeen-year locust was the only thing that spoke of animation, and that ground on as if only animated and enlivened by the sickening, destroying heat. The sun was like hot brass, and the wind that blew up from the south was hotter still. But Tommy knew that wind was their only chance. Miss Jessica began to feel that unless she could stop and get some water she was not much longer for this vale of tears. She suggested this possibility to Tommy, but Tommy only shook her head, "Take too much time," and bent over her handle bars, never lifting her eyes from the road in front of her. It flashed upon Miss Jessica that Tommy was not only very unkind, but that she sat very badly on her wheel and looked aggressively masculine and professional when she bent her shoulders and pumped like that. But just then Miss Jessica found it harder than ever to breathe, and the bluffs across the river began doing serpentines and skirt dances, and more important and personal considerations occupied the young lady.

When they were fairly over the first half of the road, Tommy took out her watch. "Have to hurry up, Jess, I can't wait for you."

"O, Tommy, I can't," panted Miss Jessica, dismounting and sitting down in a little heap by the roadside. "You go on, Tommy, and tell him—tell him I hope it won't fail, and I'd do anything to save him."

By this time the discreet Miss Jessica was reduced to tears, and Tommy nodded as she disappeared over the hill laughing to herself. "Poor Jess, anything but the one thing he needs. Well, your kind have the best of it generally, but in little affairs of this sort my kind come out rather strongly. We're rather better at them than at dancing. It's only fair, one side shouldn't have all."

Just at twelve o'clock, when Jay Ellington Harper, his collar crushed and wet about his throat, his eye glass dimmed with perspiration, his hair hanging damp over his forehead, and even the ends of his moustache dripping with moisture, was attempting to reason with a score of angry Bohemians, Tommy came quietly through the door, grip in hand. She went straight behind the grating, and standing screened in the bookkeeper's desk, handed the bag to Harper and turned to the spokesman of the Bohemians,

"What's all this business mean, Anton? Do you all come to bank at once nowadays?"

"We want 'a money, want 'a our money, he no got it, no give it," bawled a big beery Bohemian.

"O, don't chaff 'em any longer, give 'em their money and get rid of 'em, I want to see you," said Tommy carelessly, as she went into the consulting room.

When Harper entered half an hour later, after the rush was over, all that was left of his usual immaculate appearance was his eyeglass and the white flower in his buttonhole.

"This has been terrible!" he gasped. "Miss Theodosia, I can never thank you."

"No," interrupted Tommy. "You never can, and I don't want any thanks. It was rather a tight place, though, wasn't it? You looked like a ghost when I came in. What started them?"

"How should I know? They just came down like the wolf

on the fold. It sounded like the approach of a ghost dance."

"And of course you had no reserve? O, I always told you this would come, it was inevitable with your charming methods. By the way, Jess sends her regrets and says she would do anything to save you. She started out with me, but she has fallen by the wayside. O, don't be alarmed, she is not hurt, just winded. I left her all bunched up by the road like a little white rabbit. I think the lack of romance in the escapade did her up about as much as anything; she is essentially romantic. If we had been on fiery steeds bespattered with foam I think she would have made it, but a wheel hurt her dignity. I'll tend bank; you'd better get your wheel and go and look her up and comfort her. And as soon as it is convenient, Jay, I wish you'd marry her and be done with it. I want to get this thing off my mind."

Jay Ellington Harper dropped into a chair and turned a shade whiter.

"Theodosia, what do you mean? Don't you remember what I said to you last fall, the night before you went to school? Don't you remember what I wrote you—"

Tommy sat down on the table beside him and looked seriously and frankly into his eyes.

"Now, see here, Jay Ellington, we have been playing a nice little game, and now it's time to quit. One must grow up sometime. You are horribly wrought up over Jess, and why deny it? She's your kind, and clean daft about you, so there is only one thing to do. That's all."

Jay Ellington wiped his brow, and felt unequal to the situation. Perhaps he really came nearer to being moved down to his stolid little depths than he ever had before. His voice shook a good deal and was very low as he answered her.

"You have been very good to me. I didn't believe any woman could be at once so kind and clever. You almost made a man of even me."

"Well, I certainly didn't succeed. As to being good to you, that's rather a break, you know; I am amiable, but I am only flesh and blood after all. Since I have known you I have not been at all good, in any sense of the word, and I suspect I have been anything but clever. Now, take mercy upon Jess—and me—and go. Go on, that ride is beginning to tell on me. Such things strain one's nerve. Thank Heaven he's gone at last and had sense enough not to say anything more. It was growing rather critical. As I told him I am not at all super-human."

After Jay Ellington Harper had bowed himself out, when Tommy sat alone in the darkened office, watching the flapping blinds, with the bank books before her, she noticed a white flower on the floor. It was the one Jay Ellington Harper had worn in his coat and had dropped in his nervous agitation. She picked it up and stood holding it a moment, biting her lip. Then she dropped it into the grate and turned away, shrugging her thin shoulders.

"They are awful idiots, half of them, and never think of anything beyond their dinner. But O, how we do like 'em!"

❧ The Count of Crow's Nest

published as a two-part serial in *The Home Monthly*,
September and October, 1896

[The choice of subject matter and characters in this story shows the influence of Henry James. The attitudes of the viewpoint character, Buchanan, are those of Willa Cather at the age of twenty-two, and pretty much a forecast of the later Cather. Of course, behind both Cather and James are the French influences—the impact of their interest in historical romances. For Cather, Alphonse Daudet was very important at this time.

Willa Cather showed this story to Harold Dundy, a reader on *Cosmopolitan*, who offered her $100 for it, but she was not free to sell it, needing to fill the pages of her own magazine. However, his encouragement made her feel she was making progress.]

Crow's Nest was an over-crowded boarding house on West Side, over-crowded because there one could obtain shelter and sustenance of a respectable nature cheaper than anywhere else in ante-Columbian Chicago. Of course the real name of the place was not Crow's Nest; it had, indeed, a very euphuistic name; but a boarder once called it Crow's Nest, and the rest felt the fitness of the title, so after that the name clung to it. The cost of existing had been reduced to its minimum there, and it was for that reason that Harold Buchanan found the Count de Koch among the guests of the house. Buchanan himself was there from the same cause, a cause responsible for most of the disagreeable things in this world. For Buchanan was just out of college, an honor man of whom great things were expected, and was waiting about Chicago to find a drive wheel to which to apply his undisputed genius. He found this waiting to see what one is good for one of the most trying tasks allotted to the sons of men. He hung about studios, publishing houses and concert halls hunting a medium, an opportunity. He knew that he was gifted in more ways than one, but he knew equally well that he was painfully immature, and that between him and success of any kind lay an indefinable, intangible something which only time could dispose of.

[This was very much Cather's feeling about herself, expressed in letters to friends that same year before she went to Pittsburgh.]

Once it had been a question of which of several professions he should concentrate his energies upon; now the problem was to find any one in which he could gain the slightest foothold. When he had begun his search it was a quest of the marvelous, of the pot of fairy gold at the rainbow's end; but now it was a quest for gold of another sort, just the ordinary prosaic gold of the work-a-day world that will buy a man his dinner and a coat to his back.

In the meantime, among the tragic disillusionments of his first hazard of fortune, Buchanan had to live, and this he did at Crow's Nest because existence was much simplified there, almost reduced to first principles, and one could dine in a sack coat and still hold up his head with assurance among his fellow men. So there he had his study, where he began pictures and tragedies that were never completed, and wrote comic operas that were never produced, and hated humanity as only a nervous sensitive man in a crowded boarding house can hate it. The rooms above his were occupied by a prima donna who practiced incessantly, a thin, pale, unhappy-looking woman with dark rings under her eyes, whose strength and salary were spent in endeavoring to force her voice up to a note which forever eluded her. On his

left lived a discontented man, bearded like a lion, who had intended to be a novelist and had ended by becoming a very
ordinary reviewer, putting the reproach of his failure entirely
upon a dull and unappreciative public.

The occupants of the house were mostly people of this sort,
who had come short of their own expectations and thought that
the world had treated them badly and that the time was out of
joint.

[In spite of her success, Willa Cather came in her old
age to feel something of this sort of bitterness, complaining
that the future held nothing for people of her generation.]

The atmosphere of failure and that peculiar rancor which it
begets seemed to have settled down over the place. It seemed
to have entered into the very walls; it was in the close reception
room with its gloomy hangings, clammy wall paper, hard sofas
and bad pictures. It was in the old grand piano, with the worn
yellow keys that clicked like castanets as they gave out their
wavering, tinny treble notes in an ineffectual staccato. It was
in the long, dark dining room, where the gas was burning all day,
in the reluctant chairs that were always dismembering themselves under one, in the inevitable wan chromo of the sad-eyed
Cenci [Beatrice Cenci, the "Beautiful Parricide," portrait probably by Guido Reni] who is daily martyred anew at the hands of
relentless copyists, in the very clock above the sideboard whose
despairing, hopeless hands never reached the hour at the proper
time, and which always struck plaintively, long after all the other
clocks were through.

The prima donna sneered at the chilly style of the great
Australian soprano who was singing for a thousand dollars a
night down at the Auditorium, the reviewer declared that literature had stopped with Thackeray, the art student railed day and
night against all pictures but his own.

Buchanan sometimes wondered if this were a dark prophecy
of his own future. Perhaps he, too, would some day be old and
poor and disappointed, would have touched that wall which

marks the limitations of men's lives, and would hate the name of
a successful man as the dwarfs of the underworld hated the
giants in the golden groves of Asgard. He felt it would be better
to contrive to get capsized in the lake some night. Could there
be any greater degradation than to learn to hate an art and its
exponents merely because one had failed in it himself? He fer-
vently hoped that some happy accident would carry him off
before he reached that stage.

Day after day he sat down in that dining room that was so
conducive to pessimistic reflection, with the same distasteful
people: The blonde stenographer who giggled so that she often
had to leave the table, the cadaverous art student who talked of
originating a new school of landscape painting, and who meantime taught clay modeling in a design school to defray his modest
expenses at the Nest, the reviewer, the prima donna, the languid
old widow who wore lilacs in her false front and coquetted with
the fat man with the ear trumpet. She had, in days gone by, made
coy overtures to Buchanan and the surly reviewer, but as they
were more unresponsive and would have none of her, she now
devoted herself exclusively to the deaf man, though undoubtedly
ear trumpets are an impediment to coquetry. But as the deaf
man could not hear her at all, he stood it very well. He might
also be short sighted, Buchanan reflected.

In all that vista of faces, there were some twenty in all,
there was but one which was not unpleasant; that of the courtly
old gentleman who ate alone at a small table at the end of the
dining room. He was only there at dinner, his breakfast and
luncheon were always sent to his room. He had no acquaintances
in the house and spoke to no one, yet every one knew that he
was Paul, Count de Koch, and during breakfast and luncheon
hours he and his possible history had furnished the *pièce de
résistance* of conversation for some months. In that absorbing
theme even the decadence of French art and English letters and
the execution of the Australian soprano were forgotten. The
stenographer called attention to the fact that his coat was of a
prehistoric cut, though she acknowledged its fit was above criti-

cism. The widow had learned from the landlady that he shaved himself and blacked his own boots. She was certain he had been a desperately wicked man and lost all his money at Monte Carlo, for unless Counts were very reprehensible indeed they were always rich. This scrutinizing gossip about a courteous and defenseless old gentleman was the most harassing of all Buchanan's table trials, and it savored altogether too much of the treatment of Père Goriot in Madame Vauquar's "Pension Bourgeoise."

He was always glad at dinner when the Count's presence put a stop at least to audible queries, and his calm patrician face again made its strange contrast with the sordid unhappy ones about him. His clear gray eyes, his slight erect figure, and white, tapering hands seemed quite as anomalous there as his name. That gentlemanly figure made life at Crow's Nest possible to Buchanan; it was like seeing a Vandyke portrait in the gallery of daubs. The Count's whole conduct, like his person, was simple, dignified and artistic. It was a cause for much indignation among the boarders, particularly so in the case of the widow and prima donna, that he met no one. Yet his manner was never one of superiority, simply of amiable and dignified reserve. He might at all times have stood the scrutiny of a court drawing room, yet he was perfectly unostentatious and unconscious. There was something regal about his gestures. When he held back the swinging door for the hurried maid with her groaning tray of dishes, you half expected to see the Empress Eugenie and her train sweep through, or gay old Ludwig with his padded calves and painted cheeks and enormous wig, his troupe of poets and dancers behind him. He drank his pale California claret as if it were Madeira of one of those priceless vintages of the last century.

In his college days Buchanan had been a good deal among well-bred people, but he had never seen any one so quietly and faultlessly correct. Sometimes he met him walking by the Lake Shore, and he thought he would have noticed his carriage and walk among a thousand. In watching him that phrase of

Lang's, "A gentleman among *canaille*," constantly occurred to him.

One of the saddest defects of that ponderous machinery which we call society is the impenetrable wall which is built up between personalities; one of the saddest of our finite weaknesses is our incapacity to recognize and know and claim the people who are made for us. Every day we pass men who want us and whom we bitterly need, unknowing, unthinking, as friends pass each other at a masked ball: pursuing the tinkle of the harlequin's bells, not knowing that under the friar's hood is the *camaraderie* they seek. Following persistently the fluttering hem of the priestly gown, never dreaming that the heart of gold is under the spangled corsage of Folly there, sitting tired out on the stairway. It seems as if there ought to be a floor manager to arrange these things for us. However, given a close proximity and continue it long enough, and the right people will find each other out as certainly as the satellites know their proper suns. It was impossible that, in such a place as Crow's Nest, Buchanan's relations to the Count should continue the same as those of the other boarders. It was impossible that the Count should not notice that one respectful glance that was neither curious nor vulgar, only frankly interested and appreciative.

One evening as Buchanan sat in the reception room reading a volume of Gautier's romances while waiting for the dinner that was always late, he glanced up and detected the Count looking over his shoulder.

"I must ask your pardon for my seeming discourtesy, but one so seldom sees those delightful romances read in this country, that for the moment I quite forgot myself. And as I caught the title 'La Morte Amoureuse,' an old favorite of mine, I could scarcely refrain from glancing a second time."

Buchanan decided that since chance had thrown this opportunity in his way, he had a right to make the most of it. He closed the book and turned, smiling.

"I am only too glad to meet some one who is familiar with

it. I have met the idea before, it has been imitated in English, I think."

"Ah, yes, doubtless. Many of those things have been imitated in English, but—"

He shrugged his shoulders expressively. "Yes. I understand your hiatus. These things are quite impossible in English, especially the one we are speaking of. Some way we haven't the feeling for absolute and specific beauty of diction. We have no sense for the aroma of words as they have. We are never content with the effect of material beauty alone, we are always looking for something else. Of course we lose by it, it is like always thinking about one's dinner when one is invited out."

[Willa Cather's admiration for French literature and French precision of expression began early and continued throughout her life.]

The Count nodded. "Yes, you look for the definite, whereas the domain of pure art is always the indefinite. You want the fact under the illusion, whereas the illusion is in itself the most wonderful of facts. It is a mistake not to be content with perfection and not find its sermon sufficient. As opposed to chaos, harmony was the original good, the first created virtue.

[This idea of harmony comes from Henry James' "Altar of the Dead."]

And of course a great production of art must be the perfection of harmony. Even in the grotesque the harmony of the whole must be there. To be impervious to this indicates a certain bluntness toward the finer spiritual laws."

"And yet," said Buchanan, "we have been accustomed to look at all this as quite the opposite of spiritual. Our standpoint is certainly rather inconsistent, but I believe it is honest enough."

The Count smiled. "Certainly. It is a question of whether you want your sermon in a flower or in a Greek word, in poetry or in prose, whether you want the formula of goodness or goodness itself. So many of your authors write formulae. There was, however, one of your *littérateurs* who knew the distinction, even if he was something of a charlatan in using it. Poe surpassed even Gautier in using some effects of that character," pointing to the book in Buchanan's hand. "Perhaps under happier circumstances he might have done so in all. You had there a true stylist, who knew the value of an effect; a master of single and graceful conceptions, who was content to leave them as such, unexplained and without apology."

"Perhaps that is the reason we say he was crazy," said Buchanan, sadly.

> [In one of her book-review columns of this period, Willa Cather praised Poe, denying that he killed himself with drink and saying that he died of starvation.]

"Perhaps," said the Count as he lighted his cigar. "I hope to have the pleasure of discussing this again with you. You have read 'Fortunio'? No? When you have read 'Fortunio' I will wish to see you." He smiled and went out for his wintery walk on the Lake Shore.

After that Buchanan met the Count frequently, in the hallway, on the veranda, on his walks. They always had some conversation during these encounters, but their remarks were generally of a very casual nature. Buchanan felt some hesitancy about pushing the acquaintance lest he should exhaust it too soon.

> [This is Cather's own feeling, which she expressed in writing about marriage in particular—that the relationship deteriorated with time. For example, notice the lack of any depth of feeling between the professor and his wife in *The Professor's House.*]

His tendency had always lain that way. In his intemperate youth he had plunged hot-headed and rapacious into friendship after friendship, giving more than any one cared to receive and exacting more than any one had leisure to give, only to reach that almost inevitable point where, independent of any volition of his own, the impetus slackened and stopped, the wells of sweet water were dry and the cisterns were broken. These promising oases that flourish among monotonous humanity dry up so quickly, most of them. They are verdant to us but a night. There are so few minds that are fitted to race side by side, to wrestle and rejoice together, even unto the paean. And after all that is the base of affinities, that mental brotherhood. The glamour of every other passion and enthusiasm fades like the brilliance of an afterglow, leaving shadow and chill and a nameless ennui.

[Willa Cather did not find such mental brotherhood in any eligible man, and she would not settle for less.]

One evening Buchanan stopped the Count in the hall.

"May I trouble you for a moment, sir? A friend of mine who is something of a bibliomaniac has sent me from Munich a copy of Rabelais stamped with the Bavarian arms. There is an autograph on the fly leaf, indeed, two of them, and he suspects that one of them may be Ludwig's."

The Count adjusted his eye glasses and looked thoughtfully at the faded writing: "Lola M.," and further down the page, "Ludwig." "You have certainly every reason for such a supposition. Ludwig was one of the few monarchs who really cared enough for books to put his name in one, and Lola Montes' name, too, for that matter. However, in these autographs one can never tell. If you will step upstairs with me we can soon assure ourselves."

"O, I did not mean to trouble you; you were just going out, were you not?"

"It was nothing of importance, nothing that I would not gladly abandon for the prospect of your company."

Buchanan followed him up the stuffy stairway and down the narrow hall. He was conscious of a subdued thrill of quickened curiosity upon entering the Count's apartments. But as his host lit the gas one covert glance about him told him that he need not exercise rigid surveillance over his eyes. Beyond a number of books and pictures, portraits, most of them, there was little to distinguish the room from the ordinary furnished apartment. There was the usual faded moquette carpet, the same cheap rugs and the inevitable shiny oak furniture. The silver fittings of the writing table, engraved with a crest and monogram, were the only suggestions of the rank of the occupant.

"Be seated there, on the divan, and I will find a signature I know to be authentic. We will compare them." As he spoke he tugged at the unwilling drawers of a chiffonier in the corner.

"This furniture," he remarked apologetically, "partakes somewhat of the sullen nature of the house. There, we have it at last."

He lifted from the drawer a small steel chest and placed it upon the table. After opening it with a key attached to his watch-guard, he drew out a pile of papers and began sorting them. Buchanan watched curiously the various documents as they passed through his hands. Some of them were on parchment and suggested venerable histories, some of them were encased in modern envelopes, and some were on tinted note paper with heavily embossed monograms, suggesting histories equally alluring if less venerable. If these notes could speak the import of their contents, what a roar of guttural bassos, soaring sopranos, and impassioned contraltos and tenors there would be! And would the dominant note of the chorus be of Ares or Eros, he wondered?

He was aroused from his speculations by the Count's slight exclamation when he found the paper he was hunting for. He unfolded a stiff sheet of note paper, and then folding it back so that only the signature was visible, sat down beside his guest. The signature, "Ludwig W.", stood out clearly from the paper he held.

"Not Ludwig's, evidently," said the Count, "now we will look as to the other. I am sorry to say we have that, too."

He opened the other paper he held, and folded it as he

THE COUNT OF CROW'S NEST

had done the first. The signature in this case was simply "Lola." "They seem to be identical. I fancied as much. It was Madame Montes' custom to take whatever she wanted from the royal library, and she seldom troubled herself to return it. The second name is only another evidence of her inordinate vanity, and they are too numerous to be of any especial interest. I must apologize for showing you the signatures in this singularly unsatisfactory manner, but the contents of these communications were strictly personal, and, of course, were not addressed to me. I remember very little of the reign of the first Ludwig myself. There are a number of names among those papers that might interest you, if you care to see them and will omit the body of the documents. They are, many of them, papers that should never have been written at all. Such things are inevitable in very old families, though I could never understand their motive for preserving them. There is only one way to handle such things, and that is with absolute and unvarying care. To show them even to an appreciative friend is a form of blackmail. I dislike the responsibility of knowing their contents myself. I have not read any of them for years."

"And yet you, too, keep them?"

"Certainly, inbred tradition, I suppose. I have often intended to destroy them, but I have always deferred the actual doing of it. Since they have enabled me to be of some service to you, I am glad I have delayed the holocaust."

[The second-rate people of Crow's Nest, the old European with his family pride and secret, the fear of publicity— all are of Henry James; but they are Cather too. She was concerned with the European in America, James with the American in Europe. Her work abounds in descriptions setting off the artistic or genuine person against the second rate; for example, "The Sculptor's Funeral," *One of Ours*, *Lucy Gayheart*. In Cather the dark secret is incidental—explained more immediately: Peter and Pavel in *My Ántonia*, Magdalena in *Death Comes for the Archbishop*—while in Henry James the secret is more likely to be the resolving factor of the story, as in *The American* or *Portrait of a Lady*.

As for letters and personal papers, James asked his family to destroy his personal letters, which they did not do. Willa Cather asked the same—a great many of her letters have been destroyed—and her will provides that none of her letters may ever be published. Here at the age of twenty-two when this story was written, she had already begun to put up fences around her personality.]

The conventional ring of the last remark seemed to politely close all further serious discussion of the subject. Buchanan checked the question he had already mentally uttered, and taking a chair by the table, looked at the signatures his host selected. They were names that consumed him with an overwhelming curiosity and made his ears tingle and his cheeks burn; single names, most of them, those single names that Balzac said made the observer dream. As the Count took another package of documents from the box his fingers caught a small gold chain attached to some metallic object that rang sharply against the sides of the box as he lifted his hand.

"The iron cross!" cried Buchanan involuntarily, with a quick inward breath.

"Yes, it is one that I won on the field of Gravelotte years ago. It is my only contribution to this box. I have been a very ordinary man, Mr. Buchanan. In families like ours there must be some men who neither make nor break, but try to keep things together. That my efforts in that direction were somewhat futile was not entirely my fault. I had two brothers who bore the title before me; they were both talented men, and when my turn came there was very little left to save."

"I fancied you had been more a student than a man of affairs."

"Student is too grave a word. I have always read; at one time I thought that of itself gave one a sufficient purpose, but like other things it fails one at last, at least the living interest of it. At present I am only a survivor. Here, where every one plays for some stake, I realize how nearly extinct is the class to which I belong, and that I am a sort of survival of the unfit, with no duty but to keep an escutcheon that is only a name and a sword that the world no longer needs. An old pagan back in Julian's time who still clung to a despoiled Olympus and a vain philosophy, dead as its own abstruse syllogisms, might have felt as I do when the new faith, throbbing with potentialities, was coming in. The life of my own father seems to be as far away as the lives of the ancient emperors. It is not a pleasant thing to be the last of one's kind. The *tedium vitae* descends heavily upon one."

[Of course Cather's sympathies are for the old man and his "precious . . . incommunicable past." We find the same type again in the professor of *The Professor's House*. He felt he had "fallen out of his place in the human family."]

As the Count was speaking, they heard a ripple of loud laughter on the stairs and a rustle of draperies in the hall, and a tall blonde woman, dressed in a tight fitting tailor-made gown, with a pair of long lavender gloves lying jauntily over her shoulder, entered and bowed graciously to the Count.

"*Bon soir, mon père,* I was not aware you had company." There was in her voice that peculiarly hard throat tone that stage people so often use in conversation.

"Mr. Buchanan, my daughter, Helena."

Buchanan bowed and muttered a greeting, uncertain by just what title he should address her.

"No Countess, if you please, Mr. Buchanan. Just plain Helena De Koch. Titles are out of date, and more than absurd in our case. I come from a rehearsal of a concert where I sing for money, attired in a ready-made gown, botched over by a tailor, to visit my respected parent in a fourth-rate lodging house, and you call me Countess! Could anything be more innately funny? Titles only go in comic opera now. I have often tried to persuade my father to content himself with Paul De Koch."

The Count smiled, "My name was not mine to make, Helena, and I am not at all ashamed of it."

The young lady's keen but rather indifferent eyes had dwelt on Buchanan but a moment, but he felt as though he had been inspected by a drill sergeant, and that no detail of his person or attire had escaped her.

She glanced at the table and then at the Count. "So you have decided to become practical at last?"

A shade of extreme annoyance swept quickly over the Count's face. He replied stiffly,

"I have merely been showing Mr. Buchanan an autograph he wished to see."

"O, so that is all! I might have known it. People do not recover from a mania in a day." She laughed rather unpleasantly and turned graciously to Buchanan. "Have you persuaded him to show you any of them? The contents are much more interesting than the autographs, rather side lights on history, you know." Her eyelid drooped a little with an insinuating glance, just enough to suggest a wink that did not come to pass, but he felt strangely repelled by even the suggestion. It must have been the connection that made it so objectionable, he reflected. She seemed to cheapen the Count and all his surroundings.

[Rosamond, the professor's daughter, is such a person.]

"No, my interest goes no further than the autographs."

"A polite prevarication I imagine. You will have to get more in the shadow if you hide the curiosity in your eyes. I don't blame you, he found me reading them once, and all the old Koch temper came out. I never knew he had it until then. Our tempers and our title are the only remnants of our former glory. The one is quite as ridiculous as the other, since we have no one to get angry at but each other. Poverty has no right to indignation at all. I speak respectfully even to a cabman. Papa shows his superiority by having no cabman at all."

"I think neither of you need do anything at all to show that," said Buchanan politely.

"O, come, you are all like impressarios, you Americans, and the further West one goes the worse it is. I never saw a manager who could resist a title; I only use mine on such occasions."

Buchanan saw that his host looked ill at ease, so he endeavored to change the subject.

"You sing, I believe?"

"O, yes, in oratorio and concert. *Cher papa* will not hear of the opera. Oratorio seems to be the special retreat of decayed gentility. I don't believe in those distinctions myself; I have found that a title dating from the foundation of the Empire does not buy one a spring bonnet, and that one of the oldest names in Europe will not keep one in gloves. One of your clever Frenchmen said there is nothing in the world but money, the gallows excepted. But His Excellency here never quotes that. Papa is an aristocrat, while I am bourgeoise to the tips of my fingers." She waved her highly polished nails toward Buchanan.

He thought that she could not have summarized herself better. The instinctive dislike he had always felt for her had been steadily growing into an aversion since she entered the room. It was by no means the first time he had seen her, she was almost a familiar figure about the boarding house, and often came to dine with the Count. Her florid coloring and elaborately waved blonde hair might have been said to be a general expression of her style. Under that yellow bang was a low straight forehead, and straight brows from behind which looked out a pair of blue eyes, large and full but utterly without depth, and cold as icicles, which seemed to be continually estimating the pecuniary value of the world. The cheeks were full and the chin decided in spite of its dimple. The upper lip was full and short and the nostril spare. They were scarcely the features one would expect to find in the descendant of an ancient house, seeming more accidental than formed by any perpetuated tendencies of blood. Her hands were broad and plump like her wrists.

Mademoiselle was on almost familiar terms with the landlady of Crow's Nest, and Buchanan fancied that she was responsible for the bits of gossip concerning the Count that floated about the house and were daily rehearsed by the languid widow. The widow had gone so far as to darkly express her doubts as to this effulgent blonde being the Count's daughter at all, and

Buchanan had been guilty of rather hoping that she was right. It would be rather less of a reflection on the Count, he thought. But to-night's conversation left him no room for doubt, and in watching the contrast between her full, florid countenance and the chastened face across the table, he wondered if the materialists of this world were always hale and full-fed, while the idealists were pale and gray as the shadows that kept them company. But one did not find time to muse much about anything in Mademoiselle De Koch's presence.

"By the way, *cher papa,* you are coming to-morrow night to hear me sing that waltz song of Arditti's?"

"Certainly, if you wish, but I am not fond of that style of music."

"O, certainly not, that's not to be expected or hoped for, nothing but mossbacks. But, seriously, one cannot sing Mendelssohn or Haydn forever, and all the modern classics are so abominably difficult," said Mademoiselle, beginning to draw on her gloves, which Buchanan noticed were several sizes too small and required a great deal of coaxing. Indeed everything that Mademoiselle wore fit her closely. She was of that peculiar type of blonde loveliness which impresses one as being always on the verge of *embonpoint,* and its possessor seems always to be in a state of nervous apprehension lest she should cross the dead line and openly and fearlessly be called stout.

At this juncture a gentle knock was heard at the door, and Mademoiselle remarked carelessly, "That's only Tony. Come in!"

A gentleman entered and bowed humbly to Mademoiselle. He was a little tenor whom Buchanan remembered having seen before, and whose mild dark eyes and swarthy skin had given him a pretext to adopt an Italian stage name. He was a slight, narrow chested man and had a receding chin and a generally "professional" and foreign air which was unmistakably cultivated.

"A charming evening, Count. Chicago weather is so seldom genial in the winter."

After presenting him to Buchanan the Count answered him,

"I have not been out, but it seems so here."

"Doubtless, in Mademoiselle's society. But you are busy?"

He glanced inquiringly at Mademoiselle. Buchanan fancied that the question was addressed to her rather than to the Count, and thought he intercepted an answering glance.

"Not at all, we were merely amusing ourselves. Must you leave us already?"

"I think Mademoiselle has another rehearsal. You know what it means to presume to keep pace with an art, eternal vigilance. There is no rest for the weary in our profession—not, at least, in this world." This was said with a weighty sincerity that almost provoked a smile from Buchanan. There are two words which no Chicago singer can talk ten minutes without using: "art" and "Chicago," and this gentleman had already indulged in both.

> [Cather had developed a more sympathetic attitude toward both Chicago and Chicago musicians by the time she wrote *Lucy Gayheart;* even by the time she wrote *Song of the Lark*. However, both Thea and Lucy are genuine, whereas the Countess and her tenor are counterfeits. Willa Cather did not make the counterfeits leading characters in her work.]

"O, yes, we must be gone to practice the despised Arditti. Come to-morrow night if you can. Tony here will give you tickets. And if Mr. Buchanan should have nothing better to do, pray bring him with you."

Buchanan assured her that he could have nothing more agreeable at any rate, and would be delighted to go. She took possession of the tenor and departed.

II

Harold Buchanan accompanied the Count next evening, and his impressions of Mademoiselle Helena De Koch were only intensified. She sang floridly and with that peculiar confidence which always seems to attend uncertain execution. She had a peculiar trick of just seeming to catch a note by the skirts and then falling back from it, just touching it, as it were, but totally unable to sustain it. More than that, her very unconsciousness of this showed that she had absolutely no musical sense. Buchanan was inclined to think that, next to her coarse disapprecia- tion of her father, her singing was rather the worst feature about her. To sing badly and not to have perception enough to know it was such a bad index of one's mental and aesthetic constitu- tion.

After the concert they went up on the stage to see her, and she came forward to meet them, accompanied by the tenor, and greeted them graciously, bearing her blushing honors quite as thick upon her as if she had sung well.

"It was nice of you to come. Did you catch my eye?"

"I am still glowing with the pleasure of thinking I did so, but I was afraid perhaps it was only a delusion. One so often goes about puffed up over favors that were meant for the fellow back of him."

"O, I hoped mine were more intelligible than that. But now you shall be rewarded for your patience. Tony and I are going to have a little supper down at Kingsley's and you must come, just us, you know. Papa may come to chaperone us, if it is not too late for him."

The Count hastily excused himself, and indeed he must have been very dense to have accepted such a hostile invitation, even from his own daughter. But Buchanan had already bowed his acceptance, and felt that it was too late to retreat. Reluctantly he accompanied Mademoiselle and the silent tenor, and saw the Count depart alone. And yet, he reflected, this merciful inter- vention would relieve him from the awkward necessity of discuss- ing the concert with his friend.

When they were seated at Kingsley's and had given their orders, it struck him that Mademoiselle had some purpose in bringing him, for it soon became obvious that the tenor's charms were of that nature which one usually prefers to enjoy alone.

What this might be, however, did not at once appear. She discussed current music and light opera in quite an amiable and disinterested manner, and for a time contented herself with this.

"You are a journalist, I believe, Mr. Buchanan?"

"Scarcely, yet. That is one of the many things I would like to be."

"You are a Chicago man, at any rate?" inquired the tenor.

"Well, one of the queer things about Chicago is that no one is really a native. I have lived here a good deal, off and on. My father used to be in business here before I went East to school. Just at present I want to get into something, and I think that lightning is about as likely to strike one here as any where."

"More likely! Chicago is the place for young talent. I have found it so. They want new blood and new ideas. Success comes sooner and more directly here than elsewhere in your profession as in my own. I would rather sing to a Chicago audience than any other, and I think I have been before most of the best ones in this country." When the taciturn gentleman spoke at all it was of one all-important theme. Indeed, do tenors ever talk of anything else? *Art et moi; l'art, c'est moi!*

[Lucy Gayheart's Sebastian was a baritone.]

"O, Tony here takes things too seriously. 'Life is a plaything, life is a toy!' You have sung that often enough to believe it a little by this time. By the way, Mr. Buchanan, have you been down to hear the thread-bare Robin Hood? O, no, I never go; there are no light operas worth hearing except those of the Viennese. Think of that odious waltz song, ta, ta, ta-ta-te, ta; ta-ta-te, ta, ta, ta!"

Buchanan looked apprehensively about at the other supper parties in the room, and wished she would not sing so loud. But she went merrily on.

"I can endure everything American except American music, and the less said of it the better. By the way, don't you think I have taken to your language rather kindly? Of course I learned

English when I was a child, but I had to learn American after arriving, and I assure you that is quite another language."

"I was just thinking that you were quite wonderful in that respect. I should never know you were not one of us; you have all the *sermo familiaris* even to our local touches."

"O yes, I went at your slang as conscientiously as if it were grammar. That is the characteristic part of a language, anyway."

When their order arrived, the drift of the talk changed.

"You see a good deal of papa, Mr. Buchanan?"

"Not half so much as I want to."

"I am glad you like him; he is very lonely and has those antiquated class notions about mixing up with people."

"I have always felt that and have been a little bit backward. I don't want to seem to intrude."

"O, you need never be afraid of that; he likes you immensely. We've heard lots about you, haven't we, Tony?"

"Most enthusiastic and flattering accounts," responded that gentleman, looking up a moment from his lobster.

"We have thought about suggesting something, Mr. Buchanan, that might be immensely to your advantage. You are a young literary man, waiting to make a hit like all the rest of us. Now let me tell you something; if you can work papa, your fame is ready made for you."

"Well, if I could find any fame of that variety, I would be willing to pay pretty dearly for it. I had about decided that the virgin article was not lying about in very extensive deposits."

"Well, it is, just in chunks, inside of that box you saw the other night. He has hundreds of papers there that would turn the court history of Europe for the last century upside down. I know whereof I speak. His friends have urged him to publish them for the last twenty years, and I—but, of course, men never listen to their daughters. Of course he wouldn't care to edit them himself, his everlasting name, you know. But you are a practical literary man and know what *fin de siècle* taste demands, and if you could sort of combine forces, I have an idea it would be a great thing for both of you."

"But," protested Buchanan, "your father assured me those documents were of a wholly private nature."

"Of course they are. That's the sort of history that goes now-a-days. It's the sort of thing that sells and that people read, 'something spicy,' they call it. You could edit them with historical notes to give tone to the thing, you know. Of course you would have to overcome innumerable scruples on papa's part. Go at it in the name of art and history and all that. He is unyielding in his notions about such things, but if there is any living man who can do it, you are the man!" She had quite forgotten now the calm indifference of her first method of attack; her lips were set and her eyes biting keen. Buchanan could not help noticing how she leaned forward and how tightly she held her fork. Evidently this plan was not a new one. There was a purpose in those hard eyes that could not be new. He shifted his position slightly.

"I would rather you would leave me and my interests out of the question, Miss De Koch, though don't think I don't appreciate your kindness in thinking of me. If there is anything in the papers themselves to justify their publication, why does your father object to it?"

"O, he considers people's feelings—much they've ever considered ours! Of course it would make big scandals all over Europe, and no end of a fuss. There would be answers, denials, refutations; the national museums would be ransacked for counter-proofs. That one book would bring out a dozen. Just think of it, a grand wholesale *exposé* of all the courts of Europe, hailing from image-breaking Chicago! It's your chance for fame, young man, and as for money, we'd all be throwing it at the birdies in six months."

She had dropped the pass word of the conspiracy. Buchanan began to feel less at sea.

[Here we have the economic pressures of the decayed aristocracy with which Henry James so often deals.]

"Of course there would be grave considerations attending the publication of such matter."

"Not a bit of it. This is an age of disillusionment. William Tell was a myth, Josephine only a Creole coquette, and Shakespeare wasn't Shakespeare at all. This generation wants to get at the bottom of things. Now it's not the man who can invent a romance, but the man who can explode one who holds the winning card," she touched him lightly on the shoulder.

"It's a good deal as you say, undoubtedly. But I doubt the dignity, or even the decency of it."

She put her glass down impatiently. "That all may be, but when we are in Rome we must be either Romans or provincials. You must give the people what they want. Really, now, don't you like to get a tip on those old figurehead guys yourself, just to get even with them by shaking them off their pedestals a little? They were all very common clay like the rest of us."

Buchanan leaned back in his chair and decided to gain time and measure, if he could, the depth of the conspiracy sprung upon him. Mademoiselle was aglow with excitement, and even her gentleman-in-waiting had forgotten his supper, and his mild eyes were flashing with the first animation he had displayed.

"Well," he said, amused in spite of himself, "I have often thought I should like to get behind the scenes in history and see how all the great effects were really produced. How the tragic buskin is worn to make men look taller than they are, by what wires the angels are carried up to their apotheosis, and where the unfortunates go when they disappear through the trap. It would be a satisfaction to know just how often simpletons are cast for heroic parts, and great men for trivial ones, how often Hamlet and the grave digger ought to change places. I have even thought I would like to go into the dressing-room, and see just how the conventional historic puppets were made up; see the real head under the powdered wig and the real cheek under the rouge. And yet I am not anxious to be wholly disillusioned. If Caesar without his toga would not be Caesar, I would rather stay down in the orchestra chairs. I don't care to read a history of Napoleon written by his valet."

[In her youth Willa Cather was very fond of historical romances—the well written ones like Dumas'. She liked glitter and pomp—a good show.]

"Come, you know all this is moonshine. Nobody believes those things now-a-days. The more you take the halo from those fellows, the more popular you make them. A new scandal about Napoleon gives him a new lease of life. It revives the interest. Who would ever know anything about Rousseau, if it wasn't for his 'Confessions'? That keeps him popular; even my hair-dresser reads it."

"Of course it is something to have immortality among hair-dressers."

[Cather felt that art is not for the common person, that it would be better if the common person couldn't even read. When Orpheus sings on the street corner, he delivers no soul from hell. Yet when she received letters from hundreds of soldiers after *One of Ours*, and many concerning other books during the recent war, she did not regret that the common man could read.]

"It's very much better than having none at all, and being on the shelf all around. You are a young man with your mark to make, and you've got to meet the world on its own ground and give it what it wants, or it'll have none of you. If you take the people's money, you ought to cater to their tastes, that's fair enough. You cannot afford to be an old fogy, you have too much future. You see where it has put papa. Do you want to be stranded in Crow's Nest all your life, say fifty years of it? Chances to take the world by the horns do not occur every day; if you let them go by, you have a good long time for reflection, a lifetime, generally. One chance for one man, you know."

"I know that only too well, but I can't see that this is in any sense my chance. It's wholly your father's affair."

"Make it yours. Let's get to something definite; don't let him put you off with high sounding words; they aren't in the modern vocabulary and don't mean anything. Now you'll take up this matter? There is only one man in a thousand I would speak to openly in this way, but I have every faith in your ability. When things become definite, if papa is elusive about the business features of it, you and I can arrange that together."

Buchanan crumpled his napkin and threw it on the table.

"I am sorry, but I am afraid that you have misplaced your confidence; that is, you have expected too much of me. I am not an enterprising man, or a very practical one; if I were I would already have some legitimate occupation. I seem to be rather another case of the round block versus the square hole, and decidedly I can't fit into this. I could never propose such a thing to your father. If he ever speaks to me on the subject I will be frank enough, I promise you, but further than that I cannot pledge myself. Moreover, I doubt my own ability to either gauge the popular taste or fill its demands."

[This speech, it seems, expresses in part the way Willa felt about her job on *The Home Monthly*. She wrote friends that the magazine was full of trash, but apparently trash that people wanted to read. She wrote an article on the private lives of Mrs. McKinley and Mrs. William Jennings Bryan, when their husbands were prospective presidents, but she did not sign her own name. And later for *McClure's* she worked on the Mary Baker Eddy articles; this must have been a difficult assignment for one who felt as Cather did.]

Mademoiselle's amiability at once disappeared, and she took no pains to conceal the fact that she considered him both ungracious and ungrateful, though she vented her displeasure principally upon her dusky minion, the tenor, who was struggling with her rubbers. From the dogged look on his face, Buchanan imagined that this silent gentleman would one day avenge the tyrannies of his apprenticeship. Feeling very much as though he had obtained a supper under false pretenses, he said good night.

As he lit his cigar in the street, and faced the cold wet wind that blew in from the lake, he muttered to himself, "Of all the mercenary creatures! it's loathsome enough in a man, but in a woman—bah, it's positively reptilian! I don't believe she has a drop of the old man's blood in her body."

III

Some way his very aversion to the daughter drew Buchanan's sympathies more than ever to the Count. He found himself in the evening instinctively pausing at the Count's door, and when he went out to hear music or to see a play he felt more at ease when the Count was with him. He was of that temperament which quickly learns to depend on others. During their talks and rambles about the theatres he learned a good deal of the Count's history. Not directly, as the old gentleman seldom talked about himself, but in scrappy fragments that he mentally sorted and expanded into a biography. He learned how Paul had been born in the Winter Palace at St. Petersburg, where his father had superintended the education of the Czar Nicholas' sons. He had been considered rather dull socially in his youth, and had been kept in the background in a military school at Leipsic, while his two elder brothers spent his substance and amassed colossal debts in a manner that demonstrated their social talents to the world. After a good deal of reckless living, William had been killed in a duel about some vague diplomatic matter, and Nicholas by some accident at the races. When Paul at last came in to his shorn and parceled patrimony, he did something that established all the charges of imbecility that had been made against him; he sold the Koch estates and paid the Koch debts, the first time they had been paid in three centuries. By such an unheard of proceeding he at once lost caste in the diplomatic circles of the continent. To part with his family estates, to sell the home of the Counts De Koch to pay tradespeople and laborers, it was really more than well conducted society could be expected to condone. So Paul drifted to America, not until after the death of his wife, though of his wife he never spoke except formally. When he considered the daughter, Buchanan could not wonder at his reticence.

The man's quiet charm, his distinctive fineness of life and thought meant a great deal to a young man like Buchanan. They helped him to keep his standards and his tastes clean at a despondent age when that is sometimes difficult to do. It was certainly a strange thing to find this instinctive autocrat, this type of an effete nobility in that city of all cities, in Chicago, where the Present and the Practical are apotheosized and paid divine honors. But then, what can one not find in Chicago? He never stepped, without feeling the contrast, from the hurried world of barter and trade into the quiet of that little room where memories and souvenirs of other times and another world were kept hidden, as, in the days of their far captivity in the city of Baal, the Jews kept the sacred vessels of their pillaged temple.

One night, as he was indulging in his reprehensible habit of reading in bed, Buchanan heard a hurried knock at his door. At his bidding the Count entered. He was still in street dress, hat in hand, pale and in evident excitement. His hair was disordered and his forehead shone with moisture. He would not sit down, but went straight up to the bed and grasped Buchanan's hand. Buchanan felt that his was trembling and cold.

"My friend," he spoke thickly, "I need you to-night, the letters . . . the box . . . it is gone."

"The box? O, yes, the steel chest, but how, where, what do you mean?"

"When I came to my rooms to-night, I opened the drawer of the chiffonier. It was a most unusual thing, it must have been instinct, those letters are the only things left to watch. They should have been in a vault, I know, but I kept delaying. When I opened the drawer they were gone."

"This is serious. What can you do?"

"I must go out at once. You have retired and I would not

disturb you for any trivial matter, but this—this is the honor of
my family! Great God! The descendants of those people are living in Europe to-day, living honorably and bearing great names.
You hear me? Those letters must not get abroad. They would
shake men's faith in God and make them curse their mothers."

Buchanan was already dressing. Suddenly he stopped short
and dropped his shoe on the floor.

"Who knew where you kept them? Do you suspect any one
who was interested?"

The Count's voice was almost inaudible as he answered, "I
think, Mr. Buchanan, we must first go to my daughter's rooms.
It is with regret and shame that I drag you into this; it is terrible enough for me." He stood with his eyes downcast, like one
in bitter shame. Buchanan had never noticed that he was so old
a man before.

He felt that nothing could be said that would not be more
than superfluous. When he finished dressing, the Count remarked, "Put on your ulster, it is cold."

They went softly down stairs and hailed a cab. During the
drive the Count said nothing. Buchanan could see by the flash
of the street lights as they passed them that his head was sunk
on his breast. Only once he broke the silence by a sort of despairing groan. Buchanan guessed that some memory which bore immediately upon the grief of the moment had suddenly arisen
before him. Perhaps it was one of those causal actions which we
scatter so recklessly in our youth, and which, grown monstrous
like the creature of Frankenstein, rise up to shame us in our age
and spread desolation which we are powerless to check.

When they reached the house, Buchanan saw that the windows of the third floor were lighted, while the rest of the house
was in darkness. It was easy to guess on which floor Mademoiselle De Koch resided. After repeated ringing, a sleepy servant
maid opened the door. The Count asked no questions, but simply gave his name and passed up stairs, while the maid gathered
her disheveled robes about her and stumbled down the hallway. The knock at Mademoiselle De Koch's door was greeted

by a cheerful "Entrez!"

The open door revealed Mademoiselle attired in a traveling dress with a pile of letters on the desk before her, and a pen in her hand. A half packed valise lay open on the bed, and her trunks were strapped as though for sudden departure.

On seeing her visitors she gave a start of surprise, followed by a knowing glance, and then was quite at her ease. She would make a good defence, Buchanan suspected.

"Ah, it is you, *cher papa*, and you have brought company. Well, it is not exactly a conventional hour, but you are always welcome. I am delighted, Mr. Buchanan. Papa's chaperonage is certainly sufficient, even at three in the morning, so be seated."

The Count closed the door and met her. "Helena, you know why I have come and what you must do. There is no need of expletives."

"Not for you, perhaps, but I insist upon an explanation. What do you mean? I am at your service, as always, but I do not understand."

"This scene is disgraceful enough. I will allow you to spare yourself any explanations. I want the letters you took from my room. I will have them, so make no ado about it."

"You speak to me, sir, as though I were a chambermaid; you accuse me of taking your letters. What letters? I did not know you had correspondence so delicate now. Fie, papa! D'Albert said you were in your dotage ten years ago, but I have done you the honor to think him mistaken. Please do not altogether destroy my faith in you, I have so few illusions left at best." The sneer in that last sentence made Buchanan shiver as with a chill.

"I have not come to bandy words with you, Helena, nor to sermonize. You have never known what honor means. That is a distinction which cannot be taught. Don't try to act with me. I will take what I have come for, and leave you to your own felicitous philosophy of life, which I thank God is not mine. Give me the key of your trunk."

"Really, Your Excellency, this is quite too much. I shall do nothing of the sort. Come back to-morrow and I will do anyth\ng within reason. At present you are simply insane with anger, after the charming manner of your house."

"Then in just three minutes Mr. Buchanan will call an officer."

She started visibly, "You would not dare, pride—if nothing else—"

"I have no pride but the honor of my house. Quick, there is a law which can touch even you. Law was made for such as you."

The man of pale reflection was no more. This was the man of the iron cross who had led the charge on the field of Gravelotte.

Slowly, sullenly, she reached for her purse, and biting her lips handed him the key.

"Now, Mr. Buchanan, if you will assist me." He went quickly and deftly to the bottom of the trunk, almost without disturbing the clothing, and drew out the box, wrapped in numberless undergarments. After opening it and assuring himself as to the contents, he closed the trunk and Buchanan strapped it up.

Mademoiselle, who had returned to her seat and was making a pretense of writing, dropped her pen with a fierce exclamation.

"What is this honor you are always ranting about? Is it to leave your daughter to pick up her living as she may, to whine about beasts of managers, and go begging for fourth-rate engagements, when you might have supported her by the sale of a few scandalous letters? A fine sort of code to make all this racket about! Fine words will not conceal ugly facts."

The Count straightened himself as under a blow, "Stop! since you will drag out this whole ugly matter; you know that if you would have lived as I have had to live there would have been enough. As long as there was a picture, a vase, a jewel left, you know where they went. You took until there was no more to take. I simply have nothing but the pension. Even now my home is open to you, but I cannot keep you in yours. Will you never understand, I simply have no money! You know why I came here and why I must die here. When there was money what use did you make of it? Why is it that neither of us will ever dare to show our faces on the Continent again, that we tremble at the name of a continental newspaper? You remember that heading in *Figaro*? It will stare me in my grave! 'Adventuress' Great God, it was true!"

His voice broke, and his white head sank on his breast in an attitude of abject shame and anguish. Buchanan put his hand before his eyes to shut out the sight of it. But again that rasping pitiless woman's voice broke on his ear.

"And who began it all, by selling my inheritance over my head? Was it yours to sell?"

The Count spoke quietly now and his voice was steady.

"For the moment you brought back the old shame, and I almost pitied you and myself again. Generally I simply forget it; you have exhausted my power to suffer. I never feel. Helena, there is nothing I can say to you, for we have no language in common. Words do not mean the same to us. Good night."

She sprang from her seat and stood with clenched hands. "Those papers do not belong to you. They are ancient history, and they belong to the world!"

"They are the follies of men, and they belong to God," said the Count as he closed the door. As they reached the cab he spoke heavily, "It was ungenerous of me to drag you into this, but I did not feel equal to it alone."

"I think that good friends need not explain why they need each other, even if they know themselves," said Buchanan gently.

When they were in the cab he felt as though he ought to speak of something. He was afraid that perhaps the Count had not noticed it. "Miss De Koch's trunks were packed. Is she going away?"

The Count sighed wearily and leaned back in his seat, speaking so low that Buchanan had to lean forward to catch his words above the rumble of the cab.

"Yes, I saw. It is probably an elopement—the tenor. But I am helpless. I have no money. What she said was true enough;

I am no more successful as a father than I was as a nobleman. And I have been mad enough to wish that I had sons! It is a terrible thing, this degeneration of great families. You are very happy to see nothing of it here. The rot begins inside and is hidden for a time, but it demonstrates itself even physically at last. My ancestors had the frames of giants, field marshals and generals, all of them. We were all dwarfs, exhausted physically from the first, frayed ends of the strands of a great skein. Even my father was a slight man, always ill. My brothers were men of no principle, but they at least preserved the traditions. Nicholas was killed at the races, like a common jockey. In me it showed itself in my marriage. Before that the men of our house had at least chosen gentlewomen as their wives; they acknowledged the obligation. But this, even I never thought it would come to this. My mother would have starved with my father, begged in the streets, even lived at Crow's Nest, but she would never have thought of this. The possibility would never have occurred to her. I am the last of them. Helena will hardly choose a domestic career. Our little comedy is over, it is time the lights were out; the fifth act has dragged out too long. I am in haste to give back to the earth this blood I carry and free the world from it. In it is inherent failure, germinal weakness, madness, and chaos. When all sense of honor dies utterly out of an old stock, there is nothing left but annihilation. It should be buried deep, deep as they bury victims of a plague, blotted out like the forgotten dynasties of history."

A Resurrection

published in *The Home Monthly*, April, 1897

[On August 12, 1894 an article appeared in the *Nebraska State Journal* signed W. C. It was about Brownville. The material for the article had been gathered in a trip made by Willa Cather and Mariel Gere, daughter of the founder and owner of the *Journal*. Mariel was the photographer, Willa the reporter, and they were shown around the town by ex-Governor Furnas. To Mariel's distress, Willa seemed interested only in the decay and disintegration of the town, even posing some of the photographs to make things worse than they were. Brownville people were not too happy about the article.

Fifty-one years later Willa Cather in a letter to Mariel Gere mentioned the trip to Brownville, and particularly the terrible heat. In the following story, though the month is April, the heat is unbearable.

This is quite frankly a love story with a happy ending. The only other love story of this period is "On the Divide," which shows more frustration than this one.]

"I contend that you ought to have set them house plants different, Margie, closer around the pulpit rail." Mrs. Skimmons retreated to the back of the church to take in the full effect of the decorations and give further directions to Margie. Mrs. Skimmons had a way of confining her services as chairman of the decorative committee to giving directions, and the benefit of her artistic eye.

Miss Margie good naturedly readjusted the "house plants" and asked, "How is that?"

"Well, it's some better," admitted Mrs. Skimmons, critically, "but I contend we ought to have had some evergreens, even if they do look like Christmas. And now that you've used them

147

hy'cinths for the lamp brackets, what are you goin' to put on the little stand before the pulpit?"

"Martin Dempster promised to bring some Easter lilies up from Kansas City. I thought we'd put them there. He ought to be here pretty soon. I heard the train whistle in a bit ago."

"That's three times he's been to Kansas City this month. I don't see how he can afford it. Everybody knows the old ferry boat can't pay him very well, and he wasn't never much of a business man. It beats me how some people can fly high on nothing. There's his railroad fare and his expenses while he is there. I can't make out what he's doin' down there so much. More'n likely it's some girl or other he's goin' down the river after agin. Now that you and your mother have brought up his baby for him, it would be just like Mart Dempster to go trapesin' off and marry some giddy thing and maybe fetch her up here for you to bring up too. I can't never think he's acted right by you, Margie."

"So long as I'm satisfied, I can't see why it should trouble other people, Mrs. Skimmons."

"O, certainly not, if you are goin' to take offense. I meant well."

Margie turned her face away to avoid Mrs. Skimmons' scrutinizing gaze, and went on quietly with the decorations.

[Mrs. Livery Johnson of *Song of the Lark* and Lucy Gayheart's sister Pauline are both women of the type of Mrs. Skimmons.]

Miss Margie was no longer a girl. Most of the girls of her set who had frolicked and gone to school with her had married and moved away. Yet, though she had passed that dread meridian of thirty, and was the village schoolmistress to boot, she was not openly spoken of as an old maid. When a woman retains much of her beauty and youthful vigor the world, even the petty provincial world, feels a delicacy about applying to her that condemning title that when once adopted is so irrevocable. Then

Miss Marjorie Pierson had belonged to one of the best families in the old days, before Brownville was shorn of its glory and importance by the railroad maneuvers that had left everybody poor. She had not always taught tow-headed urchins for a living, but had once lived in a big house on the hill and gone to boarding school and driven her own phaeton, and entertained company from Omaha. These facts protected her somewhat.

She was a tall woman, finely, almost powerfully built and admirably developed. She carried herself with an erect pride that ill accorded with the humble position as the village schoolmistress. Her features were regular and well cut, but her face was comely chiefly because of her vivid coloring and her deeply set gray eyes, that were serious and frank like a man's. She was one of those women one sometimes sees, designed by nature in her more artistic moments, especially fashioned for all the fullness of life; for large experiences and the great world where a commanding personality is felt and valued, but condemned by circumstances to poverty, obscurity and all manner of pettiness. There are plenty of such women, who were made to ride in carriages and wear jewels and grace first nights at the opera, who, through some unaccountable blunder of the stage management in this little *comédie humaine*, have the wrong parts assigned them, and cook for farm hands, or teach a country school like this one, or make gowns for ugly women and pad them into some semblance of shapeliness, while they themselves, who need no such artificial treatment, wear cast-offs; women who were made to rule, but who are doomed to serve. There are plenty of living masterpieces that are as completely lost to the world as the lost nine books of Sappho, or as the Grecian marbles that were broken under the barbarians' battle axes. The world is full of waste of this sort.

[Two of these living masterpieces Willa Cather saved for the world: Alexandra of *O Pioneers* and Tony of *My Ántonia*. Willa Cather came to understand that serving was not after all such a doom, as at twenty-three she felt it to be.]

While Margie was arranging the "house plants" about the pulpit platform, and the other member of the committee was giving her the benefit of her advice, a man strode lazily into the church carrying a small travelling bag and a large pasteboard box.

"There you are, Miss Margie," he cried, throwing the box on the platform; and sitting down in the front pew he proceeded to fan himself with his soft felt hat.

"O, Martin, they are beautiful! They are the first things that have made me feel a bit like Easter."

"One of 'em is for you, Miss Margie, to wear to-morrow," said Martin bashfully. Then he hastened to add, "I feel more like it's Fourth of July than Easter. I'm right afraid of this weather, Mrs. Skimmons. It'll coax all the buds out on the fruit trees and then turn cold and nip 'em. And the buds'll just be silly enough to come out when they are asked. You've done well with your decorations, Mrs. Skimmons."

Mrs. Skimmons looked quizzically at Martin, puzzled by this unusual loquaciousness.

"Well, yes," she admitted, in a satisfied tone, "I think we've done right well considerin' this tryin' weather. I'm about prostrated with the heat myself. How are things goin' down in Kansas City? You must know a good deal about everything there, seein' you go down so much lately."

" 'Bout the same," replied Martin, in an uncommunicative tone which evidently offended Mrs. Skimmons.

"Well," remarked that lady briskly, "I guess I can't help you no more now, Margie. I've got to run home and see to them boys of mine. Mr. Dempster can probably help you finish." With this contemptuous use of his surname as a final thrust, Mrs. Skimmons departed.

Martin leaned back in the pew and watched Margie arranging the lilies. He was a big broad-chested fellow, who wore his broad shoulders carelessly and whose full muscular throat betrayed unusual physical strength. His face was simple and

honest, bronzed by the weather, and with deep lines about the
mild eyes that told that his simple life had not been altogether
negative, and that he had not sojourned in this world for forty
years without leaving a good deal of himself by the wayside.

[Instead of the passing years piling up some store of
wisdom and memory, Cather felt that the passage of time
is always a loss. She felt this most strongly about her own
life. Each book she wrote was made of pieces of her own
flesh and blood, gone forever.]

"I didn't thank you for the lilies, Martin. It was very kind
of you," said Margie, breaking the silence.

"O, that's all right. I just thought you'd like 'em," and he
again relapsed into silence, his eyes following the sunny path of
the first venturesome flies of the season that buzzed in and out
of the open windows. Then his gaze strayed back to where the
sunlight fell on Miss Margie and her lilies.

"The fact is, Miss Margie, I've got something to tell you.
You know for a long time I've thought I'd like to quit the ferry
and get somewhere where I'd have a chance to get ahead. There's
no use trying to get ahead in Brownville, for there's nothing to
get ahead of. Of late years I wanted to get a job on the lower
Mississippi again, on a boat, you know. I've been going down
to Kansas City lately to see some gentlemen who own boats
down the river, and I've got a place at last, a first rate one that
will pay well, and it looks like I could hold it as long as I want
it."

Miss Margie looked up from the lilies she was holding and
asked sharply, "Then you are going away, Martin?"

"Yes, and I'm going away this time so you won't never have
to be ashamed of me for it."

"I ought to be glad on your account. You're right, there's
nothing here for you, nor anybody else. But we'll miss you very
much, Martin. There are so few of the old crowd left. Will you
sell the ferry?"

"I don't just know about that. I'd kind of hate to sell the old ferry. You see I haven't got things planned out very clear yet. After all it's just the going away that matters most."

"Yes, it's just the going away that matters most," repeated Miss Margie slowly, while she watched something out of the window. "But of course you'll have to come back often to see Bobbie."

"Well, you see I was counting on taking Bobbie with me. He's about old enough now, and I don't think I could bear to be apart from him."

"You are not going to take Bobbie away from us, Martin?" cried Miss Margie in a tone of alarm.

"Why yes, Miss Margie. Of course I'll take him, and if you say so—"

"But I don't say so," cried Miss Margie in a tone of tremulous excitement. "He is not old enough, it would be cruel to take a bit of a child knocking around the world like that."

"I can't go without Bobbie. But, Miss Margie—"

"Martin," cried Miss Margie—she had risen to her feet now and stood facing him, her eyes full of gathering anger and her breast rising and falling perceptibly with her quick-drawn breathing—"Martin, you shall not take Bobbie away from me. He's more my child than yours, anyway. I've been through everything for him. When he was sick I walked the floor with him all night many a time and went with a headache to my work next morning. I've lived and worked and hoped just for him. And I've done it in the face of everything. Not a day passes but some old woman throws it in my face that I'm staying here drivelling my life out to take care of the child of the man who jilted me. I've borne all this because I loved him, because he is all my niggardly life has given me to love. My God! a woman must have something. Every woman's got to have. And I've given him everything, all that I'd starved and beat down and crucified in me. You brought him to me when he was a little wee baby, the only thing of your life you've ever given to mine. From the first time I felt his little cheek on mine I knew that a new life had come into me, and through another woman's weakness and selfishness I had at least one of the things which was mine by right. He was a helpless little baby, dependent on me for everything, and I loved him for just that. He needed my youth and strength and blood, and the very warmth of my body, and he was the only creature on earth who did. In spite of yourself you've given me half my womanhood and you shall not take it from me now. You shall not take it from me now!"

[Willa Cather had a special feeling for her youngest brother, John, affectionately called Jack. During those early Pittsburgh years, she often mentioned him, and suffered acute loneliness for the little boy.]

Martin heard her going, he heard the sob that broke as she reached the door but he did not stir from his seat or lift his bowed head. He sat staring at the sunlit spot in front of the pulpit where she had stood with the lilies in her hand, looking at him, somehow, despite her anger, like the pictures of the Holy woman who is always painted with lilies.

When the twilight began to fall and the shadows in the church grew dim he got up and went slowly down to the river toward the ferry boat. Back over the horse-shoe shaped gulch in which the town is built the sky was glorious with red splotches of sunset cloud just above the horizon. The big trees on the bluffs were tossing their arms restlessly in the breeze that blew up the river, and across on the level plains of the Missouri side the lights of the farm houses began to glow through the soft humid atmosphere of the April night. The smell of burning grass was everywhere, and the very air tasted of spring.

[*My Ántonia:* "There was only—spring itself; the throb of it, the light restlessness, the vital essence of it everywhere; in the sky, in the swift clouds, in the pale sunshine, and in the warm, high wind—rising suddenly, sinking suddenly, impulsive and playful like a big puppy that pawed you and then lay down to be petted. . . . Everywhere now there was the smell of burning grass."]

The boat hands had all gone to supper, and Martin sat down on the empty deck and lit his pipe. When he was perplexed or troubled he always went to the river. For the river means everything to Brownville folk; it has been at once their making and their undoing.

Brownville was not always the sleepy, deserted town that it is to-day, full of empty buildings and idle men and of boys growing up without aim or purpose. No, the town has had a history, a brief, sad little history which recalls the scathing epigram that Herr Heine once applied to M. Alfred de Musset; it is a young town with a brilliant past. It was the first town built on the Nebraska side of the river, and there, sheltered by the rugged bluffs and washed by the restless Missouri, a new state struggled into existence and proclaimed its right to be. Martin Dempster was the first child born on the Nebraska side, and he had seen the earth broken for the first grave. There, in Senator Tipton's big house on the hillside, when he was a very little boy, he had heard the first telegraph wire ever stretched across the Missouri click its first message that made the blood leap in all his boyish veins, "Westward the course of Empire takes it way."

In the days of his boyhood Brownville was the head of river navigation and the old steamboat trade. He had seen the time when a dozen river steamers used to tie up at the wharves at one time, and unload supplies for the wagon trains that went overland to Pike's Peak and Cherry Creek, that is Denver now.

[*Death Comes for the Archbishop:* "Wandering prospectors had found large deposits of gold along Cherry Creek, and the mountains that were solitary a year ago were now full of people. Wagon trains were streaming westward across the prairies from the Missouri River." This discovery of gold and the consequent rush of people was the reason for Father Vaillant's move to Colorado.]

He had sat on the upper veranda of the old Marsh House and listened to the strange talk of the foreign potentates that the "Montana" and "Silver Heels" used to bring up the river and who stopped there on their way into the big game country. He had listened with them to the distant throbbing of the engines that once stirred the lonely sand-split waters of the old river, and watched the steamers swing around the bend at night, glittering with lights, with bands of music playing on their decks and the sparks from the smokestacks blowing back into the darkness. He had sat under the gigantic oak before the Lone Tree saloon and heard the teamsters of the wagon trains and the boat hands exchange stories of the mountains and alkali deserts for stories of the busy world and its doings, filling up the pauses in conversation with old frontier songs and the strumming of banjos. And he could remember only too well when the old "Hannibal" brought up the steel rails for the Union Pacific Railroad, the road that was to kill Brownville.

Brownville had happened because of the steamboat trade, and when the channel of the river had become so uncertain and capricious that navigation was impossible, the prosperity that the river had given it took back in its muddy arms again and swept away. And ever since, overcome by shame and remorse, it had been trying to commit suicide by burying itself in the sand. Every year the channel [had] grown narrower and more treacherous and its waters more turbid. Perhaps it does not even remember any more how it used to hurry along into the great aorta of the continent, or the throb of the wheels of commerce that used to beat up the white foam on its dark waters, or how a certain old Indian chief desired to be buried sitting bolt upright upon the bluff that he might always watch the steamers go up and down the river.

> [One is reminded of the place where Myra Henshawe died: "From a distance I could see her leaning against her tree and looking off to sea, as if she were waiting for something. A few steamers passed below her, and the gulls dipped and darted about the headland . . ."]

So it was that the tide went out at Brownville, and the village became a little Pompeii buried in bonded indebtedness.

The sturdy pioneers moved away and the "river rats" drifted in, a nondescript people who came up the river from nowhere, and bought up the big houses for a song, cut down the tall oaks and cedars in the yards for firewood, and plowed up the terraces for potato patches, and were content after the manner of their kind.

[The defacing of nature is always painful to Willa Cather. She portrays Lucy Gayheart's suffering when the orchard is to be cut. The villainy of Ivy Peters in *A Lost Lady* is measured thus: "By draining the marsh Ivy had obliterated a few acres of something he hated, though he could not name it, and had asserted his power over the people who had loved those unproductive meadows for their idleness and silvery beauty."]

The river gypsies are a peculiar people; like the Egyptians of old their lives are for and of the river. They each have their skiff and burn driftwood and subsist on catfish and play their banjos, and forget that the world moves—if they ever knew it. The river is the school and religion of these people.

And Martin Dempster was one of them. When most of the better people of the town moved away Martin remained loyal to the river. The feeling of near kinship with the river had always been in him, he was born with it. When he was a little boy he had continually run away from school, and when his father hunted for him he always found him about the river. River boys never take kindly to education; they are always hankering for the water. In summer its muddy coolness is irresistibly alluring, and in winter its frozen surface is equally so. The continual danger which attends its treacherous currents only adds to its enticing charm. They know the river in all its changes and fluctuations as a stock broker knows the markets.

[Willa, her brothers, and her other playmates had played on the banks of and in the waters of the Republican River, just south of Red Cloud, Nebraska.]

When Martin was a boy his father owned a great deal of Brownville real estate and was considered a wealthy man. Town property was a marketable article in those days, though now no real estate ever sells in Brownville—except cemetery lots. But Martin never cared for business. The first ambition he was ever guilty of was that vague yearning which stirs in the breasts of all river boys, to go down the river sometime, clear down, as far as the river goes. Then, a little later, when he heard of an old stump speaker who used to end all his oratorical flights with a figure about "rearing here in the Missouri Valley a monument as high as the thought of man," he had determined to be a great navigator and to bring glory and honor to the town of Brownville. And here he was, running the old ferry boat that was the last and meanest of all the flock of mighty river crafts. So it goes. When we are very little we all dream of driving a street car or wearing a policeman's star or keeping a peanut stand; and generally, after catching at the clouds a few times, we live to accomplish our juvenile ambitions more nearly than we ever realize.

When he was sixteen Martin had run away as cabin boy on the "Silver Heels." Gradually he had risen to the pilot house on the same boat. People wondered why Marjorie Pierson should care for a fellow of that stamp, but the fact that she did care was no secret. Perhaps it was just because he was simple and unworldly and lived for what he liked best that she cared.

Martin's downfall dated back to the death of the steamboat trade at Brownville. His fate was curiously linked with that of his river. When the channel became so choked with sand that the steamers quit going up to Brownville Martin went lower down the river, making his headquarters at St. Louis. And there the misfortune of his life befell him. There was a girl of French extraction, an Aimée de Mar, who lived down in the shipping district. She lived by her wits principally. She was just a wee mite of a thing, with brown hair that fluffed about her face and eyes that were large and soft like those of Guido's penitent Magdalen, and which utterly belied her. You would wonder how so small a person could make so much harm and trouble in the world. Not that she was naturally malignant or evil at all. She simply wanted the nice things of this world and was determined to have them, no matter who paid for them, and she enjoyed life with a frank sort of hedonism, quite regardless of what her pleasure might cost others. Martin was a young man who stood high in favor with the captains and boat owners and who seemed destined to rise. So Aimée concentrated all her energies to one end, and her project was not difficult of accomplishment under the circumstances. A wiser or worse man would have met her on her own ground and managed her easily enough. But Martin was slow at life as he had been at books, heady and loyal and foolish, the kind of man who pays for his follies right here in this world and who keeps his word if he walks alive into hell for it. The upshot of it was that, after writing to Margie the hardest letter he ever wrote in his life, he married Aimée de Mar.

Then followed those three years that had left deep lines in Martin's face and gray hairs over his temples. Once married Aimée did not sing *"Toujours j'aimais!"* any more. She attired herself gorgeously in satins and laces and perfumed herself heavily with *violettes de l'arme* and spent her days visiting her old friends of the milliners' and hair dressers' shops and impressing them with her elegance. The evenings she would pass in a box at some second rate theatre, ordering ices brought to her between the acts. When Martin was in town he was dragged willy-nilly through all these absurdly vulgar performances, and when he was away matters went even worse. This would continue until Martin's salary was exhausted, after which Aimée would languish at home in bitter resentment against the way the world is run, and consoling herself with innumerable *cigarettes de Caporale* until pay day. Then she would blossom forth in a new outfit and the same program would be repeated. After running him heavily into debt, by some foolish attempt at a flirtation with a man on board his own boat, she drove Martin into a quarrel which resulted in a fierce hand to hand scrimmage on board ship and was the cause of his immediate discharge. In December, while he was hunting work, living from hand to mouth and hiding from his creditors, his baby was born. "As if," Aimée remarked, "the weather were not disagreeable enough without that!"

[There is a character similar to Aimée in *Shadows on the Rock,* 'Toinette Gaux, the mother of little Jacques. She too had married a sailor, borne a son, and then returned to her old life.]

In the spring, at Mardi-Gras time, Martin happened to be out of town. Aimée was thoroughly weary of domesticity and poverty and of being shut up in the house. She strained her credit for all it was worth for one last time, and on the first night of the fête, though it was bitterly cold, she donned an airy domino and ran away from her baby, and went down the river in a steam launch, hung with colored lights and manned by some gentlemen who were neither sober nor good boatmen. The launch was overturned a mile below the Point, and three of the party went to the bottom. Two days later poor little Aimée was picked up in the river, the yellow and black velvet of her butterfly dress covered with mud and slime, and her gay gauze wings frozen fast to her pretty shoulders.

[There is a suggestion here of Madame Bovary.]

So Martin spoke the truth when he said that everything that had ever affected his life one way or the other was of the river. To him the river stood for Providence, for fate.

Some of the saddest fables of ancient myth are of the fates of the devotees of the River Gods. And the worship of the River Gods is by no means dead. Martin had been a constant worshipper and a most faithful one, and here he was at forty, not so well off as when he began the world for himself at sixteen. But let no one dream that because the wages of the River God cannot be counted in coin or numbered in herds of cattle, that they are never paid. Its real wages are of the soul alone, and not visible to any man. To all who follow it faithfully, and not for gain but from inclination, the river gives a certain simpleness of life and freshness of feeling and receptiveness of mind not to be found among the money changers of the market place. It feeds his imagination and trains his eye, and gives him strength and courage. And it gives him something better than these, if aught can be better. It gives him, no matter how unlettered he may be, something of that intimate sympathy with inanimate nature that is the base of all poetry, something of that which the high-faced rocks of the gleaming Sicilian shore gave Theocritus.

[Again Cather seems to say that education would spoil the best qualities in such a person as Martin.]

Martin had come back to Brownville to live down the memory of his disgrace. He might have found a much easier task without going so far. Every day for six years he had met the reproachful eyes of his neighbors unflinchingly, and he knew that his mistake was neither condoned nor forgotten. Brownville people have nothing to do but to keep such memories perennially green. If he had been a coward he would have run away from this perpetual condemnation. But he had the quiet courage of all men who have wrestled hand to hand with the elements, and who have found out how big and terrible nature is. So he stayed.

[Martin is one with Eric Hermannson and Canute Canuteson. Later we have Emil Bergson in *O Pioneers* and Claude Wheeler in *One of Ours*, both with education, but remaining the same type of frustrated personality.]

Miss Margie left the church with a stinging sense of shame at what she had said, and wondered if she were losing her mind. For the women who are cast in that tragic mould are always trying to be like their milder sisters, and are always flattering themselves that they have succeeded. And when some fine day the fire flames out they are more astonished and confounded than anyone else can be. Miss Margie walked rapidly through the dusty road, called by courtesy a street, and crossed the vacant building lots unmindful that her skirts were switching among the stalks of last year's golden rods and sunflowers. As she reached the door a little boy in much abbreviated trousers ran around the house from the back yard and threw his arms about her. She kissed him passionately and felt better. The child seemed to justify her in her own eyes. Then she led him in and began to get supper.

"Don't make my tea as strong as you did last night, Margie. It seems like you ought to know how to make it by this time," said the querulous invalid from the corner.

"All right, mother. Why mother, you worked my button-holes in black silk instead of blue!"

"How was I to tell, with my eyes so bad? You ought to have laid it out for me. But there is always something wrong about everything I do," complained the old lady in an injured tone.

"No, there isn't, it was all my fault. You can work a better button-hole than I can, any day."

"Well, in my time they used to say so," said Mrs. Pierson somewhat mollified.

Margie was practically burdened with the care of two children. Her mother was crippled with rheumatism, and only at rare intervals could "help about the house." She insisted on doing a little sewing for her daughter, but usually it had to come out and be done over again after she went to bed. With the housework and the monotonous grind of her work at school, Miss Margie had little time to think about her misfortunes, and so perhaps did not feel them as keenly as she would otherwise have done. It was a perplexing matter, too, to meet even the modest expenses of their small household with the salary paid a country teacher. She had never touched a penny of the money Martin paid for the child's board, but put it regularly in the bank for the boy's own use when he should need it.

After supper she put her mother to bed and then put on the red wrapper that she always wore in the evening hour that she had alone with Bobbie. The woman in one dies hard, and after she had ceased to dress for men the old persistent instinct made her wish to be attractive to the boy. She heard him say his "piece" that he was to recite at the Easter service to-morrow, and then sat down in the big rocking chair before the fire and Bobbie climbed up into her lap.

[Miss Margie is a little past thirty, yet to twenty-three-year-old Willa her life as a woman is about over.]

"Bobbie, I want to tell you a secret that we mustn't tell grandma yet. Your father is talking about taking you away."

"Away on the ferry boat?" his eyes glistened with excitement.

"No dear, away down the river; away from grandma and me for good."

"But I won't go away from you and grandma, Miss Margie. Don't you remember how I cried all night the time you were away?"

"Yes, Bobbie, I know, but you must always do what your father says. But you wouldn't like to go, would you?"

"Of course I wouldn't. There wouldn't be anybody to pick up chips, or go to the store, or take care of you and grandma, 'cause I'm the only boy you've got."

"Yes, Bobbie, that's just it, dear heart, you're the only boy I've got!" And Miss Margie gathered him up in her arms and laid her hot cheek on his and fell to sobbing, holding him closer and closer.

Bobbie lay very still, not even complaining about the tears that wetted his face. But he wondered very much why any one should cry who had not cut a finger or been stung by a wasp or trodden on a sand-burr. Poor little Bobbie, he had so much to learn! And while he was wondering he fell asleep, and Miss Margie undressed him and put him to bed.

During the five years [earlier in the story the time is six years] since that night when Marjorie Pierson and her mother, in the very face of the village gossips had gone to the train to meet Martin Dempster when he came back to Brownville, worn and weak with fever, and had taken his wailing little baby from his arms, giving it the first touch of womanly tenderness it had ever known, the two lonely women had grown to love it better than anything else in the world, better even than they loved each other. Marjorie had felt every ambition of her girlhood die out before the strength of the vital instinct which this child awakened and satisfied within her. She had told Martin in the church that afternoon that "a woman must have something." Of women of her kind this is certainly true. You can find them everywhere, slaving for and loving other women's children. In this sorry haphazard world such women are often cut off from the natural outlet of what is within them; but they always make one. Sometimes it is an aged relative, sometimes an invalid sister, sometimes a waif from the streets no one else wants, sometimes it is only a dog. But there is something, always.

> [In the Cather home there was a cousin of Willa's, Bess Seymour, who was just such a person. Alexandra Bergson of *O Pioneers* and Rachel Blake of *Sapphira and the Slave Girl* come to mind also.]

When the child was in his bed Miss Margie took up a bunch of examination papers and began looking through them. As she worked she heard a slow rapping at the door, a rap she knew well indeed, that had sent the blood to her cheeks one day. Now it only left them white.

She started and hesitated, but as the rap was repeated she rose and went to the door, setting her lips firmly.

"Good evening, Martin, come in," she said quietly. "Bobbie is in bed. I'm sorry."

Martin stood by the door and shook his head at the proffered chair. "I didn't come to see Bobbie, Margie. I came to finish what I began to say this afternoon when you cut me off. I know I'm slow spoken. It's always been like it was at school, when the teacher asked a question I knew as well as I knew my own name, but some other fellow'd get the answer out before me. I started to say this afternoon that if I took Bobbie to St. Louis I couldn't take him alone. There is somebody else I couldn't bear to be apart from and I guess you've known who that is this many a year."

A painful blush overspread Miss Margie's face and she turned away and rested her arm on the mantle. "It is not like you to take advantage of what I said this afternoon when I was angry. I wouldn't have believed it of you. You have given me pain enough in years gone by without this—this that makes me sick and ashamed."

"Sick and ashamed? Why Margie, you must have known what I've been waiting in Brownville for all these years. Don't tell me I've waited too long. I've done my best to live it down. I haven't bothered you nor pestered you so folks could talk. I've just stayed and stuck it out till I could feel I was worthy. Not that I think I'm worthy now, Margie, but the time has come for me to go and I can't go alone."

He paused, but there was no answer. He took a step nearer. "Why Margie, you don't mean that you haven't known I've been loving you all the time till my heart's near burst in me? Many a night down on the old ferry I've told it over and over again to the river till even it seemed to understand. Why Margie, I've"— the note of fear caught in his throat and his voice broke and he stood looking helplessly at his boots.

Miss Margie still stood leaning on her elbow, her face from him. "You'd better have been telling it to me, Martin," she said bitterly.

"Why Margie, I couldn't till I got my place. I couldn't have married you here and had folks always throwing that other woman in your face."

"But if you had loved me you would have told me, Martin, you couldn't have helped that."

He caught her hand and bent over it, lifting it tenderly to his lips. "O Margie, I was ashamed, bitter ashamed! I couldn't forget that letter I had to write you once. And you might have had a hundred better men than me. I never was good enough for you to think of one minute. I wasn't clever nor ready spoken like you, just a tramp of a river rat who could somehow believe better in God because of you."

Margie felt herself going and made one last desperate stand. "Perhaps you've forgotten all you said in that letter, perhaps you've forgotten the shame it would bring to any woman. Would you like to see it? I have always kept it."

He dropped her hand.

"No, I don't want to see it and I've not forgot. I only know I'd rather have signed my soul away than written it. Maybe you're right and there are things a man can't live down—not in this world. Of course you can keep the boy. As you say he is more yours than mine, a thousand times more. I've never had anything I could call my own. It's always been like this and I ought to be used to it by this time. Some men are made that way. Good night, dear."

"O Martin, don't talk like that, you could have had me any day for the asking. But why didn't you speak before? I'm too old now!" Margie leaned closer to the mantle and the sobs shook her.

He looked at her for a moment in wonder, and, just as she turned to look for him, caught her in his arms. "I've always been slow spoken, Margie—I was ashamed—you were too good for me," he muttered between his kisses.

"Don't Martin, don't! That's all asleep in me and it must not come, it shan't come back! Let me go!" cried Margie breathlessly.

"O I'm not near through yet! I'm just showing you how young you are—it's the quickest way," came Martin's answer muffled by the trimmings of her gown.

"O Martin, you may be slow spoken, but you're quick enough at some things," laughed Margie as she retreated to the window, struggling hard against the throb of reckless elation that arose in her. She felt as though some great force had been unlocked within her, great and terrible enough to rend her asunder, as when a brake snaps or a band slips and some ponderous machine grinds itself in pieces. It is not an easy thing, after a woman has shut the great natural hope out of her life, to open the flood gates and let the riotous, aching current come throbbing again through the shrunken channels, waking a thousand undreamed-of possibilities of pleasure and pain.

Martin followed her to the window and they stood together leaning against the deep casing while the spring wind blew in their faces, bearing with it the yearning groans of the river.

"We can kind of say goodbye to the old place tonight. We'll be going in a week or two now," he said nervously.

"I've wanted to get away from Brownville all my life, but now I'm someway afraid to think of going."

"How did that piece end we used to read at school, 'My chains and I—' Go on, you always remember such things."

"My very chains and I grew friends,
So much a long communion tends
To make us what we are. Even I
Regained my freedom with a sigh," quoted Margie softly.

"Yes, that's it. I'm counting on you taking some singing lessons again when we get down to St. Louis."

"Why I'm too old to take singing lessons now. I'm too old for everything. O Martin, I don't believe we've done right. I'm afraid of all this! It hurts me."

He put his arm about her tenderly and whispered: "Of course it does, darling. Don't you suppose it hurts the old river down there to-night when the spring floods are stirring up the old bottom and tearing a new channel through the sand? Don't you suppose it hurts the trees to-night when the sap is climbing up and up till it breaks through the bark and runs down their sides like blood? Of course it hurts."

"Oh Martin, when you talk like that it don't hurt any more," whispered Margie.

Truly the service of the river has its wages and its recompense, though they are not seen of men. Just then the door opened and Bobby came stumbling sleepily across the floor, trailing his little night gown after him.

"It was so dark in there, and I'm scared of the river when it sounds so loud," he said, hiding his face in Margie's skirts.

Martin lifted him gently in his arms and said, "The water

won't hurt you, my lad. My boy must never be afraid of the river."

And as he stood there listening to the angry grumble of the swollen waters, Martin asked their benediction on his happiness. For he knew that a river man may be happy only as the river wills.

The Prodigies

published in *The Home Monthly*, July, 1897

[At first glance this story might seem to be an imitation
of Henry James, with his typical devouring woman. Actually,
it reflects Willa Cather's understanding of the problems
inherent in the education and care of gifted children. It was
written thirty-three years before Willa Cather met the Menuhin children, yet it parallels many—certainly not all—of their
problems.]

"I am ready at last, Nelson. Have I kept you very long?"
asked Mrs. Nelson Mackenzie as she came hurriedly down the
stairs. "I'm sorry, but I just had one misfortune after another in
dressing."

"You don't look it," replied her husband, as he glanced up
at her admiringly.

"Do you like it? O, thank you! I am never quite sure about
this shade of green, it's so treacherous. I have had such a time.
The children would not stay in the nursery and poor Elsie has
lost her 'Alice in Wonderland' and wails without ceasing because
nurse cannot repeat 'The Walrus and the Carpenter' off hand."

[Willa Cather had read *Alice in Wonderland* to her
small brothers and sister.]

"I should think every one about this house could do that.
I know the whole fool book like the catechism," said Mackenzie
as he drew on his coat.

"Is the carriage there?"

Mackenzie didn't answer. He knew that Harriet knew perfectly well that the carriage had been waiting for half an hour.

169

[This is the sort of harmless perversity we find in Victoria Templeton of "Old Mrs. Harris." In Myra of *My Mortal Enemy* the perversity develops into the vicious.]

"I hope we shant be late," remarked Harriet as they drove away. "But it's just like Kate to select the most difficult hour in the day and recognize no obstacles to our appearing. She admits of no obstacles either for herself or other people. You've never met her except formally, have you? We saw a great deal of each other years ago. I took a few vocal lessons from her father and was for a time the object of her superabundant enthusiasm. If there is anything in the world that has not at some time been its object I don't know it. One must always take her with a grain of allowance. But even her characteristic impracticability does not excuse her for inviting busy people at four o'clock in the afternoon."

"I suppose it's the only hour at which the prodigies exhibit."

"Now don't speak disrespectfully, Nelson. They really are very wonderful children. I fancy Kate is working them to death, that's her way. But I don't think I ever heard two young voices of such promise. They sang at Christ Church that Sunday you didn't go, and I was quite overcome with astonishment. They have had the best instruction. It's wonderful to think of mere children having such method. As a rule juvenile exhibitions merely appeal to the maternal element in one, but when I heard them I quite forgot that they were children. I assure you they quite deserve to be taken seriously."

"All the same I shouldn't like to be exhibiting my children about like freaks."

"Poor Nelson! there's not much danger of your ever being tempted. It's extremely unlikely that poor Billy or Elsie will ever startle the world. Really, do you know when I heard those Massey children and thought of all they have done, of all they may do, I envied them myself? To youth everything is possible —when anything at all is possible."

[The feeling that youth is the most important part of life, the almost frantic effort to postpone growing older, the changing of her birth date three times to cut off another year—all these show Cather's belief that to youth everything is possible.]

Harriet sighed and Mackenzie fancied he detected a note of disappointment in her voice. He had suspected before that Harriet was disappointed in her children. They suited him well enough, but Harriet was different.

If Harriet Norton had taken up missionary work in the Cannibal Islands her friends could not have been more surprised than when she married Nelson Mackenzie. They had slated her for a very different career. As a girl she had possessed unusual talent. After taking sundry honors at the New England Conservatory, she had studied music abroad. It had been rumored that Leschetizky was about to launch her on a concert tour as a piano virtuoso, when she had suddenly returned to America and married the one among all her admirers who seemed particularly unsuited to her. Mackenzie was a young physician, a thoroughly practical, methodical Scotchman, rather stout, with a tendency to baldness, and with a propensity for playing the cornet. This latter fact alone was certainly enough to disqualify him for becoming the husband of a pianiste. When it reached Leschetizky's ears that Miss Norton had married a cornet-playing doctor, he "recorded one lost soul more," and her name never passed his lips again. Even her former rivals felt that they could now afford to be generous, and with one accord sent their congratulations to herself and husband "whom they had heard was also a musician."

Harriet received these neat sarcasms with great amusement. She had known when she married him that Mackenzie played the cornet, that he even played "Promise Me"; but she considered it one of the most innocent diversions in which a married man could indulge. But Harriet had not married him to inaugurate a romance or to develop one. She had seen romances enough abroad and knew by heart that fatal fifth act of marriages between artists. She was sometimes glad that there was not a romantic fiber in Mackenzie's substantial frame. She had married him because for some inexplicable reason she had always been fond of him, and since her marriage she had never been disappointed or disillusioned in him. He was not a brilliant man, and his chief merits were those of character—virtues not always fascinating, but they wear well in a husband and are generally about the safest things to be married to.

[In April of 1897 Willa Cather wrote a friend concerning a young doctor who wanted to marry her, admitting that she was not fond of him but adding that this fact didn't matter.]

So, in Mackenzie's phraseology, they had "pulled well enough together." Of course Mrs. Mackenzie had her moments of rebellion against the monotony of the domestic routine, and felt occasional stirrings of the old restlessness for achievement and the old thirst of the spirit. But knowing to what unspiritual things this soul-thirst had led women aforetime, she resolved to live the common life at least commonly well.

But her married life had held one very bitter disappointment, her children. Someway she had never doubted that her children would be like her. She had settled upon innumerable artistic careers for them. Of course they would both have her talent for music, probably talent of a much finer sort than her own, and the boy would do all the great things that she had not done. She knew well enough that if the cruelly exacting life of art is not wholly denied a woman, it is offered to her at a terrible price.

[This was an oft-repeated belief of Willa Cather, which kept her from recognizing what great happiness she really had.]

She had not chosen to pay it. But with the boy it would be different. He should realize all the dreams that once stirred in the breast on which he slept.

She had awaited impatiently the time when his little fingers were strong enough to strike the keys. But although he had heard music from the time he could hear at all, the child displayed neither interest nor aptitude for it. In vain his papa tooted familiar airs to him on the cornet; sometimes he recognized them and sometimes he did not. It was just the same with the little girl. The poor child could never sing the simplest nursery air correctly. They were both healthy, lively children, unusually truthful and well conducted, but thoroughly commonplace. Harriet could not resign herself to this, she could not understand it. There was always a note of envy in her voice when she spoke of the wonderful Massey children, whose names were on every one's lips. It seemed just as though Kate Massey had got what she should have had herself.

When the Mackenzies arrived at the Masseys' door Mrs. Massey rushed past the servant and met them herself.

"I'm so glad you've come, Harriet, dear. We were just about to begin and I didn't want you to miss Adrienne's first number. It's the waltz song from *Romeo et Juliette;* she had special drill on that from Madame Marchesi you know, and in London they considered it one of her best. I know this is a difficult hour, but they have to sing again after dinner and I don't want to tax them too much. Poor dears! there are so many demands on their time and strength that I sometimes feel like fleeing to the North Pole with them. To the left, upstairs, Mr. Mackenzie. Harriet, you know the way." And their animated hostess dashed off in search of more worlds to conquer. Mrs. Massey's manner was always that of a conqueror fresh from the fray. She demanded of everyone absolute capitulation and absolute surrender to the object of her particular enthusiasm, whatever that happened to be at the moment. Usually it was her wonderful children.

When the Mackenzies descended, Kate met them with a warning gesture and ushered them into the music room where the other guests were seated silently and expectantly. When they were seated she herself sank into a chair with an air of rapt and breathless anticipation.

The accompanist took her seat and a very pale, languid little

girl came forward and stood beside the piano. She looked to be
about fourteen but was unusually small for her age. She was a
singularly frail child with apparently almost no physical reserve
power, and stood with a slight natural stoop which she quickly
corrected as she caught her mother's eye. Her great dark eyes
seemed even larger than they were by reason of the dark circles
under them. She clasped her little hands and waited until the
brief prelude was over. She seemed not at all nervous, but very
weary. Even the spirited measures of that most vivacious of
arias could not wholly dispel the listlessness from those eyes that
were so sad for a child's face. As to the merit or even the "wonder" of her singing, there was no doubt. Even the unmusical
Mackenzie, who could not have described her voice in technical
language, knew that this voice was marvellous from the throat
of a child. The volume of a mature singer was of course not there,
but her tones were pure and limpid and wonderfully correct.
The thing that most surprised him was what his wife had called
the "method" of the child's singing. Gounod's waltz aria is not
an easy one, and the child must have been perfectly taught. It
seemed to him, though, that the little dash of gaiety she threw
into it had been taught her, too, and that this child herself had
never known what it was to be gay.

"O Kate, how I envy you!" sighed Harriet in a burst of admiration too sincere to be concealed.

Her hostess smiled triumphantly; she expected every one
to envy her, took that for granted. As Mackenzie saw the little
figure glide between the portiere, he was not quite so sure that
he envied Massey.

Massey was a practical man of business like himself, who
seemed rather overcome by the surprising talent of his children.
He always stood a little apart from the musical circle which sur-
rounded them, even in his own home, and when his wife took
them abroad for instruction he stayed at home and supplied the
funds. His natural reserve grew more marked as the years went
by, and he seemed so obliterated even at his own fireside that
Mackenzie sometimes fancied he regretted having given prodi-

gies to the world.

Mrs. Massey turned to Harriet in an excited whisper: "Hermann will only sing the 'Serenade.' He selected that because it saves his voice. The duet they will sing after dinner is very trying, it's the parting scene from *Juliette*, the one they will sing in concert next week."

The boy was the elder of the two; not so thin as his sister perhaps, but still pitifully fragile, with an unusually large head, all forehead, and those same dark tired eyes. He sang the German words of that matchless serenade of Schubert's, so familiar, yet so perennially new and strange; so old, yet so immortally young. It was a voice like those one sometimes hears in the boy choirs of the great cathedrals of the Old World,

> [Willa Cather had not yet been to Europe, yet she spoke with authenticity, the sort of ability which made possible *Death Comes for the Archbishop* and *Shadows on the Rock* and other works.]

a voice that, untrained, would have been alto rather than tenor; clear, sweet, and vibrant, with an indefinable echo of melancholy. He was less limited by his physique than his sister, and it seemed impossible that such strong, sustained tones could come from that fragile body. Although he sang so feelingly there was no fervor, rather a yearning, joyless and hopeless. It was a serenade to which no lattice would open, which expected no answer. It was as though this boy of fifteen were tired of the very name of love, and sang of a lost dream, inexpressibly sweet. He, at least, had not been taught that strange unboyish sadness, thought Mackenzie.

When the last vibrant note had died away the boy bowed, and, coughing slightly, crossed the room and stood by his father.

Every one rose and crowded about the hostess, whose enthusiasm burst forth afresh. By her side stood her father, a placid old gentleman who was thoroughly satisfied with himself, his daughter and his grandchildren. He had once been a vocal teacher himself, and it was he who accompanied his daughter and her prodigies on their trips abroad. The father and boy stood apart.

"Yes," Kate was replying to the comments of her friends, "Yes, it has always been so. When I would sing them to sleep when they were little things, just learning to talk, Hermann would take up the contralto with me and little Adrienne would form the soprano for herself. Of course it comes from my side of the house. Papa might have been a great baritone had he not devoted himself to teaching. They have never heard anything but good music. They had a nurse who used to sing Sunday school songs and street airs, and when Hermann was a little fellow of five he came to me one day and said: 'Mamma, I don't like to ask you to send Annie away, but please ask her not to sing to us, she sings such dreadful things!' We took them to Dr. Harrison's church one day and the soloist sang an aria from the Messiah. After that I had no rest; all day long it was, 'Mamma, sing Man a' Sorrows'—It was before they could talk plainly. They would do anything for me if I would only sing '*In Questa Tomba*' for them." Here she turned to her father, who was slightly deaf, and raising her voice said, "I was telling them about '*In Questa Tomba*,' father."

The old gentleman smiled serenely and nodded.

Mackenzie heard his wife say, "But Kate, it seems almost impossible that they should have cared for such music so young."

Mrs. Massey caught up the conversation with renewed energy.

"That's just what I once said to Madame Marchesi in Paris, my dear. I said, 'These children seem impossible to me. I cannot think they are my own.' 'Madame,' she replied, 'genius is just that: the impossible.' Of course, Harriet, that's Madame Marchesi, I don't claim genius for them. I'm afraid of the very word. It means such responsibility. You must not think I am too vain. Of course I speak quite freely today because only my intimate friends are present."

Mackenzie glanced apprehensively at the boy who must be hearing all this. But he did not seem to hear; he still stood holding his father's hand and looking out of the window. By this time Mackenzie had edged his way until he stood quite near the hostess, and he was thinking of something nice to say. He could say nice things sometimes, but he always had to think for them. He knew that on this occasion his speech must be sufficiently appreciative. He took his hostess' hand warmly and said in a low tone for her ear alone:

"I should think you would feel blessed among women, Mrs. Massey."

Kate beamed upon him and then turned to her father and shouted, "He says he should think I'd feel blessed among women, father."

The old gentleman smiled serenely his superior smile, his daughter's smile. Poor Mackenzie blushed violently at hearing his bit of soulful rhetoric shouted to the world and retreated. His wife smiled slyly at him. She knew Kate better than he. Kate was always beside herself; she could never be unemotional for an instant. She dined, dressed, talked, shopped, called, all at high pressure. Harriet could never imagine her passive even in sleep. She was always at white heat. Her enthusiasm was a Niagara and its supply seemed exhaustless. She threw herself and her whole self into everything, at everything, as an exhibition modeller throws his clay at his easel.

"I should think with the two of them your responsibility would be a grave one," ventured one robust old gentleman whose knowledge of music was limited, and who confined his remarks to safe generalities.

"That's just it, there are two of them! You would think that one would be care and responsibility enough. But there are two, think of it! Madame Marchesi used to say, 'A little Patti and Campanini': And I would reply 'and only one poor commonplace mortal mother to look after them.' As I say, when I hear them sing I don't feel as if they belong to me at all. I can't comprehend why I should be selected from among all other women for such a unique position."

Mackenzie cast a look of amazed inquiry at his wife. She

laughed and whispered, "O, Kate's always like this when she's excited, and she's generally excited."

The little girl had slipped quietly in and now the guests were shaking hands with the children and making them compliments. They received them with quiet indifference, only smiling when courtesy seemed to require it.

"Now Adrienne, get the handkerchief case the Princess of Wales made for you herself and show it to the ladies."

"I think they are all there on the mantle, mamma," replied the child quietly.

"So they are. And here, Mr. Mackenzie, is Jean de Reszke's photograph that he gave Adrienne with the inscription, 'To the Juliette of the future from an old Romeo.' Prettily worded, isn't it? And here is the jewelled miniature of Malibran that the Duke of Orleans gave her, and the opera glasses from Madame Marchesi. And there is the portrait of her husband that Frau Cosima Wagner gave Hermann. Of course he doesn't sing Wagnerian music yet, but *ça ira, ça ira*, as Madame used to say."

After examining trinkets enough to stock a small museum, Mackenzie said quietly:

"Aren't you just a little afraid of all this notoriety for them at their age? It seems as if there will be nothing left for them later."

He saw at once that he had touched a delicate subject and she threw herself on the defensive, "No, Mr. Mackenzie, I am afraid of nothing that will spur them to their work or make them feel the importance and weight of their art. Remember the age at which Patti began."

Mackenzie glanced at the two frail figures and ventured further. "That's just it, the weight of it. Their shoulders are young to bear it all, I'm thinking. Aren't you sometimes afraid it will exhaust them physically?"

"O, they are never ill, and," with her superior smile, "in their art one cannot begin too soon. It is the work of a lifetime, you know, a lifelong consecration. I do not feel that I have any right to curb them or to stop the flight of Pegasus. You see they are beyond me; I can only follow and help them as I may."

Mackenzie turned wearily away. He was thinking of the mother in a certain novel of Daudet's who refused to risk her son's life for a throne. Mrs. Massey shot across the room to show the rotund gentleman those trophies which were perhaps given so lightly, but were in her eyes precious beyond price.

Mackenzie saw the children slip through the portiere into the library and determined to follow them and discover whether these strange little beings were fay or human. They were standing by the big window watching a group of children who were playing in the snow outside.

"Say, Ad," said the boy, "do you suppose mamma would let us go out there and snowball for a while? Suppose you ask her."

"It would be no use to ask, Hermann. We should both be in wretched voice this evening. Besides, you know mamma considers those Hamilton children very common. They do have awfully good times though. Perhaps that's why they are so common. Most people seem to be who have a good time."

"I suppose so. We never get to do anything nice. John Hamilton has a new pair of skates and goes down on the ice in the park every day. I think I might learn to skate, anyhow."

"But you'd never get time to skate if you did learn. We haven't time to keep up our Italian, even. I'm forgetting mine."

"O bother our Italian! Ad, I'm just sick of it all. Sometimes I think I'll run away. But I'd practice forever if she'd just let us go to-morrow night. Do you suppose she would?"

"I'm awfully afraid not. You know at the beginning of the season she said we must hear that opera. I'll tell you; I'll go to the opera if she'll let you go to see them."

"No you won't either! You want to see them just as much as I do. I think we might go! We never get to do anything we want to." He struck the window casing impatiently with his clenched hand.

"What's the matter, children?" said Mackenzie, feeling that he was overhearing too much.

"O we're talking secrets, sir. We didn't know there was any

one in here."

"Well, I'm not any one much, but just an old fellow who likes little folks. Come over here on the divan and talk to me."

They followed him passively, like children who were accustomed to doing what they were told. He sat down and took the little girl on his knee and put his arm around the boy. He felt so sorry for them, these poor little prodigies who seemed so tired out with life.

[When Willa Cather came to know the Menuhin family well, she approved of their isolation from the world, although it was later to cause the young people emotional anguish. Willa Cather herself had shut out the world and had forgotten her own out-going youth.]

"Now I want you to come over and visit my little folks some day and see Billy's goats."

"Are your children musical?" asked the girl.

Mackenzie felt rather abashed. "No, they're not. But they are very nice children, at least I think so."

"Then what could we talk about?"

"O, about lots of things! What do young folks usually talk about? They have a great many books. Do you like to read?"

[Willa Cather introduced the Menuhin children to Shakespeare, formed a Shakespeare club with them, so that they might know the great English literature as well as foreign languages.]

"Yes, pretty well, but we don't often have time. What do your children read?"

"Well, they like rather old-fashioned books: Robinson Crusoe and The Swiss Family Robinson and Pilgrim's Progress. Do you like Pilgrim's Progress?"

"We never read it, did we Hermann?"

The boy shook his head.

"Never read it? then you must before you are a year older. It's a great old book; full of fights and adventures, you know."

"We have read the legends of the Holy Grail and Frau Cosima Wagner gave us a book of the legends of the Nibelung Trilogy. We liked that. It was full of fights and things. I suppose I will have to sing all that music some day; there is a great deal of it, you know," said the boy apprehensively.

"You work very hard, don't you?"

"O yes, very hard. You see there is so much to do," he replied feverishly.

"Plenty of time, my lad, plenty of time. Of course you play and take plenty of exercise to make you strong?"

"We have a gymnasium and exercise there. I fence half an hour every morning. I will need to know how some day, when I sing *Faust* and parts like that."

"And what do you do, Miss? Do you take good care of your dolls?"

"I haven't any now. I used to have a dear one, but one day when we were driving in from Fontainebleau I left her in the carriage. We advertised for her, but we never found her and I never wanted another."

"Ad cared so much for that one, you see," explained the boy. "Next day when we were taking our lesson she felt so badly about it she cried, and Madame asked what was the matter and said, 'Never mind, *ma chère*, wait a little and you will have dolls enough. Girls who sing like you never lack for toys in this world. I taught the beautiful Sybil, and behold what toys she has!' I have often wondered what she meant. But it was often very difficult to tell just what Madame meant. Sometimes I used to think she was making fun of us."

Mackenzie looked at the boy sharply and veered into safer waters.

"Aren't you glad to be home again?"

"Yes, but of course we are better abroad. There's no artistic atmosphere over here. I think we go back to Paris in the spring, or London, maybe."

"You go to the opera often, don't you?"

"Yes," replied the little girl, "we are going to the 'Damnation of Faust' to-morrow night—that is if we don't go somewhere else."

"Now Ad, don't you tell secrets," said her brother sternly.

"Well, I thought we might just tell him. Perhaps he'd coax her for us."

"You'll not laugh at us and you'll not tell?"

"On my honor," said Mackenzie.

"You see," explained Hermann, "we want to see the dog show to-morrow night. We've never been to one and I think we might. The Hamilton children go every night and they say there are just hundreds of dogs."

"And why can't you, pray?"

"Well, you see it's the only time they will sing Berlioz's 'Damnation of Faust' here this season, and we ought to hear it. Then mamma don't like us to go to such things."

Mackenzie set his teeth. "Now I'll just tell you; my children are going to the dog show and you shall go with them. I'll fix it up with your mother. And what's more I'll send you over one of our skye terrier pups. Even singers are permitted to have dogs, aren't they? At least they are always losing them. You go and ask your mother if you may keep the pup, my son."

As the boy shot off the little girl nestled closer to him. "I'm so awfully glad! Hermann has just been wild to go. And perhaps we'll see the Hamilton children. You see mamma doesn't like the Hamilton children very well. They wear lots of jewels and are not always careful about their grammar, but they do have good times. Sometimes Hermann and I play we are the Hamilton children; and he pretends he has been off skating and tells me what he saw, and I pretend I've been to school and making fancy work like Mollie Hamilton. That's a very secret play and we only play it when we're alone."

So these poor little prodigies loved to play that they were just the common children of the "new rich" next door! Mackenzie took the little hand that a single ruby made look so bloodless and his eyes were very tender.

"Why, my child, how hot your hands are, and your cheeks are all flushed. Your pulse is going like a triphammer. Are you ill?"

"O no, I'm just tired. We've been working very hard for our big concert next week. That's a very important concert, you know. But there, they are all going out to dinner, and you are to take mamma out, I think. Good-bye."

"But aren't you coming too?"

"Oh no! We sing later, so of course we can't dine now."

"O no, of course you can't dine!" said Mackenzie.

After dinner the more formal guests arrived and the party again assembled in the music room.

"They are going to sing the parting scene from *Juliette*, those babies! Why will Kate select such music for them? The effect will be little short of grotesque. But then it's just like Kate, she never admits of distinctions or conditions," whispered Mrs. Mackenzie to her husband. "Here they come. O Nelson, that boy Romeo and his baby Juliet, it's sacrilege!"

They quietly took their places, "the boy Romeo and his baby Juliet," looking earnestly at each other, and began that frenzied song of pain and parting: *"Tu die partir ohime!"* Poor little children! What could they know of the immeasurable anguish of that farewell—or of the immeasurable joy which alone can make such sorrow possible? What could they know of the fearful potency of the words they uttered—words that have governed nations and wrecked empires! They sang bravely enough, but the effect was that of trying to force the tones of a 'cello from a violin.

Suddenly a quick paleness came over the face of the little Juliet. Still struggling with the score she threw out her hand and caught her Romeo's shoulder, swaying like a flower before the breath of a hurricane.

"Ad, Ad!" shrieked the boy as he sank upon one knee with his sister in his arms.

There was wild confusion among the guests; the men threw open the doors and struggled with the windows. Mackenzie sprang to the child's side but her mother was there before him, whiter than the little Juliet herself.

"Doctor, what does it mean? She has never done like this before, she is never ill."

As she bent over the child her husband thrust her back, lifting the little girl in his arms.

"Let me take her now—you have done enough!" he said sternly, with an ominous flash in his eyes. It was the only time he was ever heard to issue a command in his own household.

"O Nelson, it is terrible!" said Mrs. Mackenzie as they drove home that night. "Kate Massey must be mad. Poor little girl! And the boy—why I wouldn't have that haunted look in Billy's eyes for the world!"

"Not even to make a tenor of him?" asked Mackenzie.

A month later Mackenzie stood again in the Masseys' music room with Kate beside him. The woman was so pale and broken that he could almost find it in his heart to be sorry for her.

"I don't think I need come again now, Mrs. Massey, unless there is a relapse."

"And you still think, Doctor, that there is no hope at all? For her voice, I mean?"

"The best specialists in New York agree with me in that. Your foreign teachers have not been content with duping you out of your money, they have simply drained your child's life out of her veins," said Mackenzie brutally.

There was a ghost of the old superior smile. "Doctor, you forget yourself. Whatever you American physicians may say, I know that the child was properly taught. This has broken my heart, but it has not convinced me that I am in error. I have said I could make any sacrifice for their art, but God knows I never thought it would be this."

The little boy entered the room with a roll of music under his arm. His mother caught him to her impulsively.

"Ah, my boy, you must travel your way alone now. I suppose the day must have come when one of you must have suffered for the other. Two of the same blood can never achieve equally. Perhaps it is best that it should come now. But remember, my son, you carry not one destiny in your throat, but two. You must be great enough for both!"

The boy kissed her and said gently, "Don't cry, mother. I will try."

His mother hid her face on his shoulder and he turned to the Doctor, who was drawing on his gloves, and shrugging his frail shoulders smiled. It was the smile which might have touched the face of some Roman youth on the bloody sand, when the reversed thumb of the Empress pointed deathward.

[The ending reminds one of a sentence from Henry James' "The Story of a Year": "He lay perfectly motionless, but for his eyes. They wandered over her with a kind of peaceful glee, like sunbeams playing on a statue. Poor Ford lay, indeed, not unlike an old wounded Greek, who at dusk has crawled into a temple to die, steeping the last dull interval in idle admiration of sculptured Artemis."]

❧ Eric Hermannson's Soul

published in *Cosmopolitan*, April, 1900

[Although this story is not smooth and the dialect is not consistent, it contains many of the Cather elements that hint of the powerful writing to come. Here is her feeling for the land, the sky, and physical perfection in man or woman. Here is her own struggle between the old and the new, between the cynicism of civilization and the vitality of barbarism; the undercurrent affinity between city culture and the natural grace of the disinherited children of older civilizations, together with the impossibility of uniting the two.

We find symbolism of the rattlesnake (sin), the wild ponies (freedom), and the breaking of the violin (the destruction of the soul to Cather, though the saving of it to Asa Skinner). We find rich allusions to mythology, music, literature and sculpture.]

It was a great night at the Lone Star schoolhouse—a night when the Spirit was present with power and when God was very near to man. So it seemed to Asa Skinner, servant of God and Free Gospeller. The schoolhouse was crowded with the saved and sanctified, robust men and women, trembling and quailing before the power of some mysterious psychic force. Here and there among this cowering, sweating multitude crouched some poor wretch who had felt the pangs of an awakened conscience, but had not yet experienced that complete divestment of reason, that frenzy born of a convulsion of the mind, which, in the parlance of the Free Gospellers, is termed "the Light." On the floor before the mourners' bench, lay the unconscious figure of a man in whom outraged nature had sought her last resort. This "trance" state is the highest evidence of grace among the Free

Gospellers, and indicates a close walking with God.

Before the desk stood Asa Skinner, shouting of the mercy and vengeance of God, and in his eyes shone a terrible earnestness, an almost prophetic flame. Asa was a converted train gambler who used to run between Omaha and Denver. He was a man made for the extremes of life; from the most debauched of men he had become the most ascetic. His was a bestial face, a face that bore the stamp of Nature's eternal injustice. The forehead was low, projecting over the eyes, and the sandy hair was plastered down over it and then brushed back at an abrupt right angle. The chin was heavy, the nostrils were low and wide, and the lower lip hung loosely except in his moments of spasmodic earnestness, when it shut like a steel trap. Yet about those coarse features there were deep, rugged furrows, the scars of many a hand-to-hand struggle with the weakness of the flesh, and about that drooping lip were sharp, strenuous lines that had conquered it and taught it to pray. Over those seamed cheeks there was a certain pallor, a grayness caught from many a vigil. It was as though, after Nature had done her worst with that face, some fine chisel had gone over it, chastening and almost transfiguring it. To-night, as his muscles twitched with emotion, and the perspiration dropped from his hair and chin, there was a certain convincing power in the man. For Asa Skinner was a man possessed of a belief, of that sentiment of the sublime before which all inequalities are leveled, that transport of conviction which seems superior to all laws of condition, under which debauchees have become martyrs; which made a tinker an artist and a cameldriver the founder of an empire. This was with Asa Skinner to-night, as he stood proclaiming the vengeance of God.

> [Asa Skinner fits his environment a little better than Lou, the prophet, and is therefore less pitiful, though less lovable. He is stupid but sincere, at least for the moment. In *One of Ours* Brother Weldon is both stupid and insincere.
>
> Willa was brought up a Baptist, but she joined the Episcopal church in 1922. That the problem of faith concerned her throughout her life is evidenced by the early "Lou, the

Prophet," culminating in *Death Comes for the Archbishop,*
and *Shadows on the Rock.* Her most generous treatment of
the protestant ministry is given Peter Kronborg in *Song of the
Lark.* But he is tiresome, and even in his genuine moments he
is inarticulate. Perhaps her feeling that what lies deepest cannot be expressed led Cather to find charm in the ritual of the
Episcopal and Catholic faiths.]

It might have occurred to an impartial observer that Asa
Skinner's God was indeed a vengeful God if he could reserve
vengeance for those of his creatures who were packed into the
Lone Star schoolhouse that night. Poor exiles of all nations; men
from the south and the north, peasants from almost every country
of Europe, most of them from the mountainous, night-bound
coast of Norway. Honest men for the most part, but men with
whom the world had dealt hardly; the failures of all countries,
men sobered by toil and saddened by exile, who had been driven
to fight for the dominion of an untoward soil, to sow where
others should gather, the advanceguard of a mighty civilization
to be.

Never had Asa Skinner spoken more earnestly than now. He
felt that the Lord had this night a special work for him to do.
To-night Eric Hermannson, the wildest lad on all the Divide, sat
in his audience with a fiddle on his knee, just as he had dropped
in on his way to play for some dance. The violin is an object
of particular abhorrence to the Free Gospellers. Their antago-
nism to the church organ is bitter enough, but the fiddle they
regard as a very incarnation of evil desires, singing forever of
worldly pleasures and inseparably associated with all forbidden
things.

Eric Hermannson had long been the object of the prayers of
the revivalists. His mother had felt the power of the Spirit
weeks ago, and special prayer-meetings had been held at her
house for her son. But Eric had only gone his ways laughing, the
ways of youth, which are short enough at best, and none too
flowery on the Divide. He slipped away from the prayer-meetings
to meet the Campbell boys in Genereau's

[Campbell is a little town northwest of the original
Cather farm.]

saloon, or hug the plump little French girls at Chevalier's dances,
and sometimes, of a summer night, he even went across the dewy
cornfields and through the wild-plum thicket to play the fiddle
for Lena Hanson, whose name was a reproach through all the
Divide country, where the women are usually too plain and too
busy and too tired to depart from the ways of virtue. On such
occasions Lena, attired in a pink wrapper and silk stockings
and tiny pink slippers, would sing to him, accompanying herself
on a battered guitar. It gave him a delicious sense of freedom
and experience to be with a woman who, no matter how, had
lived in big cities and knew the ways of town-folk, who had
never worked in the fields and had kept her hands white and
soft, her throat fair and tender, who had heard great singers in
Denver and Salt Lake, and who knew the strange language of
flattery and idleness and mirth.

[This is a preview of Lena Lingard of *My Ántonia.*]

Yet, careless as he seemed, the frantic prayers of his mother
were not altogether without their effect upon Eric. For days
he had been fleeing before them as a criminal from his pursuers,
and over his pleasures had fallen the shadow of something dark
and terrible that dogged his steps. The harder he danced, the
louder he sang, the more was he conscious that this phantom
was gaining upon him, that in time it would track him down.
One Sunday afternoon, late in the fall, when he had been drinking beer with Lena Hanson and listening to a song which made
his cheeks burn, a rattlesnake had crawled out of the side of the
sod house and thrust its ugly head in under the screen door. He
was not afraid of snakes, but he knew enough of Gospellism to
feel the significance of the reptile lying coiled there upon her
doorstep. His lips were cold when he kissed Lena good-by, and

he went there no more.

The final barrier between Eric and his mother's faith was his violin, and to that he clung as a man sometimes will cling to his dearest sin, to the weakness more precious to him than all his strength. In the great world beauty comes to men in many guises, and art in a hundred forms, but for Eric there was only his violin. It stood, to him, for all the manifestations of art; it was his only bridge into the kingdom of the soul.

> [We have already seen the poverty of the cultural background—a poverty expressed later in "A Wagner Matinee," and we now see that the problem resolves into a battle between art and salvation.]

It was to Eric Hermannson that the evangelist directed his impassioned pleading that night.

"*Saul, Saul, why persecutest thou me?* Is there a Saul here to-night who has stopped his ears to that gentle pleading, who has thrust a spear into that bleeding side? Think of it, my brother; you are offered this wonderful love and you prefer the worm that dieth not and the fire which will not be quenched. What right have you to lose one of God's precious souls? *Saul, Saul, why persecutest thou me?*"

A great joy dawned in Asa Skinner's pale face, for he saw that Eric Hermannson was swaying to and fro in his seat. The minister fell upon his knees and threw his long arms up over his head.

"O my brothers! I feel it coming, the blessing we have prayed for. I tell you the Spirit is coming! Just a little more prayer, brothers, a little more zeal, and he will be here. I can feel his cooling wing upon my brow. Glory be to God forever and ever, amen!"

The whole congregation groaned under the pressure of this spiritual panic. Shouts and hallelujahs went up from every lip. Another figure fell prostrate upon the floor. From the mourners' bench rose a chant of terror and rapture:

"Eating honey and drinking wine,
Glory to the bleeding Lamb!
I am my Lord's and he is mine,
Glory to the bleeding Lamb!"

[Charles Cather forbade his children's going to medicine
shows and revival meetings. Willa had certainly disobeyed
in regard to the latter, or she could never have written this
story.]

The hymn was sung in a dozen dialects and voiced all the
vague yearning of these hungry lives, of these people who had
starved all the passions so long, only to fall victims to the basest
of them all, fear.

A groan of ultimate anguish rose from Eric Hermannson's
bowed head, and the sound was like the groan of a great tree
when it falls in the forest.

The minister rose suddenly to his feet and threw back his
head, crying in a loud voice:

"*Lazarus, come forth!* Eric Hermannson, you are lost, going
down at sea. In the name of God, and Jesus Christ his Son, I
throw you the life-line. Take hold! Almighty God, my soul for
his!" The minister threw his arms out and lifted his quivering
face.

Eric Hermannson rose to his feet; his lips were set and
the lightning was in his eyes. He took his violin by the neck
and crushed it to splinters across his knee, and to Asa Skinner the sound was like the shackles of sin broken audibly asunder.

II

For more than two years Eric Hermannson kept the austere
faith to which he had sworn himself, kept it until a girl from
the East came to spend a week on the Nebraska Divide. She was
a girl of other manners and conditions, and there were greater
distances between her life and Eric's than all the miles which

separated Rattlesnake Creek from New York city. Indeed, she had no business to be in the West at all; but ah! across what leagues of land and sea, by what improbable chances, do the unrelenting gods bring to us our fate!

[Here again is the difference between East and West, mentioned in "Tommy, the Unsentimental."]

It was in a year of financial depression that Wyllis Elliot came to Nebraska to buy cheap land and revisit the country where he had spent a year of his youth. When he had graduated from Harvard it was still customary for moneyed gentlemen to send their scapegrace sons to rough it on ranches in the wilds of Nebraska or Dakota, or to consign them to a living death in the sagebrush of the Black Hills.

[These were known as "remittance men" because they received a check from home each month. They appear in minor roles throughout Cather's Nebraska stories: for example, Trevor and Brewster, the sheep raisers, in *One of Ours;* the bachelor rancher from Boston who took advantage of Mary Dusak in *My Ántonia;* and perhaps Frank Ellinger of *A Lost Lady.*]

These young men did not always return to the ways of civilized life. But Wyllis Elliot had not married a half-breed, nor been shot in a cow-punchers' brawl, nor wrecked by bad whisky, nor appropriated by a smirched adventuress. He had been saved from these things by a girl, his sister, who had been very near to his life ever since the days when they read fairy tales together and dreamed the dreams that never come true. On this, his first visit to his father's ranch since he left it six years before, he brought her with him.

[Willa Cather thought that the brother-sister relationship had not been sufficiently appreciated in literature. She pointed out Tom and Maggie Tulliver (*The Mill on the Floss,* by George Eliot) as a good example.]

She had been laid up half the winter from a sprain received while skating, and had had too much time for reflection during those months. She was restless and filled with a desire to see something of the wild country of which her brother had told her so much. She was to be married the next winter, and Wyllis understood her when she begged him to take her with him on this long, aimless jaunt across the continent, to taste the last of their freedom together. It comes to all women of her type—that desire to taste the unknown which allures and terrifies, to run one's whole soul's length out to the wind—just once.

It had been an eventful journey. Wyllis somehow understood that strain of gypsy blood in his sister, and he knew where to take her. They had slept in sod houses on the Platte River, made the acquaintance of the personnel of a third-rate opera company on the train to Deadwood, dined in a camp of railroad constructors at the world's end beyond New Castle, gone through the Black Hills on horseback, fished for trout in Dome Lake, watched a dance at Cripple Creek, where the lost souls who hide in the hills gather for their besotted revelry. And now, last of all, before the return to thraldom, there was this little shack, anchored on the windy crest of the Divide, a little black dot against the flaming sunsets, a scented sea of cornland bathed in opalescent air and blinding sunlight.

> [Probably Willa is here describing some of the excursions she made with her brother Douglass when he was working for the Burlington in Wyoming. She was very close to her brothers Douglass and Roscoe.]

Margaret Elliot was one of those women of whom there are so many in this day, when old order, passing, giveth place to new; beautiful, talented, critical, unsatisfied, tired of the world at twenty-four. For the moment the life and people of the Divide interested her. She was there but a week; perhaps had she stayed longer, that inexorable ennui which travels faster even than the Vestibule Limited would have overtaken her. The week she tarried there was the week that Eric Hermannson was helping Jerry Lockhart thresh; a week earlier or a week later, and there would have been no story to write.

It was on Thursday and they were to leave on Saturday. Wyllis and his sister were sitting on the wide piazza of the ranchhouse, staring out into the afternoon sunlight and protesting against gusts of hot wind that blew up from the sandy river-bottom twenty miles to the southward.

The young man pulled his cap lower over his eyes and remarked:

"This wind is the real thing; you don't strike it anywhere else. You remember we had a touch of it in Algiers and I told you it came from Kansas. It's the keynote of this country."

Wyllis touched her hand that lay on the hammock and continued gently:

"I hope it's paid you, Sis. Roughing it's dangerous business; it takes the taste out of things."

She shut her fingers firmly over the brown hand that was so like her own.

"Paid? Why, Wyllis, I haven't been so happy since we were children and were going to discover the ruins of Troy together some day. Do you know, I believe I could just stay on here forever and let the world go on its own gait. It seems as though the tension and strain we used to talk of last winter were gone for good, as though one could never give one's strength out to such petty things any more."

Wyllis brushed the ashes of his pipe away from the silk handkerchief that was knotted about his neck and stared moodily off at the sky-line.

"No, you're mistaken. This would bore you after a while. You can't shake the fever of the other life. I've tried it. There was a time when the gay fellows of Rome could trot down into the Thebaid

[Reference to Thebes in the northern part of the Nile country.]

and burrow into the sandhills and get rid of it. But it's all too complex now. You see we've made our dissipations so dainty and respectable that they've gone further in than the flesh, and taken hold of the ego proper. You couldn't rest, even here. The war-cry would follow you."

"You don't waste words, Wyllis, but you never miss fire. I talk more than you do, without saying half so much. You must have learned the art of silence from these taciturn Norwegians. I think I like silent men."

"Naturally," said Wyllis, "since you have decided to marry the most brilliant talker you know."

Both were silent for a time, listening to the sighing of the hot wind through the parched morning-glory vines. Margaret spoke first.

"Tell me, Wyllis, were many of the Norwegians you used to know as interesting as Eric Hermannson?"

"Who, Siegfried? Well, no. He used to be the flower of the Norwegian youth in my day, and he's rather an exception, even now. He has retrograded, though. The bonds of the soil have tightened on him, I fancy."

"Siegfried? Come, that's rather good, Wyllis. He looks like a dragon-slayer. What is it that makes him so different from the others? I can talk to him; he seems quite like a human being."

"Well," said Wyllis, meditatively, "I don't read Bourget as much as my cultured sister, and I'm not so well up in analysis, but I fancy it's because one keeps cherishing a perfectly unwarranted suspicion that under that big, hulking anatomy of his, he may conceal a soul somewhere. *Nicht wahr?*"

"Something like that," said Margaret, thoughtfully, "except that it's more than a suspicion, and it isn't groundless. He has one, and he makes it known, somehow, without speaking."

[Compare Eric with the Blum boys of *A Lost Lady*.]

"I always have my doubts about loquacious souls," Wyllis remarked, with the unbelieving smile that had grown habitual with him.

Margaret went on, not heeding the interruption. "I knew it from the first, when he told me about the suicide of his cousin, the Bernstein boy. That kind of blunt pathos can't be summoned at will in anybody. The earlier novelists rose to it, sometimes, unconsciously. But last night when I sang for him I was doubly sure. Oh, I haven't told you about that yet! Better light your pipe again. You see, he stumbled in on me in the dark when I was pumping away at that old parlor organ to please Mrs. Lockhart. It's her household fetish and I've forgotten how many pounds of butter she made and sold to buy it. Well, Eric stumbled in, and in some inarticulate manner made me understand that he wanted me to sing for him. I sang just the old things, of course. It's queer to sing familiar things here at the world's end. It makes one think how the hearts of men have carried them around the world, into the wastes of Iceland and the jungles of Africa and the islands of the Pacific.

[This became a favorite Cather thesis.]

I think if one lived here long enough one would quite forget how to be trivial, and would read only the great books that we never get time to read in the world, and would remember only the great music, and the things that are really worth while would stand out clearly against that horizon over there. And of course I played the intermezzo from 'Cavalleria Rusticana' for him; it goes rather better on an organ than most things do. He shuffled his feet and twisted his big hands up into knots and blurted out that he didn't know there was any music like that in the world. Why, there were tears in his voice, Wyllis! Yes, like Rossetti, I *heard* his tears.

[Here is the same type of suffering Claude Wheeler in *One of Ours* endured.]

Then it dawned upon me that it was probably the first good music he had ever heard in all his life. Think of it, to care for music as he does and never to hear it, never to know that it exists on earth! To long for it as we long for other perfect experiences that never come. I can't tell you what music means to that man. I never saw any one so susceptible to it. It gave him speech, he became alive. When I had finished the intermezzo, he began telling me about a little crippled brother who died and whom he loved and used to carry everywhere in his arms. He did not wait for encouragement. He took up the story and told it slowly, as if to himself, just sort of rose up and told his own woe to answer Mascagni's. [Composer of "Cavalleria Rusticana."] It overcame me."

"Poor devil," said Wyllis, looking at her with mysterious eyes, "and so you've given him a new woe. Now he'll go on wanting Grieg and Schubert the rest of his days and never getting them. That's a girl's philanthropy for you!"

Jerry Lockhart came out of the house screwing his chin over the unusual luxury of a stiff white collar, which his wife insisted upon as a necessary article of toilet while Miss Elliot was at the house. Jerry sat down on the step and smiled his broad, red smile at Margaret.

"Well, I've got the music for your dance, Miss Elliot. Olaf Oleson will bring his accordion and Mollie will play the organ, when she isn't lookin' after the grub, and a little chap from Frenchtown will bring his fiddle—though the French don't mix with the Norwegians much."

"Delightful! Mr. Lockhart, that dance will be the feature of our trip, and it's so nice of you to get it up for us. We'll see the Norwegians in character at last," cried Margaret, cordially.

"See here, Lockhart, I'll settle with you for backing her in this scheme," said Wyllis, sitting up and knocking the ashes out of his pipe. "She's done crazy things enough on this trip, but to talk of dancing all night with a gang of half-mad Norwegians and taking the carriage at four to catch the six o'clock train out of Riverton—well, it's tommy-rot, that's what it is!"

[Riverton is a town on the Burlington railroad, about sixteen miles cross-country south west of Campbell, about the same distance from the old Cather place.]

"Wyllis, I leave it to your sovereign power of reason to decide whether it isn't easier to stay up all night than to get up at three in the morning. To get up at three, think what that means! No, sir, I prefer to keep my vigil and then get into a sleeper."

"But what do you want with the Norwegians? I thought you were tired of dancing."

"So I am, with some people. But I want to see a Norwegian dance, and I intend to. Come, Wyllis, you know how seldom it is that one really wants to do anything nowadays. I wonder when I have really wanted to go to a party before. It will be something to remember next month at Newport, when we have to and don't want to. Remember your own theory that contrast is about the only thing that makes life endurable. This is my party and Mr. Lockhart's; your whole duty tomorrow night will consist in being nice to the Norwegian girls. I'll warrant you were adept enough at it once. And you'd better be very nice indeed, for if there are many such young valkyries as Eric's sister among them, they would simply tie you up in a knot if they suspected you were guying them."

Wyllis groaned and sank back into the hammock to consider his fate, while his sister went on.

"And the guests, Mr. Lockhart, did they accept?"

Lockhart took out his knife and began sharpening it on the sole of his plowshoe.

"Well, I guess we'll have a couple dozen. You see it's pretty hard to get a crowd together here any more. Most of 'em have gone over to the Free Gospellers, and they'd rather put their feet in the fire than shake 'em to a fiddle."

Margaret made a gesture of impatience. "Those Free Gospellers have just cast an evil spell over this country, haven't they?"

"Well," said Lockhart, cautiously, "I don't just like to pass judgment on any Christian sect, but if you're to know the chosen by their works, the Gospellers can't make a very proud showin', an' that's a fact. They're responsible for a few suicides, and they've sent a good-sized delegation to the state insane asylum, an' I don't see as they've made the rest of us much better than we were before. I had a little herdboy last spring, as square a little Dane as I want to work for me, but after the Gospellers got hold of him and sanctified him, the little beggar used to get down on his knees out on the prairie and pray by the hour and let the cattle get into the corn, an' I had to fire him. That's about the way it goes. Now there's Eric; that chap used to be a hustler and the spryest dancer in all this section—called all the dances. Now he's got no ambition and he's glum as a preacher. I don't suppose we can even get him to come in to-morrow night."

"Eric? Why, he must dance, we can't let him off," said Margaret, quickly. "Why, I intend to dance with him myself."

"I'm afraid he won't dance. I asked him this morning if he'd help us out and he said, 'I don't dance now, any more,'" said Lockhart, imitating the labored English of the Norwegian.

"'The Miller of Hoffbau, the Miller of Hoffbau, O my Princess!'" chirped Wyllis, cheerfully, from his hammock.

The red on his sister's cheek deepened a little, and she laughed mischievously. "We'll see about that, sir. I'll not admit that I am beaten until I have asked him myself."

Every night Eric rode over to St. Anne, a little village in the heart of the French settlement, for the mail. As the road lay through the most attractive part of the Divide country, on several occasions Margaret Elliot and her brother had accompanied him. To-night Wyllis had business with Lockhart, and Margaret rode with Eric, mounted on a frisky little mustang that Mrs. Lockhart had broken to the side-saddle. Margaret regarded her escort very much as she did the servant who always accompanied her on long rides at home, and the ride to the village was a silent one. She was occupied with thoughts of another world, and Eric was wrestling with more thoughts than had ever been crowded into his head before. He rode with his eyes riveted on that slight figure before him, as though he wished to absorb it through the optic nerves and hold it in his brain forever. He understood the situation perfectly. His brain worked slowly, but he had a keen sense of the values of things. This girl represented an entirely new species of humanity to him, but he knew where to place her. The prophets of old, when an angel first appeared unto them, never doubted its high origin.

Eric was patient under the adverse conditions of his life, but he was not servile. The Norse blood in him had not entirely lost its self-reliance. He came of a proud fisher line, men who were not afraid of anything but the ice and the devil, and he had prospects before him when his father went down off the North Cape in the long Arctic night, and his mother, seized by a violent horror of seafaring life, had followed her brother to America. Eric was eighteen then, handsome as young Siegfried, a giant in stature, with a skin singularly pure and delicate, like a Swede's; hair as yellow as the locks of Tennyson's amorous Prince, and eyes of a fierce, burning blue, whose flash was most dangerous to women. He had in those days a certain pride of bearing, a certain confidence of approach, that usually accompanies physical perfection. It was even said of him then that he was in love with life, and inclined to levity, a vice most unusual on the Divide. But the sad history of those Norwegian exiles, transplanted in an arid soil and under a scorching sun, had repeated itself in his case. Toil and isolation had sobered him, and he grew more and more like the clods among which he labored. It was as though some red-hot instrument had touched for a moment those delicate fibers of the brain which respond to acute pain or pleasure, in which lies the power of exquisite sensation, and had seared them quite away. It is a painful thing to watch the light die out of the eyes of those Norsemen, leaving an expression of impenetrable sadness, quite passive, quite hopeless, a shadow that is never lifted. With some this change comes almost at once, in the first bitterness of homesickness, with others it comes more slowly, according to the time it takes each man's heart to die.

Oh, those poor Northmen of the Divide! They are dead many a year before they are put to rest in the little graveyard on the windy hill where exiles of all nations grow akin.

[The same graveyard is mentioned in *O Pioneers.*]

The peculiar species of hypochondria to which the exiles of his people sooner or later succumb had not developed in Eric until that night at the Lone Star schoolhouse, when he had broken his violin across his knee. After that, the gloom of his people settled down upon him, and the gospel of maceration began its work. "*If thine eye offend thee, pluck it out,*" et cetera. The pagan smile that once hovered about his lips was gone, and he was one with sorrow. Religion heals a hundred hearts for one that it embitters, but when it destroys, its work is quick and deadly, and where the agony of the cross has been, joy will not come again. This man understood things literally: one must live without pleasure to die without fear; to save the soul it was necessary to starve the soul.

The sun hung low above the cornfields when Margaret and her cavalier left St. Anne. South of the town there is a stretch of road that runs for some three miles through the French settlement, where the prairie is as level as the surface of a lake. There the fields of flax and wheat and rye are bordered by precise rows of slender tapering Lombard poplars. It was a yellow world that Margaret Elliot saw under the wide light of the setting sun.

The girl gathered up her reins and called back to Eric, "It will be safe to run the horses here, won't it?"

"Yes, I think so, now," he answered, touching his spur to his pony's flank. They were off like the wind. It is an old saying in the West that new-comers always ride a horse or two to death before they get broken in to the country. They are tempted by the great open spaces and try to outride the horizon, to get to the end of something.

[*My Ántonia:* "The only thing very noticeable about Nebraska was that it was still, all day long, Nebraska."]

Margaret galloped over the level road, and Eric, from behind, saw her long veil fluttering in the wind. It had fluttered just so in his dreams last night and the night before. With a sudden inspiration of courage he overtook her and rode beside her, looking intently at her half-averted face. Before, he had only stolen occasional glances at it, seen it in blinding flashes, always with more or less embarrassment, but now he determined to let every line of it sink into his memory. Men of the world would have said that it was an unusual face, nervous, finely cut, with clear, elegant lines that betokened ancestry. Men of letters would have called it a historic face, and would have conjectured at what old passions, long asleep, what old sorrows forgotten time out of mind, doing battle together in ages gone, had curved those delicate nostrils, left their unconscious memory in those eyes. But Eric read no meaning in these details. To him this beauty was something more than color and line; it was as a flash of white light, in which one cannot distinguish color because all colors are there. To him it was a complete revelation, an embodiment of those dreams of impossible loveliness that linger by a young man's pillow on midsummer nights; yet, because it held something more than the attraction of health and youth and shapeliness, it troubled him, and in its presence he felt as the Goths before the white marbles in the Roman Capitol, not knowing whether they were men or gods. At times he felt like uncovering his head before it, again the fury seized him to break and despoil, to find the clay in this spirit-thing and stamp upon it. Away from her, he longed to strike out with his arms, and take and hold; it maddened him that this woman whom he could break in his hands should be so much stronger than he.

[Cather's women are always stronger than their men.]

But near her, he never questioned this strength; he admitted its potentiality as he admitted the miracles of the Bible; it enervated and conquered him. To-night, when he rode so close to her that he could have touched her, he knew that he might as well reach out his hand to take a star.

Margaret stirred uneasily under his gaze and turned questioningly in her saddle.

"This wind puts me a little out of breath when we ride fast," she said.

Eric turned his eyes away.

"I want to ask you if I go to New York to work, if I maybe hear music like you sang last night? I been a purty good hand to work," he asked timidly.

Margaret looked at him with surprise, and then, as she studied the outline of his face, pityingly.

"Well, you might—but you'd lose a good deal else. I shouldn't like you to go to New York—and be poor, you'd be out of atmosphere, some way," she said, slowly. Inwardly she was thinking: "There he would be altogether sordid, impossible —a machine who would carry one's trunks upstairs, perhaps. Here he is every inch a man, rather picturesque; why is it?" "No," she added aloud, "I shouldn't like that."

"Then I not go," said Eric, decidedly.

Margaret turned her face to hide a smile. She was a trifle amused and a trifle annoyed. Suddenly she spoke again.

"But I'll tell you what I do want you to do, Eric. I want you to dance with us to-morrow night and teach me some of the Norwegian dances; they say you know them all. Won't you?"

Eric straightened himself in his saddle and his eyes flashed as they had done in the Lone Star schoolhouse when he broke his violin across his knee.

"Yes, I will," he said, quietly, and he believed that he delivered his soul to hell as he said it.

They had reached the rougher country now, where the road wound through a narrow cut in one of the bluffs along the creek, when a beat of hoofs ahead and the sharp neighing of horses made the ponies start and Eric rose in his stirrups. Then down the gulch in front of them and over the steep clay banks thundered a herd of wild ponies, nimble as monkeys and wild as rabbits, such as horse-traders drive east from the plains of Montana to sell in the farming country. Margaret's pony made a shrill sound, a neigh that was almost a scream, and started up the clay bank to meet them, all the wild blood of the range breaking out in an instant. Margaret called to Eric just as he threw himself out of the saddle and caught her pony's bit. But the wiry little animal had gone mad and was kicking and biting like a devil. Her wild brothers of the range were all about her, neighing, and pawing the earth, and striking her with their fore feet and snapping at her flanks. It was the old liberty of the range that the little beast fought for.

"Drop the reins and hold tight, tight!" Eric called, throwing all his weight upon the bit, struggling under those frantic fore feet that now beat at his breast, and now kicked at the wild mustangs that surged and tossed about him. He succeeded in wrenching the pony's head toward him and crowding her withers against the clay bank, so that she could not roll.

[Note admiration of physical strength also found in "On the Divide."]

"Hold tight, tight!" he shouted again, launching a kick at a snorting animal that reared back against Margaret's saddle. If she should lose her courage and fall now, under those hoofs— He struck out again and again, kicking right and left with all his might. Already the negligent drivers had galloped into the cut, and their long quirts were whistling over the heads of the herd. As suddenly as it had come, the struggling, frantic wave of wild life swept up out of the gulch and on across the open prairie, and with a long despairing whinny of farewell the pony dropped her head and stood trembling in her sweat, shaking the foam and blood from her bit.

Eric stepped close to Margaret's side and laid his hand on her saddle. "You are not hurt?" he asked, hoarsely. As he raised his face in the soft starlight she saw that it was white and drawn and that his lips were working nervously.

"No, no, not at all. But you, you are suffering; they struck you!" she cried in sharp alarm.

He stepped back and drew his hand across his brow.

"No, it is not that," he spoke rapidly now, with his hands clenched at his side. "But if they had hurt you, I would beat their brains out with my hands, I would kill them all. I was never afraid before. You are the only beautiful thing that has ever come close to me. You came like an angel out of the sky. You are like the music you sing, you are like the stars and the snow on the mountains where I played when I was a little boy. You are like all that I wanted once and never had, you are all that they have killed in me. I die for you, to-night, to-morrow, for all eternity. I am not a coward; I was afraid because I love you more than Christ who died for me, more than I am afraid of hell, or hope for heaven. I was never afraid before. If you had fallen —oh, my God!" he threw his arms out blindly and dropped his head upon the pony's mane, leaning limply against the animal like a man struck by some sickness. His shoulders rose and fell perceptibly with his labored breathing. The horse stood cowed with exhaustion and fear. Presently Margaret laid her hand on Eric's head and said gently:

"You are better now, shall we go on? Can you get your horse?"

"No, he has gone with the herd. I will lead yours, she is not safe. I will not frighten you again." His voice was still husky, but it was steady now. He took hold of the bit and tramped home in silence.

When they reached the house, Eric stood stolidly by the pony's head until Wyllis came to lift his sister from the saddle.

"The horses were badly frightened, Wyllis. I think I was pretty thoroughly scared myself," she said as she took her brother's arm and went slowly up the hill toward the house. "No, I'm not hurt, thanks to Eric. You must thank him for taking such good care of me. He's a mighty fine fellow. I'll tell you all about it in the morning, dear. I was pretty well shaken up and I'm going right to bed now. Good-night."

When she reached the low room in which she slept, she sank upon the bed in her riding-dress face downward.

"Oh, I pity him! I pity him!" she murmured, with a long sigh of exhaustion. She must have slept a little. When she rose again, she took from her dress a letter that had been waiting for her at the village post-office. It was closely written in a long, angular hand, covering a dozen pages of foreign note-paper, and began:—

"My Dearest Margaret: If I should attempt to say *how like a winter hath thine absence been,* I should incur the risk of being tedious. Really, it takes the sparkle out of everything. Having nothing better to do, and not caring to go anywhere in particular without you, I remained in the city until Jack Courtwell noted my general despondency and brought me down here to his place on the sound to manage some open-air theatricals he is getting up. 'As You Like It' is of course the piece selected. Miss Harrison plays Rosalind. I wish you had been here to take the part. Miss Harrison reads her lines well, but she is either a maiden-all-forlorn or a tomboy; insists on reading into the part all sorts of deeper meanings and highly colored suggestions wholly out of harmony with the pastoral setting. Like most of the professionals, she exaggerates the emotional element and quite fails to do justice to Rosalind's facile wit and really brilliant mental qualities.

[A clever touch to show that the man Margaret is going to marry could have no concept of the emotional experience she is now undergoing. A touch as clever as that of the wild ponies to remind us of the wild desire for freedom in the most civilized of us.]

Gerard will do Orlando, but rumor says he is épris of your sometime friend, Miss Meredith, and his memory is treacherous and his interest fitful.

"My new pictures arrived last week on the 'Gascogne.' The Puvis de Chavannes is even more beautiful than I thought it in Paris. A pale dream-maiden sits by a pale dream-cow and a stream of anemic water flows at her feet. The Constant, you will remember, I got because you admired it. It is here in all its florid splendor, the whole dominated by a glowing sensuosity. The drapery of the female figure is as wonderful as you said; the fabric all barbaric pearl and gold, painted with an easy, effortless voluptuousness, and that white, gleaming line of African coast in the background recalls memories of you very precious to me. But it is useless to deny that Constant irritates me. Though I cannot prove the charge against him, his brilliancy always makes me suspect him of cheapness."

Here Margaret stopped and glanced at the remaining pages of this strange love-letter. They seemed to be filled chiefly with discussions of pictures and books, and with a slow smile she laid them by.

She rose and began undressing. Before she lay down she went to open the window. With her hand on the sill, she hesitated, feeling suddenly as though some danger were lurking outside, some inordinate desire waiting to spring upon her in the darkness. She stood there for a long time, gazing at the infinite sweep of the sky.

"Oh, it is all so little, so little there," she murmured. "When everything else is so dwarfed, why should one expect love to be great? Why should one try to read highly colored suggestions into a life like that? If only I could find one thing in it all that mattered greatly, one thing that would warm me when I am alone! Will life never give me that one great moment?"

As she raised the window, she heard a sound in the plumbushes outside. It was only the house-dog roused from his sleep, but Margaret started violently and trembled so that she caught the foot of the bed for support. Again she felt herself pursued by some overwhelming longing, some desperate necessity for herself, like the outstretching of helpless, unseen arms in the darkness, and the air seemed heavy with sighs of yearning. She fled to her bed with the words, "I love you more than Christ, who died for me!" ringing in her ears.

III

About midnight the dance at Lockhart's was at its height. Even the old men who had come to "look on" caught the spirit of revelry and stamped the floor with the vigor of old Silenus.

[In classic mythology, the foster father of Bacchus, the
god of wine—a jovial old satyr.]

Eric took the violin from the Frenchman, and Minna Oleson
sat at the organ, and the music grew more and more characteristic—rude, half-mournful music, made up of the folk-songs of
the North, that the villagers sing through the long night in ham-
lets by the sea, when they are thinking of the sun, and the spring,
and the fishermen so long away. To Margaret some of it sounded
like Grieg's Peer Gynt music. She found something irresistibly
infectious in the mirth of these people who were so seldom
merry, and she felt almost one of them. Something seemed
struggling for freedom in them to-night, something of the joy-
ous childhood of the nations which exile had not killed. The
girls were all boisterous with delight. Pleasure came to them
but rarely, and when it came, they caught at it wildly and
crushed its fluttering wings in their strong brown fingers. They
had a hard life enough, most of them. Torrid summers and freez-
ing winters, labor and drudgery and ignorance, were the portion
of their girlhood; a short wooing, a hasty, loveless marriage, un-
limited maternity, thankless sons, premature age and ugliness,
were the dower of their womanhood. But what matter? To-night
there was hot liquor in the glass and hot blood in the heart; to-
night they danced.

To-night Eric Hermannson had renewed his youth. He was
no longer the big, silent Norwegian who had sat at Margaret's
feet and looked hopelessly into her eyes. To-night he was a man,
with a man's rights and a man's power. To-night he was Siegfried
indeed. His hair was yellow as the heavy wheat in the ripe of
summer, and his eyes flashed like the blue water between the
ice-packs in the North Seas. He was not afraid of Margaret to-
night, and when he danced with her he held her firmly. She was
tired and dragged on his arm a little, but the strength of the
man was like an all-pervading fluid, stealing through her veins,
awakening under her heart some nameless, unsuspected existence that had slumbered there all these years and that went out

through her throbbing finger-tips to his that answered. She wondered if the hoydenish blood of some lawless ancestor, long
asleep, were calling out in her to-night, some drop of a hotter
fluid that the centuries had failed to cool, and why, if this curse
were in her, it had not spoken before. But was it a curse, this
awakening, this wealth before undiscovered, this music set free?
For the first time in her life her heart held something stronger
than herself, was not this worth while? Then she ceased to wonder. She lost sight of the lights and the faces, and the music was
drowned by the beating of her own arteries. She saw only the
blue eyes that flashed above her, felt only the warmth of that
throbbing hand which held hers and which the blood of his heart
fed. Dimly, as in a dream, she saw the drooping shoulders, high
white forehead and tight, cynical mouth of the man she was to
marry in December. For an hour she had been crowding back
the memory of that face with all her strength.

"Let us stop, this is enough," she whispered. His only answer
was to tighten the arm behind her. She sighed and let that masterful strength bear her where it would. She forgot that this man
was little more than a savage, that they would part at dawn. The
blood has no memories, no reflections, no regrets for the past, no
consideration of the future.

"Let us go out where it is cooler," she said when the music
stopped; thinking, "I am growing faint here, I shall be all right
in the open air." They stepped out into the cool, blue air of the
night.

Since the older folk had begun dancing, the young Norwegians had been slipping out in couples to climb the windmill tower into the cooler atmosphere, as is their custom.

"You like to go up?" asked Eric, close to her ear.

She turned and looked at him with suppressed amusement.
"How high is it?"

"Forty feet, about. I not let you fall." There was a note of
irresistible pleading in his voice, and she felt that he tremendously wished her to go. Well, why not? This was a night of the
unusual, when she was not herself at all, but was living an un-

reality. To-morrow, yes, in a few hours, there would be the Vestibule Limited and the world.

"Well, if you'll take good care of me. I used to be able to climb, when I was a little girl."

Once at the top and seated on the platform, they were silent. Margaret wondered if she would not hunger for that scene all her life, through all the routine of the days to come. Above them stretched the great Western sky, serenely blue, even in the night, with its big, burning stars, never so cold and dead and far away as in denser atmospheres. The moon would not be up for twenty minutes yet, and all about the horizon, that wide horizon, which seemed to reach around the world, lingered a pale, white light, as of a universal dawn. The weary wind brought up to them the heavy odors of the cornfields. The music of the dance sounded faintly from below. Eric leaned on his elbow beside her, his legs swinging down on the ladder. His great shoulders looked more than ever like those of the stone Doryphorus,

> [a Greek spear-bearer—considered the ideal athletic type]

who stands in his perfect, reposeful strength in the Louvre, and had often made her wonder if such men died forever with the youth of Greece.

"How sweet the corn smells at night," said Margaret nervously.

"Yes, like the flowers that grow in paradise, I think."

She was somewhat startled by this reply, and more startled when this taciturn man spoke again.

"You go away to-morrow?"

"Yes, we have stayed longer than we thought to now."

"You not come back any more?"

"No, I expect not. You see, it is a long trip, half-way across the continent."

"You soon forget about this country, I guess." It seemed to him now a little thing to lose his soul for this woman, but that she should utterly forget this night into which he threw all his life and all his eternity, that was a bitter thought.

"No, Eric, I will not forget. You have all been too kind to me for that. And you won't be sorry you danced this one night, will you?"

"I never be sorry. I have not been so happy before. I not be so happy again, ever. You will be happy many nights yet, I only this one. I will dream sometimes, maybe."

The mighty resignation of his tone alarmed and touched her. It was as when some great animal composes itself for death, as when a great ship goes down at sea.

She sighed, but did not answer him. He drew a little closer and looked into her eyes.

"You are not always happy, too?" he asked.

"No, not always, Eric; not very often, I think."

"You have a trouble?"

"Yes, but I cannot put it into words. Perhaps if I could do that, I could cure it."

He clasped his hands together over his heart, as children do when they pray, and said falteringly, "If I own all the world, I give him you."

Margaret felt a sudden moisture in her eyes, and laid her hand on his.

"Thank you, Eric; I believe you would. But perhaps even then I should not be happy. Perhaps I have too much of it already."

She did not take her hand away from him; she did not dare. She sat still and waited for the traditions in which she had always believed to speak and save her. But they were dumb. She belonged to an ultra-refined civilization which tries to cheat nature with elegant sophistries. Cheat nature? Bah! One generation may do it, perhaps two, but the third—Can we ever rise above nature or sink below her? Did she not turn on Jerusalem as upon Sodom, upon St. Anthony in his desert as upon Nero in his seraglio? Does she not always cry in brutal triumph: "I am here still, at the bottom of things, warming the roots of life; you cannot starve me nor tame me nor thwart me; I made the world, I rule it, and I am its destiny."

This woman, on a windmill tower at the world's end with a giant barbarian, heard that cry to-night, and she was afraid! Ah! the terror and the delight of that moment when first we fear ourselves! Until then we have not lived.

"Come, Eric, let us go down; the moon is up and the music has begun again," she said.

He rose silently and stepped down upon the ladder, putting his arm about her to help her. That arm could have thrown Thor's hammer out in the cornfields yonder, yet it scarcely touched her, and his hand trembled as it had done in the dance. His face was level with hers now and the moonlight fell sharply upon it. All her life she had searched the faces of men for the look that lay in his eyes. She knew that that look had never shone for her before, would never shine for her on earth again, that such love comes to one only in dreams or in impossible places like this, unattainable always. This was Love's self, in a moment it would die. Stung by the agonized appeal that emanated from the man's whole being, she leaned forward and laid her lips on his. Once, twice and again she heard the deep respirations rattle in his throat while she held them there, and the riotous force under her heart became an engulfing weakness. He drew her up to him until he felt all the resistance go out of her body, until every nerve relaxed and yielded. When she drew her face back from his, it was white with fear.

"Let us go down, oh, my God! let us go down!" she muttered. And the drunken stars up yonder seemed reeling to some appointed doom as she clung to the rounds of the ladder. All that she was to know of love she had left upon his lips.

"The devil is loose again," whispered Olaf Oleson, as he saw Eric dancing a moment later, his eyes blazing.

But Eric was thinking with an almost savage exultation of the time when he should pay for this. Ah, there would be no quailing then! If ever a soul went fearlessly, proudly down to the gates infernal, his should go. For a moment he fancied he was there already, treading down the tempest of flame, hugging the fiery hurricane to his breast. He wondered whether in ages gone, all the countless years of sinning in which men had sold and lost and flung their souls away, any man had ever so cheated Satan, had ever bartered his soul for so great a price.

It seemed but a little while till dawn.

The carriage was brought to the door and Wyllis Elliot and his sister said goodby. She could not meet Eric's eyes as she gave him her hand, but as he stood by the horse's head, just as the carriage moved off, she gave him one swift glance that said, "I will not forget." In a moment the carriage was gone.

Eric changed his coat and plunged his head into the water-tank and went to the barn to hook up his team. As he led his horses to the door, a shadow fell across his path, and he saw Skinner rising in his stirrups. His rugged face was pale and worn with looking after his wayward flock, with dragging men into the way of salvation.

"Good-morning, Eric. There was a dance here last night?" he asked, sternly.

"A dance? Oh, yes, a dance," replied Eric, cheerfully.

"Certainly you did not dance, Eric?"

"Yes, I danced. I danced all the time."

The minister's shoulders drooped, and an expression of profound discouragement settled over his haggard face. There was almost anguish in the yearning he felt for this soul.

"Eric, I didn't look for this from you. I thought God had set his mark on you if he ever had on any man. And it is for things like this that you set your soul back a thousand years from God. O foolish and perverse generation!"

Eric drew himself up to his full height and looked off to where the new day was gilding the corn-tassels and flooding the uplands with light. As his nostrils drew in the breath of the dew and the morning, something from the only poetry he had ever read flashed across his mind, and he murmured, half to himself, with dreamy exultation:

"'And a day shall be as a thousand years, and a thousand years as a day.'"

[This story was translated into German by Eugene von Tempsky who labeled it a "psychological masterpiece." A request for translation rights was not usual at that time.

In August of 1893 Willa and her brother Roscoe visited the part of Webster County in which this story is laid. They climbed a fifty-foot windmill tower, were caught there by a windstorm, and barely made the trip down, their hands blistered and bleeding from clinging to the ladder.

In the delicacy of the feeling between Eric and Margaret, one is reminded of Daudet's "Les Etoiles," where a shepherd is secretly in love with his employer's daughter. One day she brings the supplies, but in returning home she is caught in a flood and has to turn back to the shepherd's cabin. He watches over her all through the night, tells her of the stars, and of the special star that guards shepherds.]

❧ The Dance at Chevalier's

published in *The Library*, April 28, 1900

[This appeared under the pseudonym of Henry Nicklemann. We know it was Willa Cather's pseudonym because
she published an article in Pittsburgh under that name and
published the same article in Lincoln under her own name.
George Seibel, former Allegheny Library Director and long-
time friend of Willa Cather, says that the pseudonym came
from Hauptmann's *Sunken Bell:* Henry was the man who
made the bell; Nicklemann was a water sprite.
    Concerning the names in this story Elsie Cather, Willa
Cather's sister, says: "There really was an Alplosen de Mar.
She was one of Roscoe's pupils in the first school he taught.
And one of my mother's great uncles went to the Deep South
in an early day and married a French girl whose name was
Severine. The families used to visit back and forth and send
each other presents up till the Civil War. Father and Mother
used to talk about them often. Mother had an aunt named for
the French Severine—Aunt Sevie Muse. She was grandmother Seibert's sister."
    There were also Chevaliers in Webster County, not far
from the Cather farm.]

It was a dance that was a dance, that dance at Chevalier's
and it will be long remembered in our country.

But first as to what happened in the afternoon. Denis and
Signor had put the cattle in the corral and come in early to rest
before the dance. The Signor was a little Mexican who had
strayed up into the cattle country. What his real name was,
heaven only knows, but we called him "The Signor," as if he had

217

been Italian instead of Mexican. After they had put the horses away, they went into the feed room, which was a sort of stable salon, where old Chevalier received his friends and where his hands amused themselves on Sundays. The Signor suggested a game of cards, and placed a board across the top of a millet barrel for a table. Denis lit his pipe and began to mix the cards.

Little Harry Burns sat on the tool-box sketching. Burns was an eastern newspaper man, who had come to live in Oklahoma because of his lungs.

[Actually the setting is Webster County, Nebraska. Willa Cather's grandparents had moved to Webster County because their daughter had tuberculosis.]

He found a good deal that was interesting besides the air. As the game went on, he kept busily filling in his picture, which was really a picture of Denis, the Mexican being merely indicated by a few careless strokes. Burns had a decided weakness for Denis. It was his business to be interested in people, and practice had made his eye quick to pick out a man from whom unusual things might be expected. Then he admired Denis for his great physical proportions. Indeed, even with his pipe in his mouth and the fresh soil of the spring ploughing on his boots, Denis made a striking figure. He was a remarkably attractive man, that Denis, as all the girls in the neighborhood knew to their sorrow. For Denis was a ladies' man and had heady impulses that were hard to resist. What we call sentiment in cultured men is called by a coarser name in the pure animal products of nature and is a dangerous force to encounter.

[We are here reminded of Eric Hermannson, who was also physically beautiful and larger than other men. An artist in the rough.]

Burns used to say to himself that this big choleric Irishman was an erotic poet undeveloped and untamed by the processes of thought; a pure creature of emotional impulses who went about seeking rhymes and harmonies in the flesh, the original Adam. Burns wondered if he would not revel in the fervid verses of his great countryman Tom Moore—if he should ever see them. But Denis never read anything but the Sunday New York papers —a week old, always, when he got them—and he was totally untrammelled by anything of a reflective nature. So he remained merely a smiling giant, who had the knack of saying pretty things to girls. After all, he was just as happy that way, and very much more irresistible, and Harry Burns knew it, for all his theories.

[Once again the suggestion, as in "Eric Hermannson's Soul," that civilization—even knowledge—would ruin these primitive giants.]

Just as he was finishing his picture, Burns was startled by a loud exclamation.

"Stop pulling cards out of your sleeve, you confounded Mexican cheat!"

"You lie! You lie!" shouted the Signor, throwing a card on the table and attempting to rise. But Denis was too quick for him. He caught the back of the Mexican's greasy hand with the point of his belt knife and, regardless of the blood that trickled through his fingers, proceeded to search his sleeve.

"There, Signor, chuck a whole deck up, why don't you? Now the next time you try that game on me I'll run my knife clean through your dirty paw, and leave a mark that men will know."

"I'll kill you for this, you dog of an Irishman! Wait and see how I will kill you," snarled the Mexican, livid with rage and pain, as he shot out of the door. Denis laughed and lay down on a pile of corn.

[This Mexican bears no relation to Spanish Johnny or the other Mexicans of Song of the Lark. He is, however, a spiritual brother to Freymark in "The Affair at Grover Station" who killed Larry O'Toole, another engaging Irishman such as Denis.]

"Better look out for that man, Denis," said little Burns, as he lit a cigarette.

"Oh, if I was looking for a man to be afraid of I wouldn't pick the Signor."

"Look out for him, all the same. They are a nasty lot, these Greasers. I've known them down in Old Mexico. They'll knife you in the dark, any one of them. It's the only country I could never feel comfortable in. Everything is dangerous—the climate, the sun, the men, and most of all the women. The very flowers are poisonous. Why does old Chevalier keep this fellow?"

[Of course Burns is prejudiced. If Cather herself were prejudiced, she changed before *Song of the Lark*, and especially before *Death Comes for the Archbishop*, where she dealt a great deal with people of Spanish-American descent.]

"Oh, he's a good hand enough, and a first-rate man with the cattle. I don't like Greasers myself, they're all sneaks. Not many of 'em ever come up in this country, and they've always got into some sort of trouble and had to light out. The Signor has kept pretty straight around the place, though, and as long as he behaves himself he can hold his job."

"You don't think Chevalier's daughter has anything to do with his staying?"

"If I did I'd trample him like a snake!"

When the Signor left the barn he shook the blood from his wounded hand and went up to the house and straight into the sitting-room, where Severine Chevalier was shaving a tallow candle on the floor for the dance. The Signor's scowl vanished, and he approached her with an exaggerated smile.

"Come, Severine. I've cut my hand; tie it up for me, like the sweet one that you are."

"How came you to cut your hand on the day of the dance? And how on the back, too? I believe you did it on purpose."

"And so I did, to have you tie it up for me. I would cut myself all over for that." And as Severine bent over to twist the bandage he kissed her on the cheek.

"Begone, you sneak; you can tie up your own cuts, if that's the way you treat me."

"Dios mio! that is treating you very well, my sweet. If that is not good what is there in this world that is? I saw that hulking Irishman kiss you last night, and you seemed to like it well enough."

"That depends on the person, Monsieur Signor," said Severine, tartly, as she slid over the tallow shavings. But she blushed hotly, all the same.

"See here, Severine, you have played with both of us long enough. If you kiss him again I will kill you. I like to kill the things I love, do you understand?"

"Merci, monsieur! I compliment you. You have great tact. You know how to coax a sweetheart. You know all about love-making."

"You baby! women have gone mad after me before now. You see how I love you, and it does not move you. That is because you are a baby and do not know how to love. A girl who doesn't know how to love is stupid, tasteless, like—like so much water. Baby!"

The girl's eyes were hot with anger as she drew herself up and faced him.

"You fool! you think you know all about love, and yet you cannot see that I am in love all the time, that I burn up with love, that I am tortured by it, that my pillows are hot with it all night, and my hands are wet with it in the day. You fool! But it is not with you, Monsieur Signor, grace a Dieu, it is not with you."

[This is the "old hot, imperious blood of the Latins" of which Dumas writes—rather a sixteenth-century description of love.]

The swarthy little Signor looked at her admiringly a moment, and then spoke in a low voice that whistled in the air like a knife—

"Is it the Irishman? It is the Irishman!"

"Yes, stupid beast, it is. But that is my own affair."

Frightened at her own rashness, she fell to shaving the candle with trembling hands, while the Mexican watched her with a smile that showed all his white teeth. Severine had time to repent her rashness, and a sickening fear of the consequences arose within her.

"You'll keep that to yourself, Signor? You won't tell father?"

"That is my affair, Mademoiselle."

She dropped the wax and touched his arm.

"Play fair, Signor, and keep it, please."

"It is I who make terms now, Mademoiselle. Well, yes, I will keep it, and I will ask a very little price for my silence. You must come out and kiss me to-night when I ask you."

"Yes, yes, I will if you will only keep your word."

He caught her in his slender, sinewy arms.

"You said once!" she cried, in angry protest, as she broke away from him.

"This was only to show you how, my sweet," he laughed.

As he left the room he looked back over his shoulder and saw that she was still rubbing her lips with her hand, and all the way up stairs to his own room he laughed, and when he packed his belongings away in his canvas saddle bags he was still smiling. When he had finished and strapped his bags he stood looking about him. He heard a snatch of an old French song through the window and saw Severine working out in her flower bed.

He hesitated a moment, then shook his head and patted his bandaged hand. "Ah, love is sweet, but sweeter is revenge. It is the saying of my people."

And now for the dance at Chevalier's, which was a dance, indeed. It was the last before the hot season came on and everybody was there—all the French for miles around. Some came in road wagons, some in buggies, some on horseback, and not a few on foot. Girls with pretty faces and rough hands, and men in creaking boots, with broad throats tanned by the sun, reeking with violent perfumes and the odors of the soil.

At nine o'clock the dance began, the dance that was to have
lasted all night. Harry Burns played an old bass viol, and Alplosen de Mar played the organ, but the chief musician was the
old Bohemian, Peter Sadelack, who played the violin. Peter had
seen better days, and had played in a theatre in Prague until
he had paralysis and was discharged because his bowing was
uncertain. Then in some way, God knows how, he and his slat-
ternly wife and countless progeny had crossed the ocean and
drifted out into the cattle country.

> [This, it will be noted, is a reference to the Peter of two
> other stories. This cross reference is noticeable in several
> places. For example, in "Eric Hermannson's Soul" there is
> mention of the dances at Chevalier's.]

The three of them made right merry music, though the two
violinists were considerably the more skilful, and poor Alplosen
quite lost her breath in keeping up with them. Waltzes, quad-
rilles and polkas they played until the perspiration streamed
down their faces, and for the square dances little Burns "called
off." Occasionally he got down and took a waltz himself, giving
some young Frenchman his instrument. All those Frenchmen
could play a fiddle from the time they were old enough to hold
one. But dancing was bad for his lungs, and with the exception
of Severine and Marie Generaux there were very few girls he
cared to dance with. It was more amusing to saw away on the
squeaky old bass viol and watch those gleeful young Frenchmen
seize a girl and whirl her away with a dexterity and grace really
quite remarkable, considering the crowd and the roughness of
the floor, and the affectionate positions in which they insisted
upon holding their partners. They were not of pure French
blood, of course; most of them had been crossed and recrossed
with Canadians and Indians, and they spoke a vile patois which
no Christian man could understand. Almost the only traces they
retained of their original nationality were their names, and their
old French songs, and their grace in the dance. Deep down in
the heart of every one of them, uncrushed by labor, undulled

by enforced abstinence, there was a mad, insatiable love of pleasure that continually warred with the blood of dull submission they drew from their red squaw ancestors. To-night it broke out like a devouring flame, it flashed in dark eyes and glowed in red cheeks. Ah that old hot, imperious blood of the Latins! It is never quite lost. These women had long since forgotten the wit of their motherland, they were dull of mind and slow of tongue; but in the eyes, on the lips, in the temperament was the old, ineffaceable stamp. The Latin blood was there.

[The French settlement near the original Cather farm was largely French-Canadian. Her interest in them and their ancestors led to *Shadows on the Rock*.]

The most animated, and by far the most beautiful among them was Severine Chevalier. At those dances little attempt was made at evening dress, but Severine was in white, with her gown cut low, showing the curves of her neck and shoulders. For she was different from the other French girls, she had more taste and more ambition, and more money. She had been sent two years to a convent school in Toronto, and when she came back the other girls could never quite get used to her ways, though they admired and envied her from afar. She could speak the French of France, could Severine, and sometimes when it was dull and too rainy to gallop across the prairies after the cattle, or to town for the mail, and when there was nothing better to do, she used to read books. She talked with little Burns about books sometimes. But, on the whole, she preferred her pony, and the wild flowers, and the wind and the sun, and romping with her boys. She was a very human young woman, and not wise enough to disguise or to affect anything. She knew what the good things of life were, and was quite frank about them. To-night she seemed glowing with some unspoken joy, and many a French lad felt his heart thump faster as he clutched her hand with an iron grasp and guided her over the rough floor and among the swaying couples; many a lad cast timid glances at old Jean Chevalier as he sat complacently by his brandy bottle, proudly watching his daughter. For old Chevalier was a king in the cattle country, and they knew that none might aspire to his daughter's hand who had not wider acres and more cattle than any of them possessed.

And for every glance that Severine drew from the men, Denis drew a sigh from the women. Though he was only Jean Chevalier's herdman, and an Irishman at that, Denis was the lion of the French dances. He danced hard, and drank hard, and made love hardest of all. But to-night he was chary of his favors, and when he could not dance with Severine he was careless of his other partners. After a long waltz he took Severine out to the windmill in the grove. It was refreshingly cool out there, the moonlight was clear and pale, and the tall lombard poplars were rustling their cool leaves. The moon was just up and was still reflected in the long lagoon on the eastern horizon. Denis put his arms about the girl and drew her up to him. The Signor saw them so, as he slipped down to the barn to saddle his horse, and he whispered to himself, "It is high time." But what the great Irishman whispered in her ear, the Signor never knew.

As Denis led her back to the house, he felt a dizzy sensation of tenderness and awe come over him, such as he had sometimes felt when he was riding alone across the moonlit lagoons under the eyes of countless stars, or when he was driving his cattle out in the purple lights of springtide dawns.

As they entered the house, the Mexican slipped in behind them and tried to edge his way through the crowd unseen. But Marie Generaux caught him by the arm.

"This is our dance, Signor, come along."

"Make it the next, my girl," he whispered, and escaped up stairs into his own room.

His saddle bags were already on his horse, but in his chest there lay one article which belonged to him, a pint whiskey flask. He took it out and unscrewed the top, and smelt it, and held it up to the light, shaking it gently and gazing on it with real affection in his narrow, snaky eyes. For it was not ordinary liquor. An old, withered negro from the gold coast of Guinea had told him how to make it, down in Mexico. He himself had gathered rank, noxious plants and poured their distilled juices into that whiskey, and had killed the little lizards that sun themselves on the crumbling stones of the old ruined missions, and dried their bodies and boiled them in the contents of that flask. For five years that bright liquor had lain sparkling in his chest, waiting for such a time as this.

When the Signor went downstairs a quadrille was just over, and the room was echoing with loud laughter. He beckoned Severine into a corner, and whispered with a meaning glance:

"Send your Irishman up stairs to me. I must see him. And save the next dance for me. There he is. Hurry."

Reluctantly she approached Denis, blushing furiously as she accosted him.

"Go up stairs and see the Signor, please, Denis."

"What can he want with me?"

"I don't know. I wish you'd go, though."

"Well, Signor, what is it?" he asked as he reached the top of the stairs.

"I must tell you something. Take a drink to brace you, and then I'll talk. It will not be pleasant news."

Denis laughed and drank, never noticing how the hand that held out the glass to him was shaking.

"I can't say much for your whiskey," he remarked, as he set down the empty glass.

The Mexican came up to him, his eyes glittering with suppressed excitement.

"I want to tell you that we have both been fools. That French girl has played with us both. We have let her cuff us about like schoolboys, and coax us with sugar like children. To-day she promised to marry me, to-night she promises to marry you. We are decidedly fools, my friend."

[That the girl who loves him and whom he loves should
be the instrument of Denis' destruction is a Henry James
theme: love preyed on anyone who loved.]

"You liar! You say that again—"

"Tut, tut, my friend, not so fast. You are a big man, and I
am a little one. I cannot fight you. I try to do you a service, and
you abuse me. That is not unusual. But you wait here by the
window through the next dance and watch the windmill, and if
I don't prove what I say, then you may kill me at your pleasure.
Is not that fair enough?"

"Prove it, prove it!" said Denis from a dry throat.

[The poison is beginning already. For the symptoms,
see the poisoning of Charles in *Marguerite de Valois*, by
Alexandre Dumas.]

In a moment he was alone, and stood watching out of the
window, scarcely knowing why he was there. "It's all a lie; I
felt the truth in her," he kept saying to himself while he waited.
The music struck up down stairs, the squeak of the cracked organ and the screech of the violins, and with it the sound of the
heavy feet. His first impulse was to go down and join them,
but he waited. In a few minutes, perhaps two, perhaps three,
before the waltz was half over, he saw the Signor stroll down
towards the windmill. Beside him was Severine. They went
straight to that moonlit bit of ground under the poplars, the spot
where twenty minutes before he had been seized and mastered
and borne away by that floodtide of tenderness which we can
know but once in our lives, and then seek, hunger for all the rest
of our sunless days.

[Cather's one-great-moment theory of love which we
also encounter in "Eric Hermannson's Soul."]

There, in that spot, which even to his careless mind was holy
ground, he saw Severine stop and lift her little flower-like face

to another man's. Long, long he held her. God knows how long it must have seemed to the man who watched and held his breath until his veins seemed bursting. Then they were gone, and only the quivering poplar leaves cast their shadows over that moonlit spot.

He felt a deadly sickness come over him. He caught the flask on the table and drank again. Presently the door opened, and the Signor entered. He should have been gone indeed, but he could not resist one more long look at the man who sat limply on the bed, with his face buried in his hands.

"I am glad you take it patiently; it is better," he remarked, soothingly.

Then over the big Irishman, who sat with his head bowed and his eyes darkened and the hand of death already heavy upon him, there came a flood of remembrances and of remorse.

"Yes," he groaned. "I can be patient. I can take torture with my mouth shut—women have taught me how." Then suddenly starting to his feet he shouted, "Begone, you Satan, or I'll strangle ye!"

When Denis stumbled down stairs his face was burning, but not with anger. Severine had been hunting for him and came up to him eagerly. "I've been looking for you everywhere. Where have you been so long? Let's dance this; it's the one you like."

He followed her passively. Even his resentment was half dead. He felt an awful sense of weakness and isolation; he wanted to touch something warm and living. In a few minutes something would happen—something. He caught her roughly, half loving her, half loathing her, and weak, trembling, with his head on fire and his breast bursting with pain, he began to dance. Over and over again the fiddles scraped their trite measures, while Severine wondered why the hand that gripped hers grew so cold. He lost the time and then swayed back and forth. A sharp cry of alarm rang from the end of the room, and little Burns bounded from the table, and reached him just as he fell.

"What is it, Denis, my boy, what is it?"

Severine knelt on the other side, still holding one of his hands.

The man's face was drawn in horrible agony, his blue eyes were distended and shot with blood, his hair hung wet over his face, and his lips were dashed with froth. He gasped heavily from his laboring breast.

"Poison—they—she and the Mexican—they have done me.—Damn—damn—women!"

[Dumas' description of poisoning: "Great pains in the head, a feeling of burning in the stomach, as if he had swallowed hot coals, pains in the bowels and vomiting . . . parchingly thirsty." And describing Charles' poisoned dog, he says, "from his throat, contracted by pain, several drops of bile had fallen, mingled with a foamy and bloody slaver."]

He struck at Severine, but she caught his hand and kissed it.

But all the protestations, all the words of love, imperious as a whirlwind, that she poured out there on her knees fell upon deaf ears. Not even those words, winged with flame, could break the silences for him. If the lips of the living could give warmth to those of the dead, death would be often robbed, and the grave cheated of its victory.

[Severine is behaving like a Dumas heroine. *Marguerite de Valois* "almost lifeless herself, threw her arms round that beautiful head, and imprinted on his brow a kiss that was almost holy." (Her lover, La Mole, had been beheaded.) "Marguerite was on her knees before La Mole, her hair dishevelled, and eyes overflowing with tears"—"knelt down beside her lover, and with her hands glittering with jewels gently raised the head of him she had loved so well."]

Harry Burns sprang to his feet. "It's that damned Mexican. Where is he?"

But no one answered. The Signor had been in his saddle half an hour, speeding across the plains, on the swiftest horse in the cattle country.

❧ The Sentimentality of William Tavener

published in *The Library*, May 12, 1900

[This is one of Cather's best stories of this period. It shows an understanding of marriage seldom found in her work.

The name Tavener came from her Winchester, Virginia, background as do also the place names. Romney and Back Creek figure in *Sapphira and the Slave Girl*, but in that book Pewtown is spelled Peughtown. And the boy Tap, mentioned in this story, is also a character in *Sapphira*.]

It takes a strong woman to make any sort of success of living in the West, and Hester undoubtedly was that. When people spoke of William Tavener as the most prosperous farmer in McPherson County, they usually added that his wife was a "good manager." She was an executive woman, quick of tongue and something of an imperatrix. The only reason her husband did not consult her about his business was that she did not wait to be consulted.

[The dominating woman of Henry James, and to a certain extent of Willa Cather, found at her worst in *Sapphira and the Slave Girl*.]

It would have been quite impossible for one man, within the limited sphere of human action, to follow all Hester's advice, but in the end William usually acted upon some of her suggestions. When she incessantly denounced the "shiftlessness" of let-

ting a new threshing machine stand unprotected in the open, he
eventually built a shed for it. When she sniffed contemptuously
at his notion of fencing a hog corral with sod walls, he made a
spiritless beginning on the structure—merely to "show his temper," as she put it and bought enough barbed wire to complete
the fence. When the first heavy rains came on, and the pigs
rooted down the sod wall and made little paths all over it to
facilitate their ascent, he heard his wife relate with relish the
story of the little pig that built a mud house, to the minister at
the dinner table, and William's gravity never relaxed for an instant. Silence, indeed, was William's refuge and his strength.

William set his boys a wholesome example to respect their
mother. People who knew him very well suspected that he even
admired her. He was a hard man towards his neighbors, and
even towards his sons: grasping, determined and ambitious.

There was an occasional blue day about the house when
William went over the store bills, but he never objected to items
relating to his wife's gowns or bonnets. So it came about that
many of the foolish, unnecessary little things that Hester bought
for boys, she had charged to her personal account.

One spring night Hester sat in a rocking chair by the sitting
room window, darning socks. She rocked violently and sent her
long needle vigorously back and forth over her gourd, and it
took only a very casual glance to see that she was wrought up
over something. William sat on the other side of the table reading his farm paper. If he had noticed his wife's agitation, his
calm, clean-shaven face betrayed no sign of concern. He must
have noticed the sarcastic turn of her remarks at the supper
table, and he must have noticed the moody silence of the older
boys as they ate. When supper was but half over little Billy, the
youngest, had suddenly pushed back his plate and slipped away
from the table, manfully trying to swallow a sob. But William
Tavener never heeded ominous forecasts in the domestic horizon,
and he never looked for a storm until it broke.

After supper the boys had gone to the pond under the willows in the big cattle corral, to get rid of the dust of plowing.

Hester could hear an occasional splash and a laugh ringing clear through the stillness of the night, as she sat by the open window. She sat silent for almost an hour reviewing in her mind many plans of attack. But she was too vigorous a woman to be much of a strategist, and she usually came to her point with directness. At last she cut her thread and suddenly put her darning down, saying emphatically:

"William, I don't think it would hurt you to let the boys go to that circus in town to-morrow."

William continued to read his farm paper, but it was not Hester's custom to wait for an answer. She usually divined his arguments and assailed them one by one before he uttered them.

"You've been short of hands all summer, and you've worked the boys hard, and a man ought use his own flesh and blood as well as he does his hired hands. We're plenty able to afford it, and it's little enough our boys ever spend. I don't see how you can expect 'em to be steady and hard workin', unless you encourage 'em a little. I never could see much harm in circuses, and our boys have never been to one. Oh, I know Jim Howley's boys get drunk an' carry on when they go, but our boys ain't that sort, an' you know it, William. The animals are real instructive, an' our boys don't get to see much out here on the prairie. It was different where we were raised, but the boys have got no advantages here, an' if you don't take care, they'll grow up to be greenhorns."

Hester paused a moment, and William folded up his paper, but vouchsafed no remark. His sisters in Virginia had often said that only a quiet man like William could ever have lived with Hester Perkins. Secretly, William was rather proud of his wife's "gift of speech," and of the fact that she could talk in prayer meeting as fluently as a man. He confined his own efforts in that line to a brief prayer at Covenant meetings.

Hester shook out another sock and went on.

"Nobody was ever hurt by goin' to a circus. Why, law me! I remember I went to one myself once, when I was little. I had most forgot about it. It was over at Pewtown, an' I remember

how I had set my heart on going. I don't think I'd ever forgiven
my father if he hadn't taken me, though that red clay road was
in a frightful way after the rain. I mind they had an elephant
and six poll parrots, an' a Rocky Mountain lion, an' a cage of
monkeys, an' two camels. My! but they were a sight to me then!"

Hester dropped the black sock and shook her head and
smiled at the recollection. She was not expecting anything from
William yet, and she was fairly startled when he said gravely, in
much the same tone in which he announced the hymns in prayer
meeting:

"No, there was only one camel. The other was a dromedary."

She peered around the lamp and looked at him keenly.

"Why, William, how come you to know?"

William folded his paper and answered with some hesita-
tion, "I was there, too."

Hester's interest flashed up—"Well, I never, William! To
think of my finding it out after all these years! Why, you couldn't
have been much bigger'n our Billy then. It seems queer I never
saw you when you was little, to remember about you. But then
you Back Creek folks never have anything to do with us Gap
people. But how come you to go? Your father was stricter with
you than you are with your boys."

"I reckon I shouldn't 'a gone," he said slowly, "but boys will
do foolish things. I had done a good deal of fox hunting the
winter before, and father let me keep the bounty money. I hired
Tom Smith's Tap to weed the corn for me, an' I slipped off un-
beknownst to father an' went to the show."

Hester spoke up warmly: "Nonsense, William! It didn't do
you no harm, I guess. You was always worked hard enough. It
must have been a big sight for a little fellow. That clown must
have just tickled you to death."

William crossed his knees and leaned back in his chair.

"I reckon I could tell all that fool's jokes now. Sometimes I
can't help thinkin' about 'em in meetin' when the sermon's long.
I mind I had on a pair of new boots that hurt me like the mis-

chief, but I forgot all about 'em when that fellow rode the donkey. I recall I had to take them boots off as soon as I got out of sight o' town, and walked home in the mud barefoot."

"O poor little fellow!" Hester ejaculated, drawing her chair nearer and leaning her elbows on the table. "What cruel shoes they did use to make for children. I remember I went up to Back Creek to see the circus wagons go by. They came down from Romney, you know. The circus men stopped at the creek to water the animals, an' the elephant got stubborn an' broke a big limb off the yellow willow tree that grew there by the toll house porch, an' the Scribners were 'fraid as death he'd pull the house down. But this much I saw him do; he waded in the creek an' filled his trunk with water and squirted it in at the window and nearly ruined Ellen Scribner's pink lawn dress that she had just ironed an' laid out on the bed ready to wear to the circus."

"I reckon that must have been a trial to Ellen," chuckled William, "for she was mighty prim in them days."

Hester drew her chair still nearer William's. Since the children had begun growing up, her conversation with her husband had been almost wholly confined to questions of economy and expense. Their relationship had become purely a business one, like that between landlord and tenant. In her desire to indulge her boys she had unconsciously assumed a defensive and almost hostile attitude towards her husband. No debtor ever haggled with his usurer more doggedly than did Hester with her husband in behalf of her sons. The strategic contest had gone on so long that it had almost crowded out the memory of a closer relationship. This exchange of confidences to-night, when common recollections took them unawares and opened their hearts, had all the miracle of romance. They talked on and on; of old neighbors, of old familiar faces in the valley where they had grown up, of long forgotten incidents of their youth—weddings, picnics, sleighing parties and baptizings. For years they had talked of nothing else but butter and eggs and the prices of things, and now they had as much to say to each other as people who meet after a long separation.

When the clock struck ten, William rose and went over to his walnut secretary and unlocked it. From his red leather wallet he took out a ten dollar bill and laid it on the table beside Hester.

"Tell the boys not to stay late, an' not to drive the horses hard," he said quietly, and went off to bed.

Hester blew out the lamp and sat still in the dark a long time. She left the bill lying on the table where William had placed it. She had a painful sense of having missed something, or lost something; she felt that somehow the years had cheated her.

The little locust trees that grew by the fence were white with blossoms. Their heavy odor floated in to her on the night wind and recalled a night long ago, when the first whip-poor-Will of the Spring was heard, and the rough buxom girls of Hawkins Gap had held her laughing and struggling under the locust trees, and searched in her bosom for a lock of her sweetheart's hair, which is supposed to be on every girl's breast when the first whip-poor-Will sings. Two of those same girls had been her bridesmaids. Hester had been a very happy bride. She rose and went softly into the room where William lay. He was sleeping heavily, but occasionally moved his hand before his face to ward off the flies. Hester went into the parlor and took the piece of mosquito net from the basket of wax apples and pears that her sister had made before she died. One of the boys had brought it all the way from Virginia, packed in a tin pail, since Hester would not risk shipping so precious an ornament by freight. She went back to the bed room and spread the net over William's head. Then she sat down by the bed and listened to his deep, regular breathing until she heard the boys returning. She went out to meet them and warn them not to waken their father.

"I'll be up early to get your breakfast, boys. Your father says you can go to the show." As she handed the money to the eldest, she felt a sudden throb of allegiance to her husband and said sharply, "And you be careful of that, an' don't waste it. Your father works hard for his money."

The boys looked at each other in astonishment and felt that they had lost a powerful ally.

❧ The Affair at Grover Station

published in *The Library*, June 16 and June 23, 1900

[This is the first story dealing with a railroad background, a background that was to be used for Ray Kennedy
in *Song of the Lark*, Tom Outland in *The Professor's House*,
and Captain Forrester in *A Lost Lady*.

Regarding sources of the railroad material Elsie Cather,
Willa's youngest sister, wrote: "Yes, the story about Grover
Station is the one that I remember. It all came back to me as
soon as I started to read. Willa worked that one out with
Douglass (one of Willa's brothers). She always worked any-
thing that she wrote about the railroad out with him.

"Douglass got into high school very young—and was not
in the least interested in what was being taught, or the way
it was being taught. Our good neighbor, Mr. David MacFar-
land, had a brother here in Lincoln who was one of the
chief officials of the Burlington between Lincoln and Denver.
Through him, Douglass got a job at Sterling, Colorado. He
worked there for two years and then came back and finished
high school in one year. He had been half way through when
he left. After he was graduated the Burlington put him in
charge of their small station in Cheyenne. The big road there
was the Union Pacific. He had been the agent in Sterling
when he was there as a youngster. He was in Cheyenne for
six or eight years. He knew all about the Burlington in that
part of the country."

This story shows the influence of French writers. Remember Prosper Merimée's story of the statue which crushed
the bridegroom to death, *The Venus de Ille*? Although the
central theme is not one of Henry James', the blue-chalked
finger tips bring to mind the ten ghostly finger marks on the

239

throat of the jealous wife who was murdered in *Romance of Certain Old Clothes.*
But mostly it seems to be a story that a brother and sister had a great deal of fun in writing. And the theme reminds one of "The Dance at Chevalier's."]

I heard this story sitting on the rear platform of an accommodation freight that crawled along through the brown, sun-dried wilderness between Grover Station and Cheyenne. The narrator was "Terrapin" Rodgers, who had been a classmate of mine at Princeton, and who was then cashier in the B— railroad office at Cheyenne. Rodgers was an Albany boy, but after his father failed in business, his uncle got "Terrapin" a position on a Western railroad, and he left college and disappeared completely from our little world, and it was not until I was sent West, by the University with a party of geologists who were digging for fossils in the region about Sterling, Colorado, that I saw him again. On this particular occasion Rodgers had been down at Sterling to spend Sunday with me, and I accompanied him when he returned to Cheyenne.

[Remember the way the story of *My Ántonia* is introduced? Old friends meeting and talking on a train.]

When the train pulled out of Grover Station, we were sitting smoking on the rear platform, watching the pale yellow disk of the moon that was just rising and that drenched the naked, gray plains in a soft lemon-colored light. The telegraph poles scored the sky like a musical staff as they flashed by, and the stars, seen between the wires, looked like the notes of some erratic symphony. The stillness of the night and the loneliness and barrenness of the plains were conducive to an uncanny train of thought. We had just left Grover Station behind us, and the murder of the station agent at Grover, which had occurred the previous winter, was still the subject of much conjecturing and theorizing all along that line of railroad. Rodgers had been an intimate friend of the murdered agent, and it was said that he knew more about the affair than any other living man, but with that peculiar reticence which at college had won him the soubriquet "Terrapin," he had kept what he knew to himself, and even the most accomplished reporter on the New York Journal, who had traveled half-way across the continent for the express purpose of pumping Rodgers, had given him up as impossible. But I had known Rodgers a long time, and since I had been grubbing in the chalk about Sterling, we had fallen into a habit of exchanging confidences, for it is good to see an old face in a strange land. So, as the little red station house at Grover faded into the distance, I asked him point blank what he knew about the murder of Lawrence O'Toole. Rodgers took a long pull at his black-briar pipe as he answered me.

"Well, yes. I could tell you something about it, but the question is how much you'd believe, and whether you could restrain yourself from reporting it to the Society for Psychical Research. I never told the story but once, and then it was to the Division Superintendent, and when I finished the old gentleman asked if I were a drinking man, and remarking that a fertile imagination was not a desirable quality in a railroad employee, said it would be just as well if the story went no further. You see it's a gruesome tale, and someway we don't like to be reminded that there are more things in heaven and earth than our systems of philosophy can grapple with. However, I should rather like to tell the story to a man who would look at it objectively and leave it in the domain of pure incident where it belongs. It would unburden my mind, and I'd like to get a scientific man's opinion on the yarn. But I suppose I'd better begin at the beginning, with the dance which preceded the tragedy, just as such things follow each other in a play. I notice that Destiny, who is a good deal of an artist in her way, frequently falls back upon that elementary principle of contrast to make things interesting for us.

"It was the thirty-first of December, the morning of the incoming Governor's inaugural ball, and I got down to the office early, for I had a heavy day's work ahead of me, and I was going to the dance and wanted to close up by six o'clock. I had scarcely unlocked the door when I heard someone calling Cheyenne on the wire, and hurried over to the instrument to see what was wanted. It was Lawrence O'Toole, at Grover, and he said he was coming up for the ball on the extra, due in Cheyenne at nine o'clock that night. He wanted me to go up to see Miss Masterson and ask her if she could go with him. He had had some trouble in getting leave of absence, as the last regular train for Cheyenne then left Grover at 5:45 in the afternoon, and as there was an east-bound going through Grover at 7:30, the dispatcher didn't want him away, in case there should be orders for the 7:30 train. So Larry had made no arrangement with Miss Masterson, as he was uncertain about getting up until he was notified about the extra.

"I telephoned Miss Masterson and delivered Larry's message. She replied that she had made an arrangement to go to the dance with Mr. Freymark, but added laughingly that no other arrangement held when Larry could come.

"About noon Freymark dropped in at the office, and I suspected he'd got his time from Miss Masterson. While he was hanging around, Larry called me up to tell me that Helen's flowers would be up from Denver on the Union Pacific passenger at five, and he asked me to have them sent up to her promptly and to call for her that evening in case the extra should be late. Freymark, of course, listened to the message, and when the sounder stopped, he smiled in a slow, disagreeable way, and saying, 'Thank you. That's all I wanted to know.' left the office.

"Lawrence O'Toole had been my predecessor in the cashier's office at Cheyenne, and he needs a little explanation now that he is under ground, though when he was in the world of living men, he explained himself better than any man I have ever met, East or West. I've knocked about a good deal since I cut loose from Princeton, and I've found that there are a great many good fellows in the world, but I've not found many better than Larry. I think I can say, without stretching a point, that he was the most popular man on the Division. He had a faculty of making everyone like him that amounted to a sort of genius.

[In this respect he is like Reggie in "The Fear That
Walks at Noonday," although Larry is physically attractive.
He is personable like Jay in "Tommy, The Unsentimental"
but also worthwhile. But Larry is dead. Here is one of the
Henry James touches: that it is safe to admire a dead person
—he has crystallized into an unchanging value.]

When he first went to working on the road, he was the agent's
assistant down at Sterling, a mere kid fresh from Ireland, without a dollar in his pocket, and no sort of backing in the world but
his quick wit and handsome face. It was a face that served him
as a sight draft, good in all banks.

"Freymark was cashier at the Cheyenne office then, but he
had been up to some dirty work with the company, and when it
fell in the line of Larry's duty to expose him, he did so without
hesitating. Eventually Freymark was discharged, and Larry was
made cashier in his place. There was, after that, naturally, little
love lost between them, and to make matters worse, Helen Masterson took a fancy to Larry, and Freymark had begun to consider himself pretty solid in that direction. I doubt whether Miss
Masterson ever really liked the blackguard, but he was a queer
fish, and she was a queer girl and she found him interesting.

"Old John J. Masterson, her father, had been United States
Senator from Wyoming, and Helen had been educated at Welles-
ley and had lived in Washington a good deal. She found Cheyenne dull and had got into the Washington way of tolerating
anything but stupidity, and Freymark certainly was not stupid.
He passed as an Alsatian Jew, but he had lived a good deal in
Paris and had been pretty much all over the world, and spoke
the more general European languages fluently. He was a wiry,
sallow, unwholesome looking man, slight and meagerly built,
and he looked as though he had been dried through and through
by the blistering heat of the tropics. His movements were as lithe
and agile as those of a cat, and invested with a certain unusual,
stealthy grace. His eyes were small and black as bright jet beads;
his hair very thick and coarse and straight, black with a sort
of purple luster to it, and he always wore it correctly parted in

the middle and brushed smoothly about his ears. He had a pair
of the most impudent red lips that closed over white, regular
teeth. His hands, of which he took the greatest care, were the
yellow, wrinkled hands of an old man, and shrivelled at the finger tips, though I don't think he could have been much over
thirty. The long and short of it is that the fellow was uncanny.
You somehow felt that there was that in his present, or in his
past, or in his destiny which isolated him from other men. He
dressed in excellent taste, was always accommodating, with the
most polished manners and an address extravagantly deferen-
tial. He went into cattle after he lost his job with the company,
and had an interest in a ranch ten miles out, though he spent
most of his time in Cheyenne at the Capitol card rooms. He had
an insatiable passion for gambling, and he was one of the few
men who make it pay.

"About a week before the dance, Larry's cousin, Harry
Burns, who was a reporter on the London Times, stopped in
Cheyenne on his way to 'Frisco, and Larry came up to meet
him. We took Burns up to the club, and I noticed that he acted
rather queerly when Freymark came in. Burns went down to
Grover to spend a day with Larry, and on Saturday Larry wired
me to come down and spend Sunday with him, as he had important news for me.

"I went, and the gist of his information was that Freymark,
then going by another name, had figured in a particularly ugly
London scandal that happened to be in Burns' beat, and his
record had been exposed. He was, indeed, from Paris, but there
was not a drop of Jewish blood in his veins, and he dated from
farther back than Israel. His father was a French soldier who,
during his service in the East, had bought a Chinese slave girl,
had become attached to her, and married her, and after her death
had brought her child back to Europe with him. He had entered
the civil service and held several subordinate offices in the cap-
ital, where his son was educated. The boy, socially ambitious
and extremely sensitive about his Asiatic blood, after having
been blackballed at a club, had left and lived by an exceedingly

questionable traffic in London, assuming a Jewish patronymic to account for his oriental complexion and traits of feature. That explained everything. That explained why Freymark's hands were those of a centenarian. In his veins crept the sluggish amphibious blood of a race that was already old when Jacob tended the flocks of Laban upon the hills of Padan-Aram, a race that was in its mort cloth before Europe's swaddling clothes were made.

[This figure of speech was also used in "A Son of the Celestial." She seems to imply there that Chinese are without feelings, but in "The Conversion of Sum Loo" she proves otherwise, while here she seems to say they are without any noble sentiments. A month after this story was published, she interviewed a leading Chinese business man and gave a favorable report on him and his race.]

"Of course, the question at once came up as to what ought to be done with Burns' information. Cheyenne clubs are not exclusive, but a Chinaman who had been engaged in Freymark's peculiarly unsavory traffic would be disbarred in almost any region outside of Whitechapel. One thing was sure: Miss Masterson must be informed of the matter at once.

"'On second thought,' said Larry, 'I guess I'd better tell her myself. It will have to be done easy like, not to hurt her self-respect too much. Like as not I'll go off my head the first time I see him and call him rat-eater to his face.'

"Well to get back to the day of the dance, I was wondering whether Larry would stay over to tell Miss Masterson about it the next day, for of course he couldn't spring such a thing on a girl at a party.

"That evening I dressed early and went down to the station at nine to meet Larry. The extra came in, but no Larry. I saw Connelly, the conductor, and asked him if he had seen anything of O'Toole, but he said he hadn't, that the station at Grover was open when he came through, but that he found no train orders and couldn't raise anyone, so he supposed O'Toole had come up on 153. I went back to the office and called Grover, but got no answer. Then I sat down at the instrument and called for fifteen minutes straight. I wanted to go then and hunt up the conductor on 153, the passenger that went through Grover at 5:30 in the afternoon, and ask him what he knew about Larry, but it was then 9:45 and I knew Miss Masterson would be waiting, so I jumped into the carriage and told the driver to make up time. On my way to the Mastersons' I did some tall thinking. I could find no explanation for O'Toole's non-appearance, but the business of the moment was to invent one for Miss Masterson that would neither alarm nor offend her. I couldn't exactly tell her he wasn't coming, for he might show up yet, so I decided to say the extra was late, and I didn't know when it would be in.

"Miss Masterson had been an exceptionally beautiful girl to begin with, and life had done a great deal for her. Fond as I was of Larry, I used to wonder whether a girl who had led such a full and independent existence would ever find the courage to face life with a railroad man who was so near the bottom of a ladder that is so long and steep.

"She came down the stairs in one of her Paris gowns that are as meat and drink to Cheyenne society reporters, with her arms full of American Beauty roses and her eyes and cheeks glowing. I noticed the roses then, though I didn't know that they were the boy's last message to the woman he loved. She paused half way down the stairs and looked at me, and then over my head into the drawing room, and then her eyes questioned mine. I bungled at my explanation and she thanked me for coming, but she couldn't hide her disappointment, and scarcely glanced at herself in the mirror as I put her wrap about her shoulders.

"It was not a cheerful ride down to the Capitol. Miss Masterson did her duty by me bravely, but I found it difficult to be even decently attentive to what she was saying. Once arrived at Representative Hall, where the dance was held, the strain was relieved, for the fellows all pounced down on her for dances, and there were friends of hers there from Helena and Laramie, and my responsibility was practically at an end. Don't expect me

to tell you what a Wyoming inaugural ball is like. I'm not good
at that sort of thing, and this dance is merely incidental to my
story. Dance followed dance, and still no Larry. The dances I had
with Miss Masterson were torture. She began to question and
cross-question me, and when I got tangled up in my lies, she
became indignant. Freymark was late in arriving. It must have
been after midnight when he appeared, correct and smiling, having driven in from his ranch. He was effusively gay and insisted
upon shaking hands with me, though I never willingly touched
those clammy hands of his. He was constantly dangling about
Miss Masterson, who made rather a point of being gracious to
him. I couldn't much blame her under the circumstances, but it
irritated me, and I'm not ashamed to say that I rather spied on
them. When they were on the balcony I heard him say:

" 'You see I've forgiven this morning entirely.'

"She answered him rather coolly:

" 'Ah, but you are constitutionally forgiving. However, I'll
be fair and forgive too. It's more comfortable.'

"Then he said in a slow, insinuating tone, and I could fairly
see him thrust out those impudent red lips of his as he said it:
'If I can teach you to forgive, I wonder whether I could not also
teach you to forget? I almost think I could. At any rate I shall
make you remember this night.

> *Rappelles-toi lorsque les destinées*
> *M'auront de toi pour jamais séparé.'*

"As they came in, I saw him slip one of Larry's red roses into
his pocket.

"It was not until near the end of the dance that the clock of
destiny sounded the first stroke of the tragedy. I remember how
gay the scene was, so gay that I had almost forgotten my anxiety
in the music, flowers and laughter. The orchestra was playing a
waltz, drawing the strains out long and sweet like the notes of
a flute, and Freymark was dancing with Helen. I was not dancing

myself then, and suddenly I noticed some confusion among the
waiters who stood watching by one of the doors, and Larry's
black dog, Duke, all foam at the mouth, shot in the side and
bleeding, dashed in through the door and eluding the caterer's
men, ran half the length of the hall and threw himself at Freymark's feet, uttering a howl piteous enough to herald any sort of
calamity. Freymark, who had not seen him before, turned with
an exclamation of rage and a face absolutely livid and kicked the
wounded brute half-way across the slippery floor. There was
something fiendishly brutal and horrible in the episode, it was
the breaking out of the barbarian blood through his mask of
European civilization, a jet of black mud that spurted up from
some nameless pest hole of filthy heathen cities. The music
stopped, people began moving about in a confused mass, and I
saw Helen's eyes seeking mine appealingly. I hurried to her, and
by the time I reached her Freymark had disappeared.

" 'Get the carriage and take care of Duke,' she said, and her
voice trembled like that of one shivering with cold.

"When we were in the carriage, she spread one of the robes
on her knee, and I lifted the dog up to her, and she took him in
her arms, comforting him.

" 'Where is Larry, and what does all this mean?' she asked.
'You can't put me off any longer, for I danced with a man who
came up on the extra.'

"Then I made a clean breast of it, and told her what I knew,
which was little enough.

" 'Do you think he is ill?' she asked.

"I replied, 'I don't know what to think. I'm all at sea,'—For
since the appearance of the dog, I was genuinely alarmed.

"She was silent for a long time, but when the rays of the
electric street lights flashed at intervals into the carriage, I could
see that she was leaning back with her eyes closed and the dog's
nose against her throat. At last she said with a note of entreaty
in her voice, 'Can't you think of anything?' I saw that she was
thoroughly frightened and told her that it would probably all
end in a joke, and that I would telephone her as soon as I heard

from Larry, and would more than likely have something amusing
to tell her.

"It was snowing hard when we reached the Senator's, and
when we got out of the carriage she gave Duke tenderly over
to me and I remember how she dragged on my arm and how
played out and exhausted she seemed.

" 'You really must not worry at all,' I said. 'You know how
uncertain railroad men are. It's sure to be better at the next
inaugural ball; we'll all be dancing together then.'

" 'The next inaugural ball,' she said as we went up the steps,
putting out her hand to catch the snow-flakes.—'That seems a
long way off.'

"I got down to the office late next morning, and before I had
time to try Grover, the dispatcher at Holyoke called me up to
ask whether Larry were still in Cheyenne. He couldn't raise
Grover, he said, and he wanted to give Larry train orders for
151, the east bound passenger. When he heard what I had to
say, he told me I had better go down to Grover on 151 myself, as
the storm threatened to tie up all the trains and we might look
for trouble.

"I had the veterinary surgeon fix up Duke's side, and I put
him in the express car, and boarded 151 with a mighty cold, un-
comfortable sensation in the region of my diaphragm.

"It had snowed all night long, and the storm had developed
into a blizzard, and the passenger had difficulty in making any
headway at all.

"When we got into Grover I thought it was the most desolate
spot I had ever looked on, and as the train pulled out, leaving
me there, I felt like sending a message of farewell to the world.
You know what Grover is, a red box of a station, section house
barricaded by coal sheds and a little group of dwellings at the
end of everything, with the desert running out on every side to
the sky line. The houses and the station were covered with a
coating of snow that clung to them like a wet plaster, and the
siding was one deep snow drift, banked against the station door.
The plain was a wide, white ocean of swirling, drifting snow,

that beat and broke like the thrash of the waves in the merciless wind that swept, with nothing to break it, from the Rockies to the Missouri.

[There was a big snowstorm in *My Ántonia* the night Mr. Shimerda shot himself. The opening scene of *O Pioneers* bears the same wintry flavor, and with it the imminent death of Mr. Bergson. The day Lucy Gayheart drowned was cold, bitter, windy.]

"When I opened the station door, the snow fell in upon the floor, and Duke sat down by the empty, fireless stove and began to howl and whine in a heart-breaking fashion. Larry's sleeping room upstairs was empty. Downstairs, everything was in order, and all the station work had been done up. Apparently the last thing Larry had done was to bill out a car of wool from the Oasis sheep ranch for Dewey, Gould & Co., Boston. The car had gone out on 153, the east bound that left Grover at seven o'clock the night before, so he must have been there at that time. I copied the bill in the copy book, and went over to the section house to make inquiries.

"The section boss was getting ready to go out to look after his track. He said he had seen O'Toole at 5:30, when the west bound passenger went through, and, not having seen him since, supposed he was still in Cheyenne. I went over to Larry's boarding house, and the woman said he must be in Cheyenne, as he had eaten his supper at five o'clock the night before, so that he would have time to get his station work done and dress. The little girl, she said, had gone over at five to tell him that supper was ready. I questioned the child carefully. She said there was another man, a stranger, in the station with Larry when she went in and that though she didn't hear anything they said, and Larry was sitting with his chair tilted back and his feet on the stove, she somehow had thought they were quarreling. The stranger, she said, was standing; he had a fur coat on and his eyes snapped like he was mad, and she was afraid of him. I asked her if she could recall anything else about him, and she said,

'Yes, he had very red lips.' When I heard that, my heart grew cold as a snow lump, and when I went out the wind seemed to go clear through me. It was evident enough that Freymark had gone down there to make trouble, had quarreled with Larry and had boarded either the 5:30 passenger or the extra, and got the conductor to let him off at his ranch, and accounted for his late appearance at the dance.

"It was five o'clock then, but the 5:30 train was two hours late, so there was nothing to do but sit down and wait for the conductor, who had gone out on the seven o'clock east bound the night before, and who must have seen Larry when he picked up the car of wool. It was growing dark by that time. The sky was a dull lead color, and the snow had drifted about the little town until it was almost buried, and was still coming down so fast that you could scarcely see your hand before you.

"I was never so glad to hear anything as that whistle, when old 153 came lumbering and groaning in through the snow. I ran out on the platform to meet her, and her headlight looked like the face of an old friend. I caught the conductor's arm the minute he stepped off the train, but he wouldn't talk until he got in by the fire. He said he hadn't seen O'Toole at all the night before, but he had found the bill for the wool car on the table, with a note from Larry asking him to take the car out on the Q. T., and he had concluded that Larry had gone up to Cheyenne on the 5:30. I wired the Cheyenne office and managed to catch the express clerk who had gone through on the extra the night before. He wired me saying that he had not seen Larry board the extra, but that his dog had crept into his usual place in the express car, and he had supposed Larry was in the coach. He had seen Freymark get on at Grover, and the train had slowed up a trifle at his ranch to let him off, for Freymark stood in with some of the boys and sent his cattle shipments our way.

"When the night fairly closed down on me, I began to wonder how a gay, expansive fellow like O'Toole had ever stood six months at Grover. The snow had let up by that time, and the stars were beginning to glitter cold and bright through the hurrying clouds. I put on my ulster and went outside. I began a minute tour of inspection, I went through empty freight cars run down by the siding, searched the coal houses and primitive cellar, examining them carefully, and calling O'Toole's name. Duke at my heels dragged himself painfully about, but seemed as much at sea as I, and betrayed the nervous suspense and alertness of a bird dog that has lost his game.

"I went back to the office and took the big station lamp upstairs to make a more careful examination of Larry's sleeping room. The suit of clothes that he usually wore at his work was hanging on the wall. His shaving things were lying about, and I recognized the silver-backed military hair brushes that Miss Masterson had given him at Christmas time, lying on his chiffonier. The upper drawer was open and a pair of white kid gloves was lying on the corner. A white string tie hung across his pipe rack, it was crumpled and had evidently proved unsatisfactory when he tied it. On the chiffonier lay several clean handkerchiefs with holes in them, where he had unfolded them and thrown them by in a hasty search for a whole one. A black silk muffler hung on the chair back, and a top hat was set awry on the head of a plaster cast of Parnell, Larry's hero. His dress suit was missing, so there was no doubt that he had dressed for the party. His overcoat lay on his trunk and his dancing shoes were on the floor, at the foot of the bed beside his everyday ones. I knew that his pumps were a little tight, he had joked about them when I was down the Sunday before the dance, but he had only one pair, and he couldn't have got another in Grover if he had tried himself. That set me to thinking. He was a dainty fellow about his shoes and I knew his collection pretty well. I went to his closet and found them all there. Even granting him a prejudice against overcoats, I couldn't conceive of his going out in that stinging weather without shoes. I noticed that a surgeon's case, such as are carried on passenger trains, and which Larry had once appropriated in Cheyenne, was open, and that the roll of medicated cotton had been pulled out and recently used. Each discovery I made served only to add to my perplexity.

Granted that Freymark had been there, and granted that he had played the boy an ugly trick, he could not have spirited him away without the knowledge of the train crew.

"'Duke, old doggy,' I said to the poor spaniel who was sniffing and whining about the bed, 'you haven't done your duty. You must have seen what went on between your master and that clam-blooded Asiatic, and you ought to be able to give me a tip of some sort.'

"I decided to go to bed and make a fresh start on the ugly business in the morning. The bed looked as though someone had been lying on it, so I started to beat it up a little before I got in. I took off the pillow and as I pulled up the mattress, on the edge of the ticking at the head of the bed, I saw a dark red stain about the size of my hand. I felt the cold sweat come out on me, and my hands were dangerously unsteady, as I carried the lamp over and set it down on the chair by the bed. But Duke was too quick for me, he had seen that stain and leaping on the bed began sniffing it, and whining like a dog that is being whipped to death. I bent down and felt it with my fingers. It was dry but the color and stiffness were unmistakably those of coagulated blood. I caught up my coat and vest and ran down stairs with Duke yelping at my heels. My first impulse was to go and call someone, but from the platform not a single light was visible, and I knew the section men had been in bed for hours. I remembered then, that Larry was often annoyed by hemorrhages at the nose in that high altitude, but even that did not altogether quiet my nerves, and I realized that sleeping in that bed was quite out of the question.

"Larry always kept a supply of brandy and soda on hand, so I made myself a stiff drink and filled the stove and locked the door, turned down the lamp and lay down on the operator's table. I had often slept there when I was night operator. At first it was impossible to sleep, for Duke kept starting up and limping to the door and scratching at it, yelping nervously. He kept this up until I was thoroughly unstrung, and though I'm ordinarily cool enough, there wasn't money enough in Wyoming to have bribed me to open that door. I felt cold all over every time I went near it, and I even drew the big rusty bolt that was never used, and it seemed to me that it groaned heavily as I drew it, or perhaps it was the wind outside that groaned. As for Duke, I threatened to put him out, and boxed his ears until I hurt his feelings, and he lay down in front of the door with his muzzle between his paws and his eyes shining like live coals and riveted on the crack under the door. The situation was gruesome enough, but the liquor had made me drowsy and at last I fell asleep.

"It must have been about three o'clock in the morning that I was awakened by the crying of the dog, a whimper low, continuous and pitiful, and indescribably human. While I was blinking my eyes in an effort to get thoroughly awake, I heard another sound, the grating sound of chalk on a wooden black board, or of a soft pencil on a slate. I turned my head to the right, and saw a man standing with his back to me, chalking something on the bulletin board. At a glance I recognized the broad, high shoulders and the handsome head of my friend. Yet there was that about the figure which kept me from calling his name or from moving a muscle where I lay. He finished his writing and dropped the chalk, and I distinctly heard its click as it fell. He made a gesture as though he were dusting his fingers, and then turned facing me, holding his left hand in front of his mouth. I saw him clearly in the soft light of the station lamp. He wore his dress clothes, and began moving toward the door silently as a shadow in his black stocking feet. There was about his movements an indescribable stiffness, as though his limbs had been frozen. His face was chalky white, his hair seemed damp and was plastered down close about his temples. His eyes were colorless jellies, dull as lead, and staring straight before him. When he reached the door, he lowered the hand he held before his mouth to lift the latch. His face was turned squarely toward me, and the lower jaw had fallen and was set rigidly upon his collar, the mouth was wide open and was *stuffed full of white cotton!* Then I knew it was a dead man's face I looked upon.

"The door opened, and that stiff black figure in stockings

walked as noiselessly as a cat out into the night. I think I went quite mad then. I dimly remember that I rushed out upon the siding and ran up and down screaming, 'Larry, Larry!' until the wind seemed to echo my call. The stars were out in myriads, and the snow glistened in their light, but I could see nothing but the wide, white plain, not even a dark shadow anywhere. When at last I found myself back in the station, I saw Duke lying before the door and dropped on my knees beside him, calling him by name. But Duke was past calling back. Master and dog had gone together, and I dragged him into the corner and covered his face, for his eyes were colorless and soft, like the eyes of that horrible face, once so beloved.

"The black board? O, I didn't forget that. I had chalked the time of the accommodation on it the night before, from sheer force of habit, for it isn't customary to mark the time of trains in unimportant stations like Grover. My writing had been rubbed out by a moist hand, for I could see the finger marks clearly, and in place of it was written in blue chalk simply,

C. B. & Q. 26387

"I sat there drinking brandy and muttering to myself before that black board until those blue letters danced up and down, like magic lantern pictures when you jiggle the slides. I drank until the sweat poured off me like rain and my teeth chattered, and I turned sick at the stomach. At last an idea flashed upon me. I snatched the way bill off the hook. The car of wool that had left Grover for Boston the night before was numbered 26387.

"I must have got through the rest of the night somehow, for when the sun came up red and angry over the white plains, the section boss found me sitting by the stove, the lamp burning full blaze, the brandy bottle empty beside me, and with but one idea in my head, that box car 26387 must be stopped and opened as soon as possible, and that somehow it would explain.

"I figured that we could easily catch it in Omaha, and wired the freight agent there to go through it carefully and report anything unusual. That night I got a wire from the agent stating that the body of a man had been found under a woolsack at one end of the car with a fan and an invitation to the inaugural ball at Cheyenne in the pocket of his dress coat. I wired him not to disturb the body until I arrived, and started for Omaha. Before I left Grover the Cheyenne office wired me that Freymark had left town, going west over the Union Pacific. The company detectives never found him.

"The matter was clear enough then. Being a railroad man, he had hidden the body and sealed up the car and billed it out, leaving a note for the conductor. Since he was of a race without conscience or sensibilities, and since his past was more infamous than his birth, he had boarded the extra and had gone to the ball and danced with Miss Masterson with blood undried upon his hands.

"When I saw Larry O'Toole again, he was lying stiff and stark in the undertakers' rooms in Omaha. He was clad in his dress clothes, with black stockings on his feet, as I had seen him forty-eight hours before. Helen Masterson's fan was in his pocket. His mouth was wide open and stuffed full of white cotton.

"He had been shot in the mouth, the bullet lodging between the third and fourth vertebrae. The hemorrhage had been very slight and had been checked by the cotton. The quarrel had taken place about five in the afternoon. After supper Larry had dressed, all but his shoes, and had lain down to snatch a wink of sleep, trusting to the whistle of the extra to waken him. Freymark had gone back and shot him while he was asleep, afterward placing his body in the wool car, which, but for my telegram, would not have been opened for weeks.

"That's the whole story. There is nothing more to tell except one detail that I did not mention to the superintendent. When I said goodbye to the boy before the undertaker and coroner took charge of the body, I lifted his right hand to take off a ring that Miss Masterson had given him and the ends of the fingers were covered with blue chalk."

❧ A Singer's Romance

published in *The Library*, July 28, 1900

[This story is a different version of "Nanette." The maid
and her background are the same; the same marital situation
exists for the artist. But here Cather makes the story more
tragic because she denies greatness to her artist, and besides
gives her the terrible blow of realizing that, compared to
her maid, she is old and unattractive. The artist at forty-two
is presented as being past her prime—an index of Willa
Cather's own youthful twenty-six.]

The rain fell in torrents and the great stream of people
which poured out of the Metropolitan Opera House stagnated
about the doors and seemed effectually checked by the black line
of bobbing umbrellas on the side walk. The entrance was fairly
blockaded, and the people, who were waiting for carriages
formed a solid phalanx, which the more unfortunate opera goers,
who had to depend on street cars no matter what the condition
of the weather, tried to break through in vain. There was much
shouting of numbers and hurrying of drivers, from whose oil
cloth covered hats the water trickled in tiny streams, quite as
though the brims had been curved just to accommodate it.
The wind made the management of the hundreds of umbrellas
difficult, and they rose and fell and swayed about like toy bal-
loons tugging at their moorings. At the stage entrance there
was less congestion, but the confusion was not proportionally
small, and Frau Selma Schumann was in no very amiable mood
when she was at last told that her carriage awaited her. As she
stepped out of the door, the wind caught the black lace mantilla
wound about her head and lifted it high in the air in such a
ludicrous fashion that the substantial soprano cut a figure much

like a malicious Beardsley poster. In her frantic endeavor to re-
place her sportive headgear, she dropped the little velvet bag
in which she carried her jewel case. A young man stationed by
the door darted forward and snatched it up from the side walk,
uncovered his head and returned the bag to her with a low bow.
He was a tall man, slender and graceful, and he looked as dark
as a Spaniard in the bright light that fell upon him from the door-
way. His curling black hair would have been rather long even for
a tenor, and he wore a dark mustache. His face had that oval
contour, slightly effeminate, which belongs to the Latin races.
He wore a long black ulster and held in his hand a wide-
brimmed, black felt hat. In his buttonhole was a single red carnation. Frau Schumann took the bag with a radiant smile, quite
forgetting her ill humor. "I thank you, sir," she said graciously.
But the young man remained standing with bared head, never
raising his eyes. "Merci, Monsieur," she ventured again, rather
timidly, but his only recognition was to bow even lower than
before, and Madame hastened to her carriage to hide her confusion from her maid, who followed close behind. Once in the
carriage, Madame permitted herself to smile and to sigh a little
in the darkness, and to wonder whether the disagreeable American prima donna, who manufactured gossip about every member of the company, had seen the little episode of the jewel bag.
She almost hoped she had.

This Signorino's reserve puzzled her more than his persist-
ence. This was the third time she had given him an opportunity
to speak, to make himself known, and the third time her timid
advance had been met by silence and downcast eyes. She was
unable to comprehend it. She had been singing in New York
now eight weeks, and since the first week this dark man, clad in
black, had followed her like a shadow. When she and Annette
walked in the park, they always encountered him in the corridors
of her hotel; when she entered the theatre he was always stationed near the stage door, and when she came out again, he
was still at his post. One evening, just to assure herself, she had
gone to the Opera House when she was not in the cast, and as

she had hoped, the dark Signior was absent. He had grown so
familiar to her that she knew the outline of his head and shoulders a square away, and in the densest crowd her eyes instantly
singled him out. She looked for him so constantly that she knew
she would miss him if he should not appear. Yet he made no
attempt whatever to address her. Once, when he was standing
near her in the hotel corridor, she made pointless and incoherent
inquiries about directions from the bell boy, in the hope that the
young man would volunteer information, which he did not. On
another occasion, when she found him smoking a cigarette at
the door of the Holland as she went out into a drizzling rain,
she had feigned impossible difficulties in raising her umbrella.
He did, indeed, raise it for her, and bowing passed quickly
down the street. Madame had begun to feel like a very bold and
forward woman, and to blush guiltily under the surveillance of
her maid. By every doorstep, at every corner, wherever she
turned, whenever she looked out of a window, she encountered
always the dark Signorino, with his picturesque face and Spanish
eyes, his broad brimmed black felt hat set at an angle on his
glistening black curls, and the inevitable red carnation in his
button hole.

When they arrived at the hotel Antoinette went to the office
to ask for Madame's mail, and returned to Madame's rooms with
a letter which bore the familiar post mark of Monte Carlo. This
threw Madame into an honest German rage, refreshing to wit-
ness, and she threw herself into a chair and wept audibly. The
letter was from her husband, who spent most of his time and
her money at the Casino, and who continually sent urgent
letters for re-enforcement.

"It is too much, 'Toinette, too much," she sobbed. "He says
he must have money to pay his doctor. Why I have sent him
money enough to pay the doctor bills of the royal family. Here
am I singing three and four nights a week—no, I will not do it."

But she ended by sitting down at her desk and writing out
a check, with which she enclosed very pointed advice, and directed it to the suave old gentleman at Monte Carlo.

Then she permitted 'Toinette to shake out her hair, and became lost in the contemplation of her own image in the mirror. She had to admit that she had grown a trifle stout, that there were many fine lines about her mouth and eyes, and little wrinkles on her forehead that had defied the arts of massage. Her blonde hair had lost its luster and was somewhat deadened by the heat of curling iron. She had to hold her chin very high indeed in order not to have two, and there were little puffy places under her eyes that told of her love for pastry and champagne. Above her own face in the glass she saw the reflection of her maid's. Pretty, slender 'Toinette, with her satin-smooth skin and rosy cheeks and little pink ears, her arched brows and long black lashes and her coil of shining black hair. 'Toinette's youth and freshness irritated her tonight: She could not help wondering— but then this man was probably a man of intelligence, quite proof against the charm of mere prettiness!

[The Cather theme of age as against youth here reflects only loss of physical charms.]

He was probably, she reflected, an artist like herself, a man who revered her art, and art, certainly, does not come at sixteen. Secretly, she wondered what 'Toinette thought of this dark Signorino whom she must have noticed by this time. She had great respect for 'Toinette's opinion. 'Toinette was by no means an ordinary ladies' maid, and Madame had grown to regard her as a companion and confidante. She was the child of a French opera singer who had been one of Madame's earliest professional friends and who had come to an evil end and died in a hospital, leaving her young daughter wholly without protection. As the girl had no vocal possibilities, Madame Schumann had generously rescued her from the awful fate of the chorus by taking her into her service.

"You have been contented here, 'Toinette? You like America, you will be a little sorry to leave?" asked Madame as she said good-night.

"Oh, yes, Madame, I should be sorry," returned 'Toinette.

"And so shall I," said Madame softly, smiling to herself.

'Toinette lingered a moment at the door; "Madame will have nothing to eat, no refreshment of any kind?"

"No, nothing to-night, 'Toinette."

"Not even the very smallest glass of champagne?"

"No, no, nothing," said Madame impatiently.

'Toinette turned out the light and left her in bed, where she lay awake for a long time, indulging in luxurious dreams.

In the morning she awoke long before it was time for 'Toinette to bring her coffee, and lay still, with her eyes closed, while the early rumble of the city was audible through the open window.

Selma Schumann was a singer without a romance. No one felt the incongruity of this more than she did, yet she had lived to the age of two-and-forty without ever having known an *affaire de coeur*. After her debut in grand opera she had married her former singing teacher, who at once decided that he had already done quite enough for his wife and the world in the placing and training of that wonderful voice, and lived in cheerful idleness, gambling her earnings with the utmost complacency, and when her reproaches grew too cutting, he would respectfully remind her that he had enlarged her upper register four tones, and in so doing had fulfilled the whole duty of man. Madame had always been industrious and an indefatigable student. She could sing a large repertoire at the shortest notice, and her good nature made her invaluable to managers. She lacked certainly, that poignant individuality which alone secures great eminence in the world of art, and no one ever went to the opera solely because her name was on the bill. She was known as a thoroughly "competent" artist, and as all singers know, that means a thankless life of underpaid drudgery. Her father had been a professor of etymology in a German university and she had inherited something of his taste for grubbing and had been measurably happy in her work. She practiced incessantly and skimped herself and saved money and dutifully supported her husband, and surely such virtue should bring its own reward. Yet when she saw other women in the company appear in a new tiara of diamonds, or saw them snatch notes from the hands of messenger boys, or take a carriage full of flowers back to the hotel with them, she had felt ill used, and had wondered what that other side of life was like. In short, from the wastes of this hum-drum existence which seems so gay to the uninitiated, she had wished for a romance. Under all her laborious habits and thrift and economy there was left enough of the unsatisfied spirit of youth for that.

Since the shadow of the dark Signorino had fallen across her path, the routine of her life hitherto as fixed as that of the planets or of a German house wife, had become less rigid and more variable. She had decided that she owed it to her health to walk frequently in the park, and to sleep later in the morning. She had spent entire afternoons in dreamful idleness, whereas she should have been struggling with the new roles she was to sing in London. She had begun to pay the most scrupulous attention to her toilettes, which she had begun to neglect in the merciless routine of her work. She was visited by many *massageurs*, for she discovered that her figure and skin had been allowed to take care of themselves and had done it ill. She thought with bitter regret that a little less economy and a little more care might have prevented a wrinkle. One great sacrifice she made. She stopped drinking champagne. The sole one of the luxuries of life she had permitted herself was that of the table. She had all her countrywomen's love for good living, and she had indulged herself freely. She had known for a long time that champagne and sweets were bad for her complexion, and that they made her stout, but she had told herself that it was little enough pleasure she had at best.

But since the appearance of the dark Signorino, all this had been changed, and it was by no means an easy sacrifice.

Madame waited a long time for her coffee, but 'Toinette did not appear. Then she rose and went into her reception room, but no one was there. In the little music room next door she heard a low murmur of voices. She parted the curtains a little, and saw 'Toinette with both her hands clasped in the hands of the dark Signorino.

"But Madame," 'Toinette was saying, "she is so lonely. I cannot find the heart to tell her that I must leave her."

"Ah," murmured the Signorino, and his voice was as caressing as Madame had imagined it in her dreams, "she has been like a mother to you, the Madame, she will be glad of your happiness."

When Selma Schumann reached her own room again she threw herself on her bed and wept furiously. Then she dried her eyes and railed at Fortune in deep German polysyllables, and gesturing like an enraged Valkyrie.

Then she ordered her breakfast—and a quart of champagne.

[Champagne for breakfast is not unusual. In *The Rainbow Bridge* (Putnam, 1954), Mary Watkins Cushing tells of her life with Madame Olive Fremstad, who served champagne to early visitors rather than endure their cigarette smoke. The book pictures the way in which a great artist depends on those who attend her.

Olive Fremstad, for Willa Cather, was one of the great —the inspiration, in part, for *Song of the Lark*.]

🍃 The Conversion
of Sum Loo

published in *The Library*, August 11, 1900

[Shortly before this story was published, Willa Cather interviewed Lee Chin, the leading Chinese importer of Pittsburgh, whose first wife had committed suicide because she could not return to the United States with him after his annual trip to China to visit her, and whose second wife had a mental breakdown.

Lee Chin said: "You must remember that to the average Chinaman the precepts of your religion seem very like those of his own, and it is difficult for him to understand why his ceremonies and forms are altogether bad. . . . He has a great literature of his own, poetry that rivals the best of yours, and he wrote novels, quite like yours in form, a thousand years before Europe had developed the novel. His integrity in trade is proverbial. He made gunpowder and discovered the art of printing and the use of anaesthetics before Europe."]

> For who may know how the battle goes,
> Beyond the rim of the world?
> And who shall say what gods survive,
> And which in the Pit are hurled?
> How if a man should burn sweet smoke
> And offer his prayers and tears
> At the shrine of a god who had lost the fight
> And been slain for a thousand years?

The purport of this story is to tell how the joy at the Mission of the Heavenly Rest for the most hopeful conversion of Sum

265

Chin and Sum Loo, his wife, was turned to weeping, and of how little Sister Hannah learned that the soul of the Oriental is a slippery thing, and hard to hold, to hold in the meshes of any creed.

Sum Chin was in those days one of the largest importers of Chinese bronzes and bric-a-brac in San Francisco and a power among his own people, a convert worth a hundred of the coolie people. When he first came to the city he had gone to the Mission Sunday School for a while for the purpose of learning the tongue and picking up something of American manners. But occidental formalities are very simple to one who has mastered the complicated etiquette of Southern Asia, and he soon picked up enough English for business purposes and so had fallen away from the Mission. It was not until his wife came to him, and until his little son was born that Sum Chin had regarded the Mission people seriously, deeming it wise to invoke the good offices of any and all gods in the boy's behalf.

Of his conversion, or rather his concession, the people of the Heavenly Rest made great show, for besides being respected by the bankers and insurance writers, who are liberal in the matter of creed, he was well known to all the literary and artistic people of the city, both professionals and devout amateurs. Norman Girrard, the "charcoal preacher" as he was called, because he always carried a bit of crayon and sketched opportunely and inopportunely, declared that Sum Chin had the critical faculty, and that his shop was the most splendid interior in San Francisco. Girrard was a pale-eyed theological student who helped the devout deaconesses at the Mission of the Heavenly Rest in their good work, and who had vacillated between art and the Church until his whole demeanor was restless, uncertain, and indicative of a deep-seated discontent.

By some strange attraction of opposites he had got into Sum Chin's confidence as far as it is ever possible to penetrate the silent, inscrutable inner self of the Oriental. This fateful, nervous little man found a sedative influence in the big, clean-limbed Chinaman, so smooth and calm and yellow, so content with all things finite and infinite, who could sit any number of hours in the same position without fatigue, and who once, when he saw Girrard playing tennis, had asked him how much he was paid for such terrible exertion. He liked the glowing primitive colors of Sum Chin's shop, they salved his feelings after the ugly things he saw in his mission work. On hot summer days, when the sea breeze slept, and the streets were ablaze with heat and light, he spent much time in the rear of Sum Chin's shop, where it was cool and dusky, and where the air smelt of spices and sandalwood, and the freshly opened boxes exhaled the aroma of another clime which was like an actual physical substance, and food for dreams. Those odors flashed before his eyes whole Orient landscapes, as though the ghosts of old-world cities had been sealed up in the boxes, like the djin in the Arabian bottle.

There he would sit at the side of a formidable bronze dragon with four wings, near the imported laquered coffin which Sum Chin kept ready for the final emergency, watching the immaculate Chinaman, as he sat at an American office desk attending to his business correspondence. In his office Sum Chin wore dark purple trousers and white shoes worked with gold, and an overdress of a lighter shade of purple. He wrote with a brush which required very delicate manipulation, scraping his ink from the cake and moistening it with water, tracing the characters with remarkable neatness on the rice paper. Years afterward, when Girrard had gone over to art body and soul, and become an absinthe-drinking, lady-killing, and needlessly profane painter of Oriental subjects and marines on the other side of the water, malicious persons said that in the tortures of his early indecision he had made the acquaintance of Sum Chin's opium pipe and had weakened the underpinning of his orthodoxy, but that is exceedingly improbable.

During these long seances Girrard learned a good deal of Sum Chin's history. Sum Chin was a man of literary tastes and had begun life as a scholar. At an early age he had taken the Eminent Degree of the Flowering Talent, and was preparing for the higher Degree of the Promoted Men, when his father had

committed some offense against the Imperial Government, and
Sum Chin had taken his guilt upon his own head and had been
forced to flee the Empire, being smuggled out of the port at
Hong Kong as the body servant of a young Englishman whom
he had been tutoring in the Chinese Classics. As a boy he had
dwelt in Nanking, the oldest city of the oldest Empire, where
the great schools are, and where the tallest pagoda in the world
rears its height of shining porcelain. After he had taken the
Eminent Degree of the Flowering Talent and been accorded an
ovation by the magistrates of his town, he had grown tired of the
place; tired of the rice paper books, and the masters in their
black gowns, and the interminable prospect of the Seven Thousand Classics; of the distant blue mountains and the shadow
of the great tower that grew longer and longer upon the yellow
clay all afternoon. Then he had gone South, down the great
canal on a barge with big red sails like dragons' wings. He came
to Soutcheofou, that is built upon the water ways of the hills of
Lake Taihoo. There the air smelt always of flowers, and the
bamboo thickets were green, and the canals were bright as quick-
silver, and between them the waving rice fields shimmered in the
sun like green watered silk. There the actors and jugglers
gathered all the year round. And there the mandarins come
to find concubines. For once a god loved a maiden of Soutcheofou and gave her the charms of Heaven and since then the
women of that city have been the most beautiful in the Middle
Kingdom and have lived but to love and be loved. There Sum
Chin had tarried, preparing for his second degree, when his trouble came upon him and the sacred duty of filial piety made him a
fugitive.

> [Part of the above paragraph is copied from "A Son of
> the Celestial." Here, however, we find the addition of the
> Oriental conception of filial duty and the idea of ancestor
> worship.]

Up to the time of his flight Sum Chin had delayed the holy
duty of matrimony because the cares of paternity conflict with

the meditations of the scholar, and because wives are expensive and scholars are poor. In San Francisco he had married a foreign-born Chinese girl out of Berkeley Place, but she had been sickly from the first and had borne him no children. She had lived a long time, and though she was both shrewish and indolent, it was said that her husband treated her kindly. She had been dead but a few months when the news of his father's death in Nanking, roused Sum Chin to his duty of begetting offspring who should secure repose for his own soul and his dead father's.

He was then fifty, and his choice must be made quickly. Then he be-thought him of the daughter of his friend and purchasing agent, Te Wing, in Canton, whom he had visited on his last trip to China, eight years before. She was but a child then, and had lain all day on a mat with her feet swathed in tight bandages, but even then he had liked the little girl because her eyes were the color of jade and very bright, and her mouth was red as a flower. He used to take her costly Chinese sweetmeats and tell her stories of the five Sea Dragon Kings who wear yellow armor, and of their yearly visit to the Middle Heaven, when the other gods are frightened away, and of the unicorn which walks abroad only when sages are born, and of the Phoenix which lays cubical eggs among the mountains, and at whose flute-like voice the tigers flee. So Sum Chin wrote to Te Wing, the Cantonese merchant, and Girrard arranged the girl's admission through the ports with the Rescue Society, and the matter was accomplished.

Now a change of dwelling place, even from one village to another, is regarded as a calamity among Chinese women, and they pray to be delivered from the curse of childlessness and from long journeys. Little Te Loo must have remembered very kindly the elegant stranger who had drunk tea in her father's home and had given her sweetmeats, that she consented to cross the ocean to wed him. Yet she did this willingly, and she kept a sharp lookout for the five Sea Dragon Kings on the way, for she was quite sure that they must be friends of her husband's. She arrived in San Francisco with her many wedding gifts and her trousseau done up in yellow bales bound with bamboo

withes, a very silly, giggly maid, with her jade-like eyes and her
flower-like mouth, and her feet like the tiny pink shells that one
picks up along the seashore.

From the day of her marriage Sum Loo began devout ceremonies before the shrine of the goddess who bestows children,
and in a little while she had a joyful announcement to make to
her husband. Then Sum Chin ceased from his desultory reading
at the Seven Thousand Classics, the last remnant in him of the
disappointed scholar, and began to prepare himself for weightier
matters. The proper reception of a son into the world, when there
are no near relatives at hand, and no maternal grandmother to
assist in the august and important functions, is no small responsibility, especially when the child is to have wealth and rank.
In many trivial things, such as the wearing of undershirts in
winter and straw hats in summer, Sum Chin had conformed to
American ways, but the birth of a man's son is the most important
event in his life, and he could take no chances. All ceremonials
must be observed, and all must transpire as it had among his
people since the years when European civilization was not even
a name. Sum Loo was cheerful enough in those days, eating
greedily, and admiring her trousseau, and always coaxing for
new bangles and stories about the five Sea Dragon Kings. But
Sum Chin was grave and preoccupied. Suppose, after all his
preparations, it should be a girl, whose feet he would have to
bind and for whom he would have to find a suitor, and what
would it all amount to in the end? He might be too old to have
other children, and a girl would not answer his purpose. Even
if it were a boy he might not live to see him grow up, and his
son might forget the faith of his fathers and neglect the necessary
devotions. He began to fear that he had delayed this responsibility too long.

But the child, when it came, was a boy and strong, and he
heaved out his chest mightily and cried when they washed his
mouth with a picture of the sun dipped in wine, the symbol of
a keen intelligence. This little yellow, waxen thing was welcomed
into the house of Sum Chin as a divinity, and indeed, he looked

not unlike the yellow clay gods in the temples frequented by expectant mothers. He was smooth and dark as old ivory, and his eyes were like little beads of black opium, and his nose was so diminutive that his father laughed every time he looked at it. He was called Sum Wing, and he was kept wrapped in a gorgeous piece of silk, and he lay all day long quite still, with his thumb in his mouth and his black eyes never blinking; and Girrard said he looked like an ivory image in his father's shop. Sum Wing had marked prejudices against all the important ceremonials which must be performed over all male infants. He spat out the ceremonial rice and kicked over the wine.

"Him Melican babee, I leckon," said his father in explanation of his son's disregard of the important rites. When the child kicked his mother's side so that she scolded him, Sum Chin smiled and bought her a new bracelet. When the child's cry reached him as he sat in his shop, he smiled. Often, at night, when the tiny Sum Wing slept on his mother's arm, Sum Chin would lean over in the dark to hear his son's breathing.

When the child was a month old, on a day that the priest at the Joss house declared was indicated as lucky by many omens, Sum Wing's head was shaven for the first time, and that was the most important thing which had yet occurred to him. Many of his father's society—which was the Society Fi, or the Guardianship of Nocturnal Vigils, a band which tried to abolish midnight "hold-ups" in Chinatown—came and brought gifts. Nine little tufts of hair were left on the back of the child's head, to indicate the number of trunks his bride would need to pack her trousseau, and nine times his father rubbed two eggs with red shells over his little pate, which eggs the members of the Society for the Guardianship of Nocturnal Vigils gravely ate, thereby pledging themselves to protect the boy, seek him if lost, and mourn for him if dead. Then a nurse was provided for Sum Wing, and his father asked Girrard to have the mission folk pray to the Jesus god for his son, and he drew a large check on his bankers for the support of the mission. Sum Chin held that when all a man's goods are stored in one ship, he should insure it with all reputable underwriters. So, surely, when a man has but one son he should secure for him the good offices of all gods of any standing. For, as he would often say to Girrard, in the language of an old Taoist proverb, "Have you seen your god, brother, or have I seen mine? Then why should there be any controversy between us, seeing that we are both unfortunates?"

Sum Wing was a year and a half old, and could already say wise Chinese words and play with his father's queue most intelligently, when fervent little Sister Hannah began to go to Sum Chin's house, first to see his queer little yellow baby and afterwards to save his wife's soul. Sum Loo could speak a little English by this time, and she liked to have her baby admired, and when there was lack of other amusement, she was not averse to talking about her soul. She thought the pictures of the baby Jesus god were cunning, though not so cunning as her Sum Wing, and she learned an English prayer and a hymn or two. Little Sister Hannah made great progress with Sum Loo, though she never cared to discuss theology with Sum Chin. Chinese metaphysics frightened her, and under all Sum Chin's respect for all rites and ceremonials there was a sort of passive, resigned agnosticism, a doubt older than the very beginnings of Sister Hannah's faith, and she felt incompetent to answer it. It is such an ancient doubt, that of China, and it has gradually stolen the odor from the roses and the tenderness from the breasts of the women.

The good little Sister, who should have had children of her own to bother about, became most deeply attached to Sum Wing, who loved to crumple her white headdress and pinch her plump, pink cheeks. Above all things she desired to have the child baptized, and Sum Loo was quite in the notion of it. It would be very nice to dress the child in his best clothes and take him to the Mission Chapel and hold him before the preacher with many American women looking on, if only they would promise not to put enough water on him to make him sick. She coaxed Sum Chin, who could see no valid objection, since the boy would be properly instructed in the ceremonials of his own religion by the Taoist priest, and since many of his patrons were among the founders of the mission, and it was well to be in the good books of all gods, for one never knew how things were going with the Imperial Dynasties of the other world.

So little Sum Wing was prayed, and sung, and wept over by the mission women, and a week later he fell sick and died, and the priest in the Joss house chuckled maliciously. He was buried in his father's costly coffin which had come from China, and at the funeral there were many carriages and mourners and roast pigs and rice and gin in bowls of real china, as for a grown man, for he was his father's only son.

Sum Chin, he went about with his queue unbraided and his face haggard and unshaven so that he looked like a wreck from some underground opium den, and he rent many costly garments and counted not the cost of them, for of what use is wealth to an old man who has no son? Who now would pray for the peace of his own soul or for that of his father? The voice of his old father cried out from the grave in bitterness against him, upbraiding him with his neglect to provide offspring to secure rest for his spirit. For of all unfilial crimes, childlessness is the darkest.

It was all clear enough to Sum Chin. There had been omens and omens, and he had disregarded them. And now the Jesus people had thrown cold water in his baby's face and with evil incantations had killed his only son. Had not his heart stood still when the child was seized with madness and screamed when the cold water touched its face, as though demons were tearing it with red hot pincers?—And the gods of his own people were offended and had not helped him, and the Taoist priest mocked him and grinned from the Joss house across the street.

When the days of mourning were over he regained his outward composure, was scrupulous as to his dress and careful to let his nails grow long. But he avoided even the men of his own society, for these men had sons, and he hated them because the gods had prospered them. When Girrard came to his shop, Sum Chin sat writing busily with his camel's hair brush, making neat characters on the rice paper, but he spoke no word. He maintained all his former courtesy toward the mission people, but sometimes, after they had left his shop, he would creep upstairs with ashen lips, and catching his wife's shoulder, would shake her rudely, crying between his teeth, "Jesus people, Jesus people, killee ma babee!"

As for poor Sum Loo, her life was desolated by her husband's grief. He no longer was gentle and kind. He no longer told her stories or bought her bracelets and sweetmeats. He let her go nowhere except to the Joss house, he let her see no one, and roughly told her to cleanse herself from the impurities of the Foreign Devils. Still, he was a broken old man, who called upon the gods in his sleep, and she pitied him. Surely he would never have any more children, and what would her father say when he heard that she had given him no grandchildren? A poor return she made her parents for all their kindness in caring for her in her infancy when she was but a girl baby and might have been quietly slipped out of the world; in binding her beautiful feet when she was foolish enough to cry about it, and in giving her a good husband and a trousseau that filled many bales. Surely, too, the spirit of her husband's father would sit heavy on her stomach that she had allowed the Jesus people to kill her son. She was often very lonely without her little baby, who used to count his toes and call her by a funny name when he wanted his dinner. Then she would cry and wipe her eyes on the gorgeous raiment in which Sum Wing had been baptized.

The Mission people were much concerned about Sum Loo. Since her child's death none of them had been able to gain access to the rooms above her husband's store, where she lived. Sister Hannah had again and again made valiant resolutions and set out with determination imprinted on her plump, rosy countenance, but she had never been able to get past the suave, smiling Asiatic who told her that his wife was visiting a neighbor, or had a headache, or was giving a teaparty. It is impossible to contradict the polite and patent fictions of the Chinese, and Sister Hannah always went away nonplussed and berated herself for lack of courage.

One day, however, she was fortunate enough to catch sight of Sum Loo just as she was stepping into the Joss house across the street, and Sister Hannah followed her into that dim, dusky place, where the air was heavy with incense. At first she could see no one at all, and she quite lost her way wandering about among the glittering tinselled gods with their offerings of meat, and rice, and wine before them. They were terrible creatures with hoofs, and horns, and scowling faces, and the little Sister was afraid of the darkness and the heavy air of the place. Suddenly she heard a droning singsong sound, as of a chant, and, moving cautiously, she came upon Sum Loo and stood watching her in terrified amazement. Sum Loo had the copy of the New Testament in Chinese which Sister Hannah had given her husband, open before her. She sat crouching at the shrine of the goddess who bestows children and tore out the pages of the book one by one, and, carefully folding them into narrow strips, she burned them in the candles before the goddess, chanting as she did so, one name over and over incessantly.

Sister Hannah fled weeping back to the Mission of the Heavenly Rest, and that night she wrote to withdraw the application she had sent in to the Board of Foreign Missions.